1973

The Last Year

THE BEATLES

Were Fab

1973
The Last Year
THE BEATLES
Were Fab

JOHN BLANEY

Paper Jukebox

CONTENTS

1. January: The Mary Whitehouse experience
2. February: Suits you, sir
3. March: Whoa oh-oh is me
4. April: Now is the time to say goodbye (goodbye)
5. May: This heavy load
6. June: An open book
7. July: On the road, again
8. August: Out the blue
9. September: The road to Lagos
10. October: Dr Winston O'Boogie goes too far
11. November: Another day, another law suit
12. December: Welcome to the three day week

INTRODUCTION

Was 1973 the last year The Beatles were fab? Lennon, McCartney, Harrison, and Starr couldn't become any more famous than they already were, but fame isn't an indicator of unprecedented success. There have been plenty of people who have been famous for being famous. That's the definition of celebrity. The Beatles' fabness was more than that. It was measured in the number of records sold and, perhaps, more importantly, the quality of the music on those records. Then, as now, people disagreed about the subjective nature of what constitutes good, bad, or indifferent music. One's taste in music is subjective. Fifty years later debates about quality still rage.

Why 1973? Surely, there are plenty more years to choose from. 1976 was a good year for The Beatles. As Punk rock went mainstream, every single The Beatles released from 1962 to 1970 re-entered the UK singles chart. During one week in April, The Beatles had an unprecedented 23 entries in the UK top 100. Now that's what I call fab. What about 1995? The year The Anthology television series aired. Accompanied by an album and single, 'Free As A Bird,' the television series triggered a new round of Beatlemania. *Anthology Vol. 1* was the first Beatles album to enter the *Billboard* 200 album chart at number one and sold 2.3 million copies in the first month. If that's not fab then what is? Wasn't 2000 the last year The Beatles were fab? The release of the compilation album *1* saw more records being broken. It became the highest-selling CD of 2000 and, eventually the entire decade. In the UK, 1 sold 319,126 copies in its first week. In the US, the response was even bigger. *1* debuted at number one on the *Billboard* 200 album chart with sales of over *1* million in the first two weeks. Fab, indeed. The Beatles will continue to be fab for many years, simply because they are The Beatles. They are the gold standard applied to every new band or solo artist who looks likely to emulate their success.

But, 1973 was different. It was the first year since the group split up in 1970 that all four Beatles released million-selling albums and singles. A feat that would never be repeated. It was the first year The Beatles were re-assessed and repackaged. The Beatles were, again, ahead of the curve. But this time they were reacting to a situation rather than preempting a change. The *Red* and *Blue* albums were a rushed attempt to combat the sale of bootleg and counterfeit records. Bootleggers were beating major record companies at their own game. However, the only way they could operate was by breaking the law. By taking the bootleggers to court

The Beatles highlighted the problem and indirectly influenced significant changes to copyright law.

The *Red* and *Blue* albums became a gateway into the music of The Beatles for a new generation of fans. They became part of the group's core canon and have become as totemic as *Revolver* and *Abbey Road*. Unlike many other Beatles compilations that have been allowed to fade into history, the *Red* and *Blue* albums have been re-issued several times. In 1978 they were issued on colour vinyl for the first time. Next, they were issued on compact disc. The compact disc edition was re-mastered and re-issued in 2010 and was followed by a re-mastered vinyl edition in 2014. In 2023, Apple issued a remixed and expanded edition. The *Red* and *Blue* albums are here to stay.

Before 1973, the greatest hits package was a budget affair, churned out to cash in. The release of the *Red* and *Blue* albums was the start of an industry that continues to this day. It's an industry that repackages the past for old and young alike. It has become increasingly sophisticated. Albums are repackaged as multi-disc affairs, re-mixed, re-mastered, and presented as important historical artefacts. They are bestowed with a gravitas that is usually reserved for documents of State like the Magna Carta or Declaration of Independence. They aren't cheap cash-ins, they are designed to give credence to the idea that the bands that made these records were of musical, social, cultural, and historical importance. Far more important than mere kings, queens, prime ministers, or presidents.

1973 was the last year in which each of The Beatles competed with one another and their former band. Paul McCartney released two number-one albums and three singles, Ringo Starr released a number-one album and two number-one singles, George Harrison released a number-one album and a number-one single, and John Lennon released a top-ten album and single. These weren't insignificant albums either. In two cases they represent the pinnacle of each artist's career. Paul McCartney and Wings *Band On The Run* is considered by many to be his best-ever album. The same can be said for Ringo Starr's *Ringo*. Not only is *Ringo* regarded as one of his best, but it was the album that reunited The Beatles (well, almost) and was the template for his All-Starr Band, which he continues to tour with to this day. George Harrison's number one album, *Living In The Material World*, is still overshadowed by his debut, *All Things Must Pass*, but is nevertheless its equal in other ways. Similarly, Lennon's *Mind Games* album is overshadowed by *Imagine*. But for all its faults *Mind Games* is full of great songwriting.

All this happened during a period of great stress in the lives of Lennon, McCartney, Harrison, and Starr. Their business relationship with Allen Klein ended as untidily as it started. Except for McCartney, their marriages were on the rocks. Nevertheless, McCartney had problems of his own. He was found guilty of possession of cannabis, again, and his band was falling apart. Lawsuits flew around like confetti. Northern Songs/ATV sued Lennon and McCartney claiming breach of their agreement. Lennon counter sued claiming conspiracy to defraud. Allen Klein sued Lennon, Harrison, Starr, and Apple over unpaid loans. In addition, Lennon faced deportation from America and McCartney and Harrison found it difficult to enter and work there because of convictions for possession of cannabis. Harrison was being sued for plagiarism, as was Lennon. Lennon and Harrison were also under investigation by the Bank of England. They had cashflow problems because most of their money was being held by the official receiver while attempts were made to resolve The Beatles' partnership agreement. Much of this nightmare would drag on for years.

McCartney's marriage was more stable than the others, but his band wasn't. It broke up on the eve of an eventful trip to Nigeria where they were due to record a new album. Having split with Ono, Lennon moved to Los Angeles to work with Phil Spector on a new album of old songs. It would be as eventful and life-threatening as McCartney's recording sessions in Lagos but for different reasons.

It's difficult to fathom how stressful their lives were. While all this was happening to them they were supposed to continue writing songs, recording albums, and making films. The fact that they achieved this and recorded some of the best music of their solo careers is a remarkable testament to their talents.

Throughout this book you will find references to the cost of records, tickets, materials, royalties etc. I have used official inflation calculators to adjust the 1973 figures to 2024 values, which are presented in brackets. I have also included the US and UK top ten charts for each month to provide some context. Lennon's, McCartney's, Harrison's, and Starr's records weren't released in a vacuum. The charts show the competition they were facing, and how different US and UK markets were. The fact that The Beatles could triumph in radically different musical environments is another remarkable achievement.

I would like to thank Peter Sims for providing me with press cuttings from his collection. A big thank you to David E. F. Gleason for digitising his archive of music business and broadcasting magazines. It is a remarkable resource and proved invaluable in the writing of this book. I would also like to thank the staff of the BBC Written Archive for allowing me access to BBC Radio 1 playlists.

CHAPTER 1
JANUARY: THE MARY
WHITEHOUSE EXPERIENCE

As the bells rang midnight on the 1st of January 1973, Britain became a member of the European Economic Community (EEC). The decision to join the EEC was as divisive as leaving just over forty years later. Some looked forward to a new, closer relationship with Europe and greater prosperity. Others looked back to an imagined golden age when Britain ruled the waves. Whatever your view, the only certainty was uncertainty. Social, economic, religious, and political instability cast a lengthening shadow across the land. In Northern Ireland, The Troubles escalated and quickly spread to the mainland. Rail workers, civil servants, firefighters, ambulance drivers, and miners withdrew their labour. Relations between Britain and Iceland became so frosty that a second Cod War ensued.

McCartney had made his views about the EEC known, and he didn't like it. His reasons were based on ignorance, fear of change, fear of the other, misunderstanding, and bloody-mindedness. "One of the worst things about the common market is that miles are going to become kilometres. That's a foreign word, another foreign word in the British language. Acres become hectares, and so on. I wouldn't mind if the British government announced we're gonna have these words, but they're still going to be English things. That pees me right off. You have a great tradition in England, and some people hate tradition. They seem to want to take it down and put something in its place. I think that people who do that without regard to the past and the validity of the tradition often make mistakes and come back in two years and think 'Blimey I wrecked that!' Whoever's going to change kilometres from miles is going to be reading a book in 10 years and say, 'ah miles they were good weren't they'."

McCartney's nationalism opposed Lennon's, sometimes confusing, internationalism. Lennon hadn't made his views about the EEC known because no one asked him. However, there was one issue that both Lennon and McCartney agreed on. Both had released songs criticising the State's intervention in Northern Ireland. Like many who reacted to 30th January 1972, it had been visceral. Neither fully understood what was happening in Northern Ireland. But both felt compelled to say something about it. Because McCartney released his song as a single, it received more public scrutiny than Lennon's, which was only available on his album *Some Time In New York City*. 'Give Ireland Back To The Irish' was banned by the BBC. But that didn't stop McCartney from performing the song when Wings embarked on a short tour of universities in February 1972. Not that it made a blind bit of difference to the political situation. Indeed, it could be argued that it heightened tensions. That was certainly the case for Henry McCullough's brother Victor, who was attacked and beaten because of Henry's involvement with the song. McCullough wisely kept his head down and didn't comment on the song publicly. He did admit that: "it was a little difficult for me, but nothing that one wasn't able to handle at the end of the day and thankfully I wasn't living in Ireland at the time or I think it could have been a lot worse".

Mixing pop and politics was one thing; mixing sex and drugs was quite another. Once again, Wings were clipped by the BBC when it decided to ban 'Hi, Hi, Hi'. But not before that bastion of rebellion, Tony Blackburn played it on his Radio 1 show. "It slipped through the net, and was played once on the *Tony Blackburn Show*, but you can take it that from now it will not be played on Radio 1 or 2" said a BBC spokesperson. McCartney claimed that: "The BBC got some of the words wrong. But I suppose it is a bit of a dirty song if sex is dirty and naughty. I was in a sensuous mood in Spain when I wrote it. To me, it was just a song to close our act and since it went down well when we toured the continent, I thought it would be a good single. I think it's the best single we've done as Wings."

The 1960s had been labelled permissive. But for every action, there is an equal and opposite reaction. The reply came in the form of Mary Whitehouse. She had been campaigning against moral decline since the early '60s. First, there was the Clean-Up TV pressure group, established in 1964, where she was the most prominent figure. Then she founded the National Viewers' and Listeners' Association, using it as a platform to criticise the BBC for what she perceived as a lack of accountability and excessive use of foul language and portrayals of sex and violence in its programmes.

McCartney might have got away with his dirty song if only he had employed innuendo. Chuck Berry had topped the charts with his risqué reading of 'My Ding-A-Ling'. Unsurprisingly, Mary Whitehouse tried to get it banned. Despite writing to the BBC's Director General that "One teacher told us of how she found a class of small boys with their trousers undone, singing the song and giving it the indecent interpretation which—despite all the hullabaloo—is so obvious ... We trust you will agree with us that it is no part of the function of the BBC to be the vehicle of songs which stimulate this kind of behaviour—indeed quite the reverse." For some reason, she failed, and the BBC continued to broadcast the song. Having faced the wrath of Whitehouse once, the BBC played it safe with Wings' dirty song and banned it before she could complain.

When recording the song, Wings struggled to capture the sensuous mood that had inspired it. What had come to them naturally on stage took forever in the sterile atmosphere of a recording studio. Although they had made several recordings of the song during their recent European tour, none of them was considered good enough to release on record. Rather than add overdubs to a live recording, Wings attempted to cut a new version in the studio. On 1st September 1972, Wings entered Morgan Studios in Wilsden, London, to begin work on the song. However, no matter how often they ran the track, they could not capture the sound McCartney heard in his head. Recording 'Hi, Hi, Hi' was abandoned in favour of 'C Moon,' which was considerably easier to capture.

Wings continued to work on 'Hi, Hi, Hi' in the second week of September. Having decided against adding overdubs to a live recording of the song, it was now agreed that that was precisely what they would do. Denny Laine and Henry McCulloch overdubbed guitars, and McCartney replaced his bass to a live recording made in Groningen. Once again, the song was put to one side while they worked on more songs for the *Red Rose Speedway* album.

On 18th September, Wings returned to EMI Studios to work on 'Hi, Hi, Hi'. All previous attempts were scrapped when it was decided to start afresh with a new arrangement. "I originally wrote it with a shuffle beat, but we decided it didn't [work] as a record that way. So we re-did it with a rockashake beat, kind of squared off a bit," McCartney explained. Even with a new beat, attempts to capture a successful take failed to materialize. Take 24 was considered the best take so far. But McCartney changed his mind and decided that take 17 was the keeper. More overdubs were added before it too was abandoned. The band laboured on deep into the night but failed to record anything of use.

Finally, on 20th September, they nailed it. Only this time, the recording was captured in a series of overdubs rather than by the band playing live in the studio. The song was built on a solid foundation of Denny Seiwell's drums supported by McCartney's bass. Guitars and vocals were added, and after days spent in the studio, take 61 was marked as 'best'. However, McCartney hadn't finished the recording yet. A week after recording take 61, Wings returned to EMI Studios on 24th September to add even more overdubs to the recording. But having filled the multi-track tape, Alan Parsons, who was engineering the recording, had to bounce several guitar tracks down to free up space for McCulloch to overdub slide guitar and for McCartney to replace his vocal. The following day, more guitars were overdubbed, replacing some that had been added previously, and percussion and background vocals were added. Once again, the recording was left to stew while McCartney considered his options. More overdubs, that's what was needed. More guitars were overdubbed in the first week of October at EMI Studios. Finally, the recording met McCartney's exacting standard and received five rough mixes, none considered good enough for the master.

If Wings thought they'd finished with 'Hi, Hi, Hi,' they were wrong. On 6th November, they returned to EMI Studios to produce a master mix of the song. However, McCartney had other plans and added organ, guitar, harmony vocals, and drums to the up-tempo coda. Finally, the track was ready to mix. However, even this relatively simple task was complicated by McCartney's perfectionism. Mixing the song to McCartney's satisfaction took four hours and eight attempts. The record's B-side was completed a few days later, and the tape was sent to be cut to lacquer for pressing at EMI's Hayes factory.

Work on the new single didn't stop there. On Saturday, 25th November, Wings headed to Southern TV studios in Northam to record promotional films for both sides of their new single. McCartney was hedging his bets. He had an inkling that the A-side stood a good chance of being banned. This time, he'd be prepared. 'C Moon' would replace the official A-side should it be needed, which is why a promotional film was made along with 'Hi, Hi, Hi'. McCartney also had independent radio and TV stations on his side. While the BBC banned the A-side, the ITV network didn't. The promotional film of Wings performing the song was broadcast in the UK on the 'Russell Harty Plus' TV show on 16th December 1972.

Wings' third single was scheduled for release on 1st December (UK) and 4th December (US). At the time of its release in the UK, Chuck Berry was top of the charts with the novelty song 'My Ding-A-Ling'. Berry's novelty hit was full of sexual innuendo, but the BBC hadn't banned it. It had done the opposite and given the song primetime airplay on its national radio stations and *Top Of The Pops* television show. The remainder of the top five included the family-friendly The Osmonds, the loud and boisterous Slade, and the singer-songwriter talents of Elton John.

The UK chart contained a mix of teenyboppers, hard rockers, glam rockers, and more traditional pop. 'Hi, Hi, Hi' had a more complex, rockier sound than Wings' previous release, but it struggled to compete with Slade's 'GudBuy T'Jane' or Alice Cooper's 'Elected'. It entered the chart at a respectable number 27. But by the following week, it had only climbed five places to number 22. The fact that 'Hi, Hi, Hi' had been banned wasn't helping. Not even the broadcast of the promotional film by the ITV network seemed to help because the following week it remained stuck at 22. McCartney and EMI must have been getting worried;

so much time, effort, and money spent on a relative flop. However, when 'C Moon' was promoted to the top side, the single started to take off. The promotional film for 'C Moon' was broadcast on 4th January 1973 by the BBC flagship music show *Top Of The Pops*. At that time, it was at number 10, four places behind 'Happy Xmas (War Is Over)' by John and Yoko/The Plastic Ono Band with the Harlem Community Choir. Little Jimmy Osmond sat at the top of the charts with his ode to The Beatles' home city, 'Long Haired Lover From Liverpool'.

'Happy Xmas (War Is Over)' started as a poster campaign launched on 15th December 1969 in 12 cities worldwide. The simple white posters proclaimed: "War Is Over! If You Want It. Happy Christmas from John & Yoko". With this germ of an idea, John and Yoko wrote a seasonal song, developing themes of peace and change that both had long championed.

Lennon often 'borrowed' motifs from other songs to kick-start his own. He'd based 'Come Together' on Chuck Berry's 'You Can't Catch Me,' 'Crippled Inside' borrowed from a folk tune, 'Black Dog Blues,' and the opening bars of 'Happy Xmas (War Is Over)' bore more than a passing resemblance to 'Stewball' by Peter, Paul & Mary. He was already being sued by Morris Levy who clamed 'Come Together' infringed the copyright on Chuck Berry's 'You Can't Catch Me,' owned by Levy's publishing company, Big Seven Music. This time, Lennon was in luck. Peter, Paul & Mary had borrowed the tune for 'Stewball' from the public domain. There was no case to answer. 'Happy Xmas (War Is Over)' also resembled The Paris Sisters' 'I Love How You Love Me,' and to add to the mix of influences, Lennon instructed his producer, Phil Spector, to make the record sound like the one he'd just produced for his wife, Ronnie Spector, George Harrison's 'Try Some, Buy Some.' Unlike the torturous sessions required to record 'Hi, Hi, Hi,' Lennon's recording sessions were the model of brevity. 'Happy Xmas (War Is Over)' was recorded on 28th October 1971 at the Record Plant in New York with a second session on 30th October to overdub Klaus Voormann's bass; he missed the session on the 28th because of a delayed flight, and the Harlem Community Choir.

Apple issued 'Happy Xmas (War Is Over)' in the USA on 1st December 1971, but the British release was held up by almost a year because of Ono's claim as co-author. The Lennons, like the McCartneys, were having problems with their music publisher, who was unhappy at Lennon's and McCartney's claims that they were writing with their wives. ATV/Northern Songs refused to accept that either Mrs Lennon or Mrs McCartney were writers. Northern Songs and Maclen sued, claiming copyright infringement, against John Lennon, Yoko Lennon, Ono Music, Inc.. Apple Records, inc., and Capitol Records, Inc. They claimed all rights, titles, and interest in Lennon's compositions 'Happy Xmas (War Is Over),' 'Woman Is The Nigger of the World,' 'Angela,' 'Attica State,' 'Sunday, Bloody Sunday,' and 'The Luck of the Irish'. Northern Songs and Maclen wanted Lennon and Ono to stop using the material and claimed royalty payments and damages of $10,000 ($69,893.24).

The real issue, as always, was money. By claiming they had co-written songs with their wives, Lennon and McCartney denied ATV/Northern Songs and their US publisher Maclen, half of the composer's royalty. ATV/Northern Songs had to tread carefully. Lennon and McCartney were never impressed with their publisher, particularly when they discovered that they were minority shareholders in a company that they were told they owned. Matters weren't helped by the way Dick James chose to dispose of his share of the company, which made the relationship between writers and publisher even worse. Northern Songs' agreement with Lennon and McCartney expired on 10th February 1973, and there was no guarantee that either would renew their contracts with the company.

Indeed, Lennon filed a counterclaim, accusing Northern Songs and Maclen of a conspiracy that allegedly defrauded him of approximately $9 million ($63,310,540.54) in royalties. He wrote directly to Jack Gill, ATV's financial director, to see if they could reach an out-of-court agreement. "I don't know exactly what's going on in London re Klein's Northern action, as far as I know nothing is supposed to be happening," he claimed. He continued: "The 'US' thing (lawsuit) should not be difficult, for ALL concerned. I told my lawyers to make a deal whereby we split the publishing 50/50 (Northern/Ono), it really does seem reasonable to me. I was surprised when my 'counteroffer' was rejected, they did tell you about it … didn't they? Please let me know what you think. It all seems so pointless."

McCartney also attempted to bypass the legal system. "I wrote Sir Lew Grade a long letter saying, "Don't you think I ought to be able to do this and do that and don't you think I've done enough and don't you think I'm OK - Hey man why have you gotta sue me? He wrote me back a very rational letter. I can't remember exactly what it said, but it was a very nice letter he's actually OK, Lew, he's alright." Both parties eventually settled out of court. A new agreement was brokered, with McCartney agreeing to a 50/50 split between Northern Songs and McCartney Music. Any songs written after February 1973 would belong solely to McCartney and be subject to an improved publishing royalty of 55/45 in McCartney's favour. Once again, McCartney proved to be a better businessman than Lennon, who had suggested a 50/50 split. McCartney also received half of the money previously payable to Lenmac

Enterprises (a company formed to collect Lennon's and McCartney's Performing Rights Society payments) for 56 songs written under the original Lenmac agreement. The deal ran until 9th February 1980. Lennon settled with ATV/Northern Songs in 1974 with a similar deal.

By the week ending 13th January, Lennon and McCartney had swapped places on the charts. 'Happy Xmas (War Is Over)' had slipped to number 15, while 'Hi, Hi, Hi'/'C Moon' had climbed to number 5. The Osmonds, T. Rex, David Bowie, and Little Jimmy Osmond prevented Wings from topping the charts. Wings stayed at number 5 for two weeks before dropping two places to number 7.

While Lennon and McCartney were battling it out in the chart and the courts, McCartney continued to stockpile tracks for the next Wings album. In the second week of January, Wings returned to EMI Studios to start mixing some of the songs they'd recorded the previous year. Seven songs were mixed this week, and five were completed the following week. During this time, Wings also recorded more overdubs onto 'Rode All Night' (originally recorded during sessions for *Ram*), 'Best Friend,' and Denny Laine's 'I Would Only Smile.' None of these songs would make the final cut.

A report in *Cash Box* claimed that Henry McCulloch would be recording with Jerry Lee Lewis when he visited London to record a new album. According to Charles Fach, Mercury VP/A&R, an all-star cast of London's rock elite was lined up to record with the Killer. It suggested that the musicians confirmed for the album included Rod Stewart and Faces, Steve Winwood, Ric Grech, Alvin Lee, Rory Gallagher, Gary Wright, Henry McCulloch of Wings, Tony Ashton, Albert Lee and members of his group, Heads Hands & Feet, Barry Gibb, Matthew Fisher, and a lone American, Delaney Bramlett. However, McCulloch was busy with Wings, so he did not play on any of the Killer's sessions.

Having spent Saturday, the 13th, mixing 'Hands Of Love,' Paul and Linda attended Eric Clapton's comeback concert at the Finsbury Park Rainbow Theatre. George Harrison and Ringo Starr were also spotted propping up the bar after the show. As the McCartneys' attendance wasn't reported, we must assume they didn't join the backstage celebrations. Indeed, such a public reunion would have been reported in the music papers.

McCartney probably wasn't in the mood to socialize with his former bandmates. Financial and legal worries had created fracture lines within the group that divided loyalties and friendships. The group's inner dynamic had always been complicated, but Harrison was about to muddle it even more. Harrison wasn't in a good place. He was ricocheting between the sacred and the profane, between sex and drugs and meditation. Like Lennon and McCartney, Harrison had to deal with the pressure of following a hit album with another. Lennon and McCartney were established hit makers. But Harrison's success had taken many by surprise. However, the triumph of 'My Sweet Lord' had quickly turned sour. The litigation surrounding the song would drag on for years and haunt him for the rest of his life. He would be permanently stained with the accusation of plagiarism, and the accusation played on his mind. Harrison claimed it became such a burden: "I don't even want to touch the guitar or piano in case I'm touching somebody's note. Somebody might own that note, so you'd better watch out."

This, combined with everything else that was happening to him at the time, hurt his mental well-being and altered this personality. His new album made it patently clear that he was a divided man. The distractions of the material world were all too readily available to a rich pop star like Harrison. He may have been a seeker after spiritual enlightenment, but he couldn't resist the sex, drugs, and rock 'n' roll lifestyle he'd grown up with.

Signs of Harrison's all too visible cognitive dissonance surfaced in 1971 with the release of Ronnie Spector's recording of his song 'Try Some, Buy Some'. Spector struggled to understand the song's meaning, as did most of those who heard it. However, with hindsight, it's evident that its author was torn between the sacred and the profane. The lyric is ambiguous and leads one to conclude that he desperately sought spiritual salvation while describing the consequences of indulging his taste for earthly thrills.

On top of everything else, his marriage was on the rocks. He had numerous short-lived affairs, including a brief fling with Ringo Starr's wife, Maureen Starkey. It takes two to tango, and the fact that Harrison and Maureen had an affair suggests that not all was well in the Starkey household. But worse still, George didn't hide it from anyone, including his wife. Maureen would visit Friar Park when Pattie was away, spend time with George in the studio, and stay overnight. He'd committed his feelings to music the previous year when he wrote 'So Sad'. "I started 'So Sad' in New York City in 1972. I like this song a lot as a melody and lyrically, except the only problem with it is that it's depressing. It is so sad. It was at the time I was splitting up with Pattie."

Pattie was no saint and had started an affair with George's best friend, Eric Clapton. Beatle relationships were as tangled as their financial affairs. Everything was in a mess and needed tidying up. The hippie idea of free love never ended happily, and as Lennon noted, years later, they all required some clean-up time.

Harrison never claimed to be perfect, and despite the spiritual pronouncements that littered his albums, which critics at the time found tiresome, if not downright boring, he could not relinquish the temptations that fame and riches brought him. He had started to act like a spoilt, entitled potentate rather than a pious disciple of Khrishna. Pattie Harrison later suggested, "George seemed torn between the deep beneath us and the glitter on the surface." This ugly dichotomy was there for all to see, reflected in the album's dramatic bible black cover. The front depicts his right hand holding a Hindu medallion; the back shows him holding three coins. Harrison is in the middle, a typical Piscean seeking enlightenment in the unseen realm but rooted in the material world.

How Ringo felt about the revelation that his best friend was having an affair with his wife isn't known. Nobody asked him about it, and he's never talked about it. Ringo was also struggling with alcohol addiction and extramarital affairs. Professionally, however, the drummer had convinced himself that he was a businessman. Speaking in late 1972 to Rex Reed of the *Chicago Tribune*, Starr claimed: "I am a businessman now. I wouldn't say it is more exciting than music, I wouldn't mind playing in a band again, but I wouldn't want to go through all the one night stands. Maybe I'll form my own band. But the best thing is I'm doing my own thing, man, and I don't have to go somewhere and beg people for money to do it my way. If being a Beatle has meant anything, it has given us the security we didn't have when we first started out. Being The Beatles was kind of like an old age pension." Ringo was right. The Beatles was the best pension plan anyone could wish for. The Beatles was, and remains, a money-making machine. The problem was that the machine hadn't been designed. It had been pieced together with little consideration for how it would function. Untangling this muddle of limited companies, corporations, and contracts would take time and money and wouldn't come easy.

Until 1973, the man with the unenviable task of untangling The Beatles' business affairs was official receiver J. D. Spooner. Much to his relief, he was replaced by Stephen Gray. However, Gray didn't find the task any easier, complaining that neither Apple nor the individual Beatles were providing full access to their financial records. His job was made more difficult by The Beatles' inability to decide on how to divide the pot. On 19th March, McCartney said: "I've been speaking to John recently. I'm not sure what is going to happen to Apple, as everyone keeps changing his mind." If The Beatles didn't know what was going on, how could the official receiver do his job? Gray also had to balance the demands of opposing parties. These included EMI, Apple Corps Ltd, Eastman and Eastman, ABCKO, ATV/Northern Songs, Maclen, Lenmac, United Artists, MPL, Lennon Music, Harrisongs, McCartney Music, Kidney Punch Music, Bag Productions, and more.

As an official receiver, it was his job to provide an accurate account of their labyrinthine business activities. Imagine trying to complete a jigsaw puzzle without the picture while somebody keeps hiding key pieces and swapping them for others. He was also responsible for paying The Beatles a monthly allowance from the partnership profits. This had been set at £1000 a month (£10,304.12). But in 1973, it was increased to £3000 a month (£30,912.36). This gave each Beatle an annual income of £36,000 (£372,580). And that didn't include income from their newly formed production companies or songwriting agreements. Money from these income streams was not paid into the partnership account. £36,000 annual income was a very nice pension indeed. The average weekly wage in the UK was £30, or £1,560 a year. The State pension was £7.75 a week or £403 a year for a single person and £12.50 a week or £650 a year for a married couple. However, as Lennon and McCartney had noted some nine years earlier, "Money can't buy me love."

Of the four, McCartney was the only Beatle in a stable, loving relationship. Like Harrison and Starr, Lennon's marriage was in trouble, with rumours circulating in the press. While Lennon faced pressures similar to those of his former bandmates, his were exacerbated by the US State Department. It wanted to deport him because of a 1968 conviction for possession of cannabis. In truth it was a flimsy excuse used to rid the administration of a thorn in its side. Lennon had campaigned against Nixon and the war in Vietnam. It was a mark of how insecure the leader of the free world was that he and his administration felt compelled to rid themselves of the former mop-top, peacenik, and, as they saw him, troublemaker.

Lennon was feeling the pressure, and something had to give. When asked in January 1973 about the state of their marriage, Ono said: "Sometimes we're very happy, sometimes we're not. We are human. There was a negative situation at one time, like Scott and Elsa [Fitzgerald], but we've overcome that because we were a bit more aware, thank God." Just how aware Lennon was is open to debate. Talking about his attitude to women before he met Ono, Lennon said: "We were raised to have a relationship with other men, on the football field or whatever it was. So I had no idea how to treat a woman. I thought she was someone you met at a party, and who you either dated or you didn't. Certainly you couldn't talk music with them or even discuss rock and roll. Like most men I was terrified of the opposite sex."

Lennon claimed that Ono helped him become a feminist, but in private, he could be as chauvinistic as any male. He certainly wasn't aware of Ono's feelings on 7th November 1972, US election night. Lennon openly committed adultery at a party held by Jerry

Rubin that was intended to celebrate the Democratic victory. A victory that didn't materialize. A few months later, in January 1973, Lennon and Ono argued at another party. Despite everything he'd said, Lennon still didn't know how to treat women. The fame and riches hadn't helped; he was as insecure as he'd always been. Speaking in 1981, Ono said of Lennon: "Jealous! My god! After we were together he made me write a list of all the men I'd slept with before we met. I started to do it quite casually, then I realised how serious it was to John. He didn't even like me knowing the Japanese language because that was part of me that didn't belong to him. After a while I couldn't even read any papers or books in Japanese."

The Lennons were growing apart. Ono's star was burning bright, while her husband's was starting to fade. Ono was releasing new music, playing concerts, and being interviewed by the press. She had gone from being demonized as the dragon lady who broke up The Beatles to being praised. Reviewed by *Phonograph Record*, her album *Approximately Infinite Universe* was claimed to be "the best Beatles-related effort to come out since The Beatles' breakup." Such praise would have been unimaginable only a few years earlier.

Ono was on a crusade, fighting for herself, her career, and women's rights. Speaking to Barbara Lewis, about her follow up album *Feeling The Space*, she said: "It's a woman's power album which I'm dedicating to those who died in pain and sorrow." She also claimed that profits from the sale of the album, if there were any, would be used to help her sisters around the world who are in mental institutions or jails because they were unable to adjust to a male-dominated society.

The only press coverage Lennon got was about his fight to avoid deportation. He had nothing to say, no record, concert, book, or exhibition to promote. When journalists interviewed Ono, they asked about him, and Ono was happy to repeat the myth of Johnandyoko. However, in truth Johnandyoko was no more. Lennon admitted as much to the cinematographer Steve Gebhardt: "I remember John saying to me that the days of everything being Johnandyoko—one word—were over." From now on, it would be John and Yoko or Yoko and John. By the end of the year, they would separate, and guess who came off the rails.

Ringo, however, was getting lots of press, thanks to his association with the hottest thing to appear on *Top Of The Pops* since The Beatles, Marc Bolan and T. Rex. The previous year, Starr had directed *Born To Boogie*, a film of T. Rex in concert augmented with some fantasy sequences and footage of T. Rex jamming with Ringo and Elton John. The film premiered at Oscar 1 in London on 14th December. *Born To Boogie* was Starr's debut as a director.

What a debut it was. Of course, it capitalized on the latest pop sensation, but so did *A Hard Day's Night*. Released at the height of T. Rextasy, it was a remarkable success for Bolan, Starr, and Apple films. It proved so popular that its run was extended at four London locations, where it opened on its initial release.

Ringo sang, "They're gonna put me in the movies," and wasn't wrong. Not only had he directed a hit movie, he'd co-starred in a second. *That'll Be The Day*, set in the 1950s. Part of the film was set in a holiday camp. The screenplay was written by music journalist Ray Connelly, who knew nothing about holiday camps, but thanks to his day job, he knew people who did. One of them was Ringo Starr. "I'd written about working in a holiday camp, but I'd never even been to one, let alone worked in one," said Connelly. "Fortunately, we knew two people who had–Ringo Starr, who'd been a drummer at a Butlins camp, and The Beatles' former road manager, Neil Aspinall, who was now the managing director of their Apple operation. So we went to see Ringo and Neil, who were so entertaining with their Butlins memories that we offered Ringo the second lead in the film, as a friendly Liverpudlian Jack-the-lad."

David Essex, then staring in the stage production of *Godspell*, was cast in the lead role. But David Putnam claims: "more important for us was getting Ringo Starr to appear in the film to play the co-lead. That was quite a long negotiation." Putnam knew the value of having a Beatle co-star in his film. The trick was getting him for the right money. The film did not have a large budget, and Putnam had to pay accordingly. Starr was paid in the region of £5,000 (£50,000) for appearing in the film. It's not a massive sum by any means. But Ringo was luckier than most because he didn't need the money; he was already receiving a Beatles pension, which made accepting the role much easier.

WEEK ENDING 6 JANUARY 1973
1. YOU'RE SO VAIN: CARLY SIMON
2. ME & MRS. JONES: BILLY PAUL
3. CLAIR: GILBERT O'SULLIVAN
4. IT NEVER RAINS IN SOUTHERN CALIFORNIA: ALBERT HAMMOND
5. ROCKIN' PNEUMONIA BOOGIE WOOGIE FLU: JOHNNY RIVERS
6. SUPERSTITION: STEVIE WONDER
7. YOU OUGHT TO BE WITH ME: AL GREEN
8. SUPER FLY: CURTIS MAYFIELD
9. FUNNY FACE: DONNA FARGO
10. YOUR MAMA DON'T DANCE: LOGGINS & MESSINA

WEEK ENDING 13 JANUARY 1973
1. YOU'RE SO VAIN: CARLY SIMON
2. SUPERSTITION: STEVIE WONDER
3. ME & MRS. JONES: BILLY PAUL
4. CLAIR GILBERT O'SULLIVAN
5. ROCKIN' PNEUMONIA BOOGIE WOOGIE FLU: JOHNNY RIVERS
6. SUPER FLY: CURTIS MAYFIELD
7. YOUR MAMA DON'T DANCE: LOGGINS & MESSINA
8. WHY CAN'T WE LIVE TOGETHER: TIMMY THOMAS
9. CROCODILE ROCK: ELTON JOHN
10. KEEPER OF THE CASTLE: FOUR TOPS

WEEK ENDING 20 JANUARY 1973
1. SUPERSTITION: STEVIE WONDER
2. YOU'RE SO VAIN: CARLY SIMON
3. CROCODILE ROCK: ELTON JOHN
4. WHY CAN'T WE LIVE TOGETHER: TIMMY THOMAS
5. YOUR MAMA DON'T DANCE: LOGGINS & MESSINA
6. SUPER FLY: CURTIS MAYFIELD
7. ME & MRS. JONES: BILLY PAUL
8. ROCKIN' PNEUMONIA BOOGIE WOOGIE FLU: JOHNNY RIVERS
9. KEEPER OF THE CASTLE: FOUR TOPS
10. I WANNA BE WITH YOU: RASPBERRIES

WEEK ENDING 27 JANUARY 1973
1. SUPERSTITION: STEVIE WONDER
2. CROCODILE ROCK: ELTON JOHN
3. YOU'RE SO VAIN: CARLY SIMON
4. WHY CAN'T WE LIVE TOGETHER: TIMMY THOMAS
5. YOUR MAMA DON'T DANCE: LOGGINS & MESSINA -
6. SUPER FLY: CURTIS MAYFIELD
7. OH BABE WHAT WOULD YOU SAY: HURRICANE SMITH
8. HI HI HI: WINGS
9. ME & MRS. JONES: BILLY PAUL
10. LOVE JONES: BRIGHTER SIDE OF DARKNESS

WEEK ENDING 6 JANUARY 1973
1. LONG HAIRED LOVER FROM LIVERPOOL: LITTLE JIMMY OSMOND
2. THE JEAN GENIE: DAVID BOWIE
3. SOLID GOLD EASY ACTION T. REX
4. CRAZY HORSES: THE OSMONDS
5. HI HI HI/C.MOON: WINGS
6. BALL PARK INCIDENT: WIZZARD
7. YOU'RE SO VAIN: CARLY SIMON
8. BIG SEVEN: JUDGE DREAD
9. GUDBUY T'JANE: SLADE
10. ALWAYS ON MY MIND: ELVIS PRESLEY

WEEK ENDING 13 JANUARY 1973
1. LONG HAIRED LOVER FROM LIVERPOOL: LITTLE JIMMY OSMOND
2. BLOCKBUSTER: THE SWEET
3. THE JEAN GENIE: DAVID BOWIE
4. YOU'RE SO VAIN: CARLY SIMON
5. HI HI HI/C.MOON: WINGS
6. BALL PARK INCIDENT: WIZZARD
7. SOLID GOLD EASY ACTION: T. REX
8. CRAZY HORSES: THE OSMONDS
9. ALWAYS ON MY MIND: ELVIS PRESLEY
10. BIG SEVEN: JUDGE DREAD

WEEK ENDING 20 JANUARY 1973
1. BLOCKBUSTER: THE SWEET
2. LONG HAIRED LOVER FROM LIVERPOOL: LITTLE JIMMY OSMOND
3. THE JEAN GENIE: DAVID BOWIE
4. YOU'RE SO VAIN: CARLY SIMON
5. DO YOU WANNA TOUCH ME? (OH YEAH!): GARY GLITTER
6. BALL PARK INCIDENT: WIZZARD
7. HI HI HI/C.MOON: WINGS
8. WISHING WELL: FREE
9. IF YOU DON'T KNOW ME BY NOW: HAROLD MELVIN AND THE
   BLUENOTES
10. DANIEL: ELTON JOHN

WEEK ENDING 27 JANUARY 1973
1. BLOCKBUSTER: THE SWEET
2. DO YOU WANNA TOUCH ME? (OH YEAH!): GARY GLITTER
3. YOU'RE SO VAIN: CARLY SIMON
4. LONG HAIRED LOVER FROM LIVERPOOL: LITTLE JIMMY OSMOND
5. THE JEAN GENIE: DAVID BOWIE
6. DANIEL: ELTON JOHN
7. PART OF THE UNION: STRAWBS
8. WISHING WELL: FREE
9. IF YOU DON'T KNOW ME BY NOW: HAROLD MELVIN AND THE
   BLUENOTES
10. BALL PARK INCIDENT: WIZZARD

CHAPTER 2
FEBRUARY: SUITS YOU, SIR

February was decision time for The Beatles. The contract that Lennon, Harrison, and Starr had signed with Allen Klein/ABKCO in 1969 was about to end. But, like many things in Beatleland, the ending would be protracted and messy. Although they knew the end was in sight, they had done little to prepare themselves for life after Klein. Lennon and Harrison were unhappy with how Klein handled recent projects, and Lennon, in particular, was dissatisfied with Klein's response to his activism. Yet, neither had looked for a new personal manager. Perhaps it was because any quest for personal representation would have quickly become public knowledge and alerted Klein to the possibility that they would not renew their management contract with him. They were so indecisive that they couldn't even commit to an end date. Although Klein's contract was coming to an end, the Threetles continued to extend it. In April, Lennon said: "The contract expired in February, and we were extending it at first on a monthly basis and then finally on a two weeks' basis and then finally we pushed the boat out."

Klein wasn't going to give up without a fight. He had one last ace up his sleeve that he thought might convince them to re-sign with him. EMI was planning a best of The Beatles. The Beatles' greatest hits packages were nothing new. Several had already been released. *A Collection of Beatles Oldies* had been issued in the UK in December 1966. *Greatest Hits 1 & 2* had been issued in Australia. Germany issued *The Beatles' Greatest*, a compilation from 1965. But this time there was a twist. Klein wanted to release a new Beatles compilation to accompany a film that Neil Aspinall had worked on since The Beatles split up. But it was the release of an unofficial greatest hits package in America that forced decisive action from Klein/ABKCO and EMI/Capitol.

In late 1972, a small company in New Jersey, Audiotape Inc., thought it could work around vague copyright laws and compiled a four-disc set, The Beatles *Alpha Omega*, advertised on television and radio. The collection featured 60 Beatles songs and several contemporary solo tracks. Before 1972, copyright law in the US stated that sound recordings were not subject to federal copyright but were subject to various applicable state torts and statutes. The Sound Recording Amendment of 1971 extended federal copyright to recordings fixed on or after 15th February 1972 (the act's effective date). Recordings released before that date would remain subject to state or standard law copyright. Audiotape Inc. was based in New Jersey, where copyright law was less stringent than in other states. Indeed, the *Philadelphia Inquirer* claimed that "New Jersey is a haven for record bootlegging because, unlike Pennsylvania and most other states, it has no state law against record piracy." By restricting the sale of the set to mail order from its New Jersey address, Audiotape could hide behind the ill-defined/non-existent law. Because the federal law was relatively new, it was untested, and like so many things concerning The Beatles, they were about to become legal guinea pigs.

However, getting a copy of *Alpha Omega* was easier said than done. Many who ordered a copy of the album were disappointed when it failed to arrive. Some wrote to Audiotape asking why it had been delayed. When they received no reply, some wrote to their local newspaper for advice. The reason for the non arrival of the album was because Audiotape was being sued. Louis Saka, the president of Audiotape, admitted that *Alpha Omega* had been made without The Beatles' permission. However, he argued that because the recordings were released before February 1972, they were not covered by Federal copyright law. He also claimed that customers orders were being dispatched. Yet, at least one disappointed fan wrote to the *Ithaca Journal* stating that they had written to Audiotape several times and still not received the album. They probably never did.

Bootlegging was big business, and the laws concerning bootleg recordings were so vague on both sides of the Atlantic that record shops sold them alongside official releases. It wasn't only independents who sold illegal recordings; chain stores like Virgin Records had them on open sale too. The Oxford Street branch of Virgin Records sold them, and its manager was happy to be interviewed about bootleg records for BBC television. The BBC also interviewed Yoko Ono at Apple's Saville Row offices about the sale of bootlegs. When asked if she was worried about bootlegs, she said: "It's very nice to see that people are stimulated enough to bootleg it. I'm sure we are losing money in all sorts of ways."1 She wasn't wrong. Her husband was also a fan of the illegal records. Talking to Charles Charlesworth about bootlegs, he said: "In a way I dig it because it's good for your ego, but I know I'm not supposed to because it's against the business." It was of course, simply rhetoric. Once they realised exactly how much they were losing their laissez-faire attitude evaporated and they started to exercise an iron grip on the rights they owned.

Having appeared on national television bragging about selling bootleg records, Virgin Records' Oxford Street shop was busted for importing and selling the dodgy discs. In March, Richard Branson was fined £1,045 (£10,815.19) for selling bootleg records. It had the desired effect. Bootlegs disappeared from Virgin Records shops overnight. Independent record shops continued to sell bootlegs, albeit under the counter or hidden away at the back of the shop. The article in the *Philadelphia Inquirer* said that the music business in the US lost over \$200 million (\$1,389,265,765.77) each year because of the sale of illegal records and tapes.

Audiotape and other New Jersey-based companies wanted a piece of this enormous pie. In 1971, the penalty for selling bootleg records in the UK was a fine of two pounds for each record sold, up to a total of £50. This was increased in 1972 to £400. This was still peanuts compared to the estimated \$200 million a year that US bootleggers were coining. With that figure ringing in his head, you can bet that Klein took a different view of bootlegging than did the Lennons.

Klein clarified his views on piracy when he spoke at the NARM (National Association of Recording Merchandisers) conference on 27th February. He rebuked manufacturers for not taking legal action against "air pirates" that advertise through radio and TV. He stated that his action against WABC and WPIX represented the first legal attempt to stop "air piracy". He said that he had gone before the RIAA (Recording Industry Association of America) board to request that labels, which were part of broadcasting groups, take action against the practice and claimed that many pirate adverts were "cloaked in respectability" when they advertised on television or in national publications. Klein gave two instances of attempting to stop radio pirate adverts, which resulted in two replies: "Go to hell" and "We have no law against it".

Klein took his role as manager seriously. After all, he was taking a cut of The Beatles' income, and if pirate records reduced that income, it would hit him just as it did The Beatles. However, business is based on trust. The higher you climb the business ladder, the more important trust becomes. It was bad enough that music fans couldn't trust Audiotape to deliver a \$15 record; it was quite another if you couldn't trust your manager with your multimillion-pound business. Trust in Klein had long departed the Lennon, Harrison, and Starr camp. A few years earlier, Klein had looked like a knight in shining armour sent to save them and their money; now, they viewed him as a badly tarnished, untrustworthy robber baron.

McCartney's 1970 lawsuit against The Beatles was based on his distrust of the American. In a statement to the judge, McCartney's barrister David Hirst said: "Mr. Klein cannot be trusted with the stewardship of the partnership, property, and assets ... Mr. Klein has paid himself commission to which he is not entitled and is asserting an entitlement to even more ... Our confidence in Mr. Klein has not been enhanced by the fact that on 29th January he was convicted on ten tax offences by a jury in a New York Federal District Court." Klein had form. He started cooking the books almost as soon as he got his feet under the desk. He had negotiated a new deal with Capitol that increased The Beatles' royalty rate in the US from 17.5 percent to 25 percent, and was contractually entitled to 20 percent of the 7.5 percent increase. But he had charged a commission of £852,000 (£8,865,959.93), 20 percent of the new 25 percent royalty, which had already been paid to him at the time of the hearing. McCartney claimed this was at least £500,000 (£5,203,028.13) too high. "And we got him! That was the only thing we caught him on, and we couldn't send him to jail for that, but at least we could get a judgment."

Klein couldn't help himself, and in March 1972, he was at it again. He was accused of skimming $1.14 from every *Concert For Bangla Desh* album. Something he denied. Not even he would take the rice from a starving child's bowl. The accusation was published in *New York Magazine*. Klein demanded a printed retraction. When that wasn't forthcoming, he called a press conference to announce his suit against the magazine and to explain where all the money had gone. This didn't go as planned. His staff made the mistake of inviting the underground press to the event. A. J. Weberman, a Rock Liberation Front member, insulted Klein and threw rotten vegetables around the plush office. It was hardly surprising that Klein had grown tired of Lennon's activism if this was how his associates acted. With mainstream media in attendance, Klein was smart enough to know not to make a big deal of the disturbance. Unfortunately, Phil Spector wasn't as smart and started exchanging verbal and physical insults with the journalists. Fong-Torres of *Rolling Stone* reported that when Weberman called Klein a "rip-off," Spector yelled back that he should "go sell hot dogs in front of Dylan's house!" None of this can have gone down well with Harrison or Lennon. To undo the damage, Klein placed ads in all the trade publications (costing an average of $1,500 a page). Finally, he filed a suit for defamation and damages.

Almost everything about the charity concert had been poorly managed, with the result that Harrison had to write a personal cheque to the Inland Revenue for £1,000,000 (£10,406,056.25) to satisfy constant tax claims by the British government. If that didn't anger Harrison, it later transpired that *New York Magazine* had been right about Klein for the wrong reason. He wasn't skimming $1.14 from every *Concert For Bangla Desh* album; instead, he was selling promotional albums to wholesalers and not accounting for them. It transpired that he was the kind of man who would take the rice from a starving child's bowl after all. In 1979, he was imprisoned for two months for not declaring income from selling Apple promotional records between 1970 and 1972.

If Klein's creative accounting and downright financial chicanery weren't worrying enough, there was the small matter of his plans to take control of Apple and, therefore, The Beatles' earnings. At the Annual Meeting of Stockholders on 15th February 1972, Klein clarified his intentions to buy Apple. He later claimed that Lennon, Harrison, and Starr were prepared to buy McCartney's 25% share of the business, which would have ended the dispute and let ABKCO take control of Apple. As they'd already lost Northern Songs to ATV, The Beatles weren't about to lose Apple to ABKCO. McCartney certainly wasn't going to let it happen. No matter how much he wanted rid of Klein. On 8th April, Klein acknowledged that McCartney had stopped his cunning plan to take control of Apple. "Paul rejected a £1 million offer by the other Beatles to buy him out of their partnership. But Paul turned it down. He wouldn't take it. He wasn't interested. He doesn't want to sell. He doesn't want to get out, and that's really the problem. Now you have a company with four partners, each of whom has a different interest, and to get each one to agree something, like whether Ringo should make a film, becomes almost impossible. How do they stay partners? It's very hard. I had hoped to arrange a takeover of Apple and The Beatles' interests, merging them with my ABKCO Industries. But my hopes were defeated by McCartney's attitude. ABKCO Industries earned about £2.6 million (£27,055,746.26) from its 20% commission on Apple earnings over the four years but in the last three months of 1972, the commission was only £100,000 (£1,040,605.63)."

Selling Apple to another business would have gone some way to disentangling The Beatles' byzantine partnership. Indeed, the idea had been floated two years earlier. It came from McCartney's legal team, and unsurprisingly, it didn't involve ABKCO. A memo from McCartney's barrister dated 13th May 1971 proposed selling Apple to EMI. The proposal was that EMI would buy 80% of Apple, with the individual Beatles retaining their 5% share of the company as a form of annuity. However, even this suggestion would have required all four to agree to a change in the partnership agreement to bring about the sale. It was also made clear that any such sale came with taxation problems and was reliant on the Inland Revenue to come to a reasonable settlement over the tax liabilities. As Harrison had learned to his cost, when he wrote a cheque to the Inland Revenue for £1 million to cover the tax owed on the *Concert For Bandga Desh* project, the chances of the Revenue coming to any reasonable settlement was unlikely.

Selling Apple to EMI was always a long shot because it would have meant The Beatles losing control of their recordings, royalties, and future releases. As they had formed Apple partly to have more control over their music, selling it to EMI was unlikely. The Beatles' relationship with their record label hadn't always run smoothly.

Could they trust EMI any more than they could trust Klien? Handing EMI control of everything they'd fought for, simply to dissolve their partnership, only made the proposition even more unpalatable. The Beatles were still selling millions of records around the world. Add to that sales of all the solo albums, and the numbers would make any self-respecting vinyl mogul blush. The previous month, *Billboard* reported: "The UK record industry, having experienced one of the best years ever, is expected to maintain its momentum in 1973. And the retail trade, too, is confident that the incredible selling bonanza which started in early summer and carried through the Christmas period will continue through January and February and well into the year." Record sales were booming around the world. *Billboard* also reported on Christmas sales in Canada. Once again, The Beatles dominated. "A&A, Sam the Record Man, and the vast Eatons merchandising group reported that Beatles' product had been one of the strongest items in this year's gift buying. Sam Sniderman said that he expected to have moved in excess of 5,000 copies of the George Harrison *All Things Must Pass* set alone in one store during December." Not bad for an album that was two years old.

This was music to the ears of one man, Allen Klein. In February 1973, at an ABKCO Industries stockholders' meeting held at the Warwick Hotel, he confirmed that The Beatles sold more than 2,000,000 LP units of their catalogue product each year. These figures would be exceeded in 1973 with the release of the *Red* and *Blue* compilations. He also claimed that in the first quarter of the year, income from The Beatles comprised only 6% of ABKCO's gross for the quarter. Only weeks earlier, *Cash Box* reported that "ABKCO Industries, Inc. had reported net income of $1,399,000 ($9,600,858.06) or $1.05 per share on revenues of $11,210,000 ($77,868,346.17) for the fiscal year ended 30th September. These amounts compare to income of $559,000 or 42¢ per share on revenues of $8,936,000 ($61,324,708.83) for the prior fiscal year. These results are equal to an increase of 63% in net income before extraordinary items, an increase of 150% in net income, and an increase of 25% in revenues."

A lot more money would have flowed Klein's way had his plans to release a Beatles film alongside the new greatest hits album become a reality. However, McCartney wasn't the only person working to stop Klein's plans. The relationship with Klein was so bad that Neil Aspinall, The Beatles gatekeeper, worked to ensure that Klein's proposal to release the film that he'd been working on came to nothing. Aspinall formed a new company, Standby Films, to take ownership of the film to ensure that they rather than Klein had control of it. Any proposed tie-in with a Beatles hits compilation wasn't going to happen if Aspinall had anything to do with it.

Klein may have lost control of the film, but until this contract to manage The Beatles/Apple expired, he still controlled what was or wasn't released. He wasted no time blocking the sale of the *Alpha Omega* album. He filed a lawsuit on behalf of George Harrison, Capitol Records, and Apple Records against Audiotapes, Inc., Elias Saka, Electro-Scanning Systems Ltd., Leon Nasar, TV Products, Inc., Economic Consultants, Inc., American Broadcasting Companies, Inc., WPIX, Inc., and John Does 1 thru 100. Klein's lawsuit demanded a permanent injunction against the defendants to stop them from duplicating The Beatles' records and tapes, from advertising and selling their records, and from using The Beatles' names, pictures or likenesses "which they are doing wrongfully and without authorization by 'pirating' the material from albums and tapes rightfully produced and sold by plaintiffs Apple and Capitol." The action also placed an injunction on The Beatles' name or likenesses being used in radio, TV, and magazine commercials in New York and other states. ABC agreed that it would not sell, advertise, or promote records or tapes in the future without obtaining prior written approval from Apple Records and would not permit the use of the names "Beatles" or portraits or pictures without similar permission from Apple.

Other charges in the action indicated that Economic Consultants, Inc. ran ads for a four-disc set, "The Story of The Beatles," in magazines such as *Motor Trend, Oui, Penthouse, Car and Driver*, and *Signature*. The lawsuit also stated that since 1st Sept 1969, Apple had paid The Beatles $19,000,000 ($133,655,585.59) in royalties and that Harrison demanded $15,000,000 ($105,517,567.57) in punitive damages for improper use of his name, portrait, picture, and/or likeness for purposes of advertising and trade. In short, the plaintiffs were in big trouble for using The Beatles' name and likeness. Because of the vagaries of US copyright law, it would be difficult to get a conviction for copyright infringement. This is why the lawsuit focused on violating name and image rights.

Klein's next move was to plan an official response to the *Alpha Omega* album. This wasn't difficult as EMI already had a greatest hits package in development, tentatively titled *The Best Of The Beatles*. Capitol Records wasted no time confirming that the new Beatles albums were intended to work alongside Klein's lawsuits to stop the sale of bootleg records. Brown Meggs, vice president of Capitol Records, said: "We will be issuing, on Apple, a two-record set of vintage Beatles songs to counteract the sale of the bootleg Beatles records, called *Alpha Omega*, which are currently being blatantly advertised on television and in newspapers across the country. We feel it will be easier to fight the bootleg product with a rival package than through the courts. It's appropriate and right that The Beatles have, on Apple, the official authorised collection put together by themselves."

Besides signing off the track listing and artwork, The Beatles had little to do with putting the albums together. Lennon explained the process: "Allen Klein knocked out the basic list for the Red and Blue albums, and then we'd just look down it and say, 'yes, no,' and so on. I made sure they put that picture which I got Linda (McCartney) [sic] to take of the same pose as our first album... No one can release old Beatles product without an okay from each of us. I like packages, you know. I approve of everything I would buy myself. I'd buy The Beatles one... I asked for George Martin to reproduce the tracks. I was involved in that respect, just checking on the condition of them because I didn't want lousy versions going out. I wanted them to be as it was. I asked Capitol/EMI to please ask George Martin to take care of this... at least he knows what to do. I don't want some strange guy, you know, making dubbed versions of it and putting it out..."

Lennon's explanation about how the *Red* and *Blue* albums came to be is only partially correct. The albums were programmed by Allan Steckler, an ABKCO employee managing Apple Records, who compiled the albums chronologically using the group's British release dates. "I was an ABKCO employee. Klein knew that my allegiance was to him, but when it came to artistic issues, I would always side with the artists if I could, and the artists knew that as well. I ran the Apple label by myself," he explained. "I didn't have anyone to help ... I ran around like crazy. Anything that had to be done, I did. I coordinated all the releases and got designers to do the art." Steckler's idea was to use the Angus McBean photos for the album covers and employ Tom Wilkes, who had recently worked on Harrison's *All Things Must Pass*, to design the sleeves. Although Lennon asked George Martin to assemble the audio masters for the album, Capitol compiled the audio for the US release. Rather than contact EMI in the UK to provide masters, Capitol decided to compile the albums using masters it held. Consequently, some tracks were issued in mono or duophonic stereo, even though actual stereo mixes existed.

Although McCartney had signed off the albums, he wasn't keen to be associated with his past. A past that remained a thorn in his side, that still hurt and shone a bright light on his current musical activities. "I don't like these old remember when things," he said. "I don't like talking about the old thing when inevitably anything I say I'm doing now won't match up to all glorious things they'll show happened in the past." When asked about the *Red* and *Blue* albums he seemed more interested in stopping the bootleggers than maintaining The Beatles' legacy. "The bootlegging thing was one of the reasons. I didn't take an awful lot of interest in them, actually. I still haven't heard them. I know what's on them because I've heard it all before, you know. I haven't really taken much interest in Beatles stuff of late just because there has been this hangover of Apple and Klein. The whole scene has gone so bloody sick. The four ex-Beatles are totally up to here with it. Everyone wants it solved so everyone can get on with being a bit peaceful with each other."

While Klein was working to stop the sale of unauthorized albums, Lennon and McCartney had been renegotiating their contracts with Northern Songs/ATV. Upon re-signing with Grade, a condition placed on McCartney and Lennon was that they would agree to work on projects closely associated with his media empire. To this end, McCartney wrote the theme music for the ATV series *Zoo Gang*, in return for which he was given his television special *James Paul McCartney*. A year later, Lennon re-signed with Northern Songs/ATV and agreed to perform on a television show celebrating the great media mogul *Salute to Sir Lew Grad*e. It would be his last live television appearance.

Sir Lew Grade wasn't the only businessman chasing lucrative songwriting contracts. McCartney may not have shown much interest in his past, but he was still very interested in his hero, Buddy Holly. In particular, he had his eye on the rocker's song catalogue. Eastman and Eastman had been working on McCartney's behalf to purchase Nor-Va-Jak Music for $100,000 ($686,265.77). Although McCartney didn't "like these old remember when things," he was keen to invest in them. McCartney had learned from his mistakes. Despite their business problems, money continued to flow into The Beatles' coffer. Once their differences had been resolved, each Beatle would receive a considerable windfall from the official receiver. Some of it had to be invested, and McCartney knew that investing in copyrights was a surefire winner. Besides, he was a fan of Buddy Holly. The Texan musician had influenced The Beatles, from their songwriting to their name. "I thought, if you're going to have to spend money on something, it might as well be something you really love rather than just, I don't know, a brush factory or something," he explained. "My business advisor was talking to me and said 'What kind of thing do you love then?' and I mentioned Buddy Holly as being one of the things. And it so happened that Buddy's music came up for sale in America, so my business advisor said, 'Why don't you buy it?' And there was nothing I'd love more, really, because that way I feel like I can protect the stuff [Buddy's music] so there's no big rip-offs for people like his widow, and also I can help popularise his music, too, just by being associated with it."

As well as the £3,000 (£31,218.17) monthly wage the official receiver paid him, McCartney had money coming in from his latest hit, 'Hi, Hi, HI'. By the second week of February, it had reached its US chart high of number 10. One place above Wings was Hurricane Smith with 'Oh Babe What Would You Say'. Hurricane Smith was none other than Norman Smith, who had engineered some of The Beatles' biggest hits, and here he was, outselling McCartney. Wings weren't only in competition with The Beatles' old sound engineer. They were up against some stiff competition. Elton John was number 1 with 'Crocodile Rock,' followed by Carly Simon and Stevie Wonder.

Wings continued adding the finishing touches to their new album, which was slowly taking shape. Songs were sequenced into running orders to see which worked best. But having worked on the album for the best part of a year, McCartney must have felt the strain. Work stopped again, and Wings went on holiday. McCartney flew his family and band to Morocco for much-needed rest and recreation. He may have even considered the television special he had agreed to make for Lew Grade's ATV. However, according to Denny Seiwell, most of the time was spent searching for and smoking hashish.

While Wings were relaxing in a haze of hashish smoke, George Harrison worked hard to complete his new album. The basic tracks had been recorded at his new home studio F.P.S.H.O.T. (Friar Park Studio Henley On Thames), with overdubs taking place at Apple's newly refurbished studio in Savile Row, namely vocals, lead guitar parts, Jim Horn's contributions, and percussion. The Indian classical instruments sitar, flute, and tabla were added to the 'spiritual sky' sections of 'Living In The Material World'. The final elements to be recorded were John Barham's orchestral and choir arrangements for 'The Day the World Gets 'Round,' 'Who Can See It' and 'That Is All.' Harrison also employed Pete Ham from Badfinger to play on the album. Pete attended several sessions at Apple Studios but wasn't credited on the album. It may be that Harrison decided not to use any of the guitar parts recorded by Ham, or he may have forgotten to give Pete the credit he was due. Although Badfinger remained signed with Apple Records, they had started to loosen their ties with the company. The previous month, they signed a long-term, worldwide publishing agreement with Warner Bros. Music, which would take effect at the termination of the group's publishing agreement with Apple.

As Harrison was putting the finishing touches to his album, he prepared a version of 'Give Me Love (Give me Peace On Earth)' for broadcast exclusively by the BBC. Standard practice was to record this kind of material at BBC studios, usually somewhere like Maida Vale Studios, London. Had Harrison recorded at the BBC, he would have faced three issues. Firstly, BBC studios weren't as sophisticated as commercial studios. Consequently, recordings made at BBC studios wouldn't have been up to Harrison's standard. He was a perfectionist when it came to audio fidelity. Secondly, if he recorded at a BBC studio, he would have to record three or four songs in one three-hour session. As he often spent that long recording a single guitar overdub, he wouldn't have wanted to work to the kind of schedule demanded by the BBC. Thirdly, if he'd recorded in a BBC studio, they would own the copyright to the sound recording. By recording outside of the BBC, he bypassed all three issues; he could spend as long as he liked recording and mixing the songs, and, more importantly, EMI/Apple would own the copyright to the sound recording. Any such recordings were valuable assets and worth considerably more than the fee he'd receive from the BBC. More importantly, this alternative version would ensure airplay on a national radio station. Played alongside the commercial version, it gave Harrison maximum exposure on the BBC's most prominent radio network.

Harrison also found time to help Nicky Hopkins to record his album. Weekdays were spent recording Harrison's album, and on weekends, the musicians worked on Nicky Hopkins' solo album, *The Tin Man Was a Dreamer*. "I wanted to record it at Apple, but George [Harrison] started doing his album, which I think turned out great. So we'd record George during the week, and I'd do my album on the weekends," Hopkins explained. On finishing the album, Harrison flew to Los Angeles to attend Beatles/Apple-related business meetings and to begin work on Ravi Shankar's Shankar Family & Friends and Ringo Starr's *Ringo*.

WEEK ENDING 3 FEBRUARY 1973
1. CROCODILE ROCK: ELTON JOHN
2. YOU'RE SO VAIN: CARLY SIMON
3. SUPERSTITION: STEVIE WONDER
4. WHY CAN'T WE LIVE TOGETHER: TIMMY THOMAS
5. YOUR MAMA DON'T DANCE: KENNY LOGGINS & JIM MESSINA
6. OH, BABE, WHAT WOULD YOU SAY?: HURRICANE SMITH
7. TROUBLE MAN: MARVIN GAYE
8. THE WORLD IS A GHETTO: WAR
9. DO IT AGAIN: STEELY DAN
10. HI, HI, HI: WINGS

WEEK ENDING 10 FEBRUARY 1973
1. CROCODILE ROCK: ELTON JOHN
2. YOU'RE SO VAIN: CARLY SIMON
3. WHY CAN'T WE LIVE TOGETHER: TIMMY THOMAS
4. OH, BABE, WHAT WOULD YOU SAY?: HURRICANE SMITH
5. SUPERSTITION: STEVIE WONDER
6. DO IT AGAIN: STEELY DAN
7. THE WORLD IS A GHETTO: WAR
8. TROUBLE MAN: MARVIN GAYE
9. DON'T EXPECT ME TO BE YOUR FRIEND: LOBO
10. COULD IT BE I'M FALLING IN LOVE: THE SPINNERS

WEEK ENDING 17 FEBRUARY 1973
1. CROCODILE ROCK: ELTON JOHN
2. YOU'RE SO VAIN: CARLY SIMON
3. OH, BABE, WHAT WOULD YOU SAY?: HURRICANE SMITH
4. DUELING BANJOS: DELIVERANCE/ERIC WEISSBERG & STEVE MANDELL
5. KILLING ME SOFTLY WITH HIS SONG: ROBERTA FLACK
6. DO IT AGAIN: STEELY DAN
7. COULD IT BE I'M FALLING IN LOVE: THE SPINNERS
8. DON'T EXPECT ME TO BE YOUR FRIEND: LOBO
9. WHY CAN'T WE LIVE TOGETHER: TIMMY THOMAS
10. ROCKY MOUNTAIN HIGH: JOHN DENVER

WEEK ENDING 24 FEBRUARY 1973
1. KILLING ME SOFTLY WITH HIS SONG: ROBERTA FLACK
2. DUELING BANJOS: DELIVERANCE/ERIC WEISSBERG & STEVE MANDELL
3. CROCODILE ROCK: ELTON JOHN
4. YOU'RE SO VAIN: CARLY SIMON
5. COULD IT BE I'M FALLING IN LOVE: THE SPINNERS
6. DO IT AGAIN: STEELY DAN
7. LAST SONG: EDWARD BEAR
8. DON'T EXPECT ME TO BE YOUR FRIEND: LOBO
9. LOVE TRAIN: THE O'JAYS
10. ROCKY MOUNTAIN HIGH: JOHN DENVER

UK

WEEK ENDING 3 FEBRUARY 1973
1. BLOCKBUSTER: THE SWEET
2. DO YOU WANNA TOUCH ME? (OH YEAH!): GARY GLITTER
3. PART OF THE UNION: STRAWBS
4. YOU'RE SO VAIN: CARLY SIMON
5. DANIEL: ELTON JOHN
6. LONG HAIRED LOVER FROM LIVERPOOL: LITTLE JIMMY OSMOND
7. WISHING WELL: FREE
8. PAPER PLANE: STATUS QUO
9. SYLVIA: FOCUS
10. ROLL OVER BEETHOVEN: ELECTRIC LIGHT ORCHESTRA

WEEK ENDING 10 FEBRUARY 1973
1. BLOCKBUSTER: THE SWEET
2. PART OF THE UNION: STRAWBS
3. DO YOU WANNA TOUCH ME? (OH YEAH!): GARY GLITTER
4. DANIEL: ELTON JOHN
5. SYLVIA: FOCUS
6. ROLL OVER BEETHOVEN: ELECTRIC LIGHT ORCHESTRA
7. WHISKY IN THE JAR: THIN LIZZY
8. YOU'RE SO VAIN: CARLY SIMON
9. LONG HAIRED LOVER FROM LIVERPOOL: LITTLE JIMMY OSMOND
10. PAPER PLANE: STATUS QUO

WEEK ENDING 17 FEBRUARY 1973
1. BLOCKBUSTER: THE SWEET
2. PART OF THE UNION: STRAWBS
3. DO YOU WANNA TOUCH ME? (OH YEAH!): GARY GLITTER
4. SYLVIA: FOCUS
5. CINDY INCIDENTALLY: THE FACES
6. WHISKY IN THE JAR: THIN LIZZY
7. DANIEL: ELTON JOHN
8. ROLL OVER BEETHOVEN: ELECTRIC LIGHT ORCHESTRA
9. LOOKING THROUGH THE EYES OF LOVE: THE PARTRIDGE FAMILY
10. BABY I LOVE YOU: DAVE EDMUNDS

WEEK ENDING 24 FEBURARY 1973
1. CUM ON FEEL THE NOIZE: SLADE
2. PART OF THE UNION: STRAWBS
3. BLOCKBUSTER: THE SWEET
4. SYLVIA: FOCUS
5. CINDY INCIDENTALLY: THE FACES
6. DO YOU WANNA TOUCH ME? (OH YEAH!): GARY GLITTER
7. WHISKY IN THE JAR: THIN LIZZY
8. BABY I LOVE YOU: DAVE EDMUNDS
9. LOOKING THROUGH THE EYES OF LOVE: THE PARTRIDGE FAMILY
10. FEEL THE NEED IN ME: DETROIT EMERALDS

CHAPTER 3
MARCH: WHOA OH-OH IS ME

In February 1973, Bhaskar Menon, president of Capitol Records, revealed what an asset the company had in The Beatles. *Billboard* magazine reported that Capitol's profits were booming. It earned $1,098,000 ($7,627,069.05) on sales of $37,956,000 ($263,654,857.03) for the second quarter of the fiscal year. Menon explained that although it represented an increase in profit, sales were down compared to the corresponding period a year previously because there had been no new "album product by The Beatles [...] released in the first half of this fiscal year." Menon had increased productivity and profitability at Capitol. However, it still depended on The Beatles, a band that had broken up three years earlier. Nevertheless, 1973 was going to be a hectic year for The Beatles and Capitol Records. Not only were there two new compilation albums, but there were also two new albums by Wings and a new album each by Lennon, Harrison, and Starr. By the end of the year, Capitol would be floating on a sea of cash.

However, sales were still being undermined by pirate and bootleg records. A report in the 10th February issue of *Billboard* stated that in Pittsburgh, many record dealers had suffered upward of a 40 percent sales loss and that some shops had been forced to either close or sell their operations. The problem was attributed to radio advertisements offering three and four-LP sets for $10.00 ($69.46).

The Beatles had taken steps to stop the advertisement of bootleg records and were winning. ABC had responded to ABKCO's lawsuit and pulled adverts for the unauthorized *Alpha Omega* 4 LP set and had agreed not to sell, advertise or promote records or tapes in the future without obtaining prior written approval from Apple Records and that it would not permit the use of the names "Beatles" or portraits or pictures without similar permission from Apple. In a statement issued by ABKCO, Klein said, "George is doing this not only for The Beatles and himself, but for all artists throughout the record industry. So much of the litigation that has taken place to date involves music publishers and the complex copyright laws, but no one has acted on behalf of the artist who is being deprived of his right of privacy, who is being deprived of his livelihood by not receiving a cent in royalties from the bootleggers, whose artistic rights are being infringed upon and whose contracts are being interfered with. I'm glad that George, on behalf of The Beatles, has taken this stand in an effort to establish precedents on behalf of all the artists who are victims of the pirates. I expect other radio and TV stations as well as magazines, especially those associated with music and record companies as well as all others, will follow ABC's fine lead in refusing advertising from pirates."

While Harrison was doing his bit to defeat the pirates, the US government was doing its best to piss him off. Harrison was due to visit the US in April to start work on a new Ravi Shankar album. However, he agreed to rearrange his schedule and fly out a month early to attend important business meetings with Lennon, Starr and Klein. Harrison took the scenic route to the US and flew via Pakistan. Arriving in the US in the second week of March, he was detained at the airport but eventually allowed into the country. Like Lennon, Harrison was on the FBI's radar and required a visa waiver to enter the US due to his reputation as a narcotics user. His visa application said he was visiting "to engage in legal consultation with his attorneys and Mr John Lennon in Los Angeles and with business manager, Mr Allen Klein, in New York." The visa stated that no extension would be granted without prior authorisation from INS Washington. Harrison was none too happy at being detained on his arrival, but he became even more annoyed when his application to extend his stay until 30th June was refused. Nevertheless, he could attend his meetings and even do a little work on the side, hopefully without the INS finding out about it.

Ringo Starr was the only Beatle who didn't have problems getting into or out of the US and had arrived a few days ahead of Harrison. On 3rd March, he was in Nashville to collect Grammy awards for the *Concert For Bangla Desh* album, which had won Album of the Year in 1972. Two weeks later, on 16th March, he was supposed to be in Holland to act as Master of Ceremonies for a TV pop show. Starr had accepted the invitation in principle. Peter Howard of Apple Films had agreed on the conditions for his appearance, but it wasn't to be. Starr was in Los Angeles recording a new album, and on the night of the 16th, he, John, and Yoko went to the movies to watch Marlon Brando in *Last Tango In Paris*.

In December 1972, Starr gave several interviews to promote the different film projects he was working on. In one interview, he complained about how busy he'd been. If he wasn't directing a film, he was acting in a film, promoting a film, or planning a film. "I haven't had a day off this year," he said. "Once you say 'go' and you're the producer, you're first in and last out." He'd also been recording with other artists, from Harry Nilsson to The Who. If anything, he'd been neglecting his recording career in favour of making films and helping others. But that was about to change. The time had come to call in a few favours and recruit an all-star band to help record his next long-playing record. Life in the fast lane is fast, and Starr had no intention of slowing down.

According to Starr, his new album came together by accident. "I worked with Harry Nilsson in London on his album (*Son Of Schmilsson*) with producer Richard Perry. So Harry and I were invited to do the Grammy awards, and Richard was saying, 'Remember you were talking to me in the club one night, you know... You'd like to do something? After the Grammys, why don't you come down to LA for a week?' And we went in. It worked so well, in ten days we had eight tracks, you see. Once we started we couldn't stop. And then I got John to write me something, and I got Paul, I got George. You know... dragged in all me friends, 'cuz I'm lucky – I got a lot of people who'll work for me. I'll work for them, but I always feel very lucky that people will come out for me."

Richard Perry remembers it differently and claims he called Starr on the telephone to remind him about their plans to work together: "Ringo was a drummer who I had long admired. Then we got friendly, and one night we were sitting together in Tramp, the London club, semi-inebriated, and I told him how wonderful I thought it would be if he were to do a solo album. I felt that it would have a tremendous audience, although he was very sceptical about it, having had the experience of Beatle albums, which apparently took a tremendous amount of time and obvious care, and he was assuming that the same sort of thing would be more of an ordeal than he wanted to go through. He appreciated my suggestion, but for the moment, decided to shelve it. [Later, I said] 'Remember you talked about going to the studio? Let's go in and see what happens'. So without any lawyers knowing anything about it, we came back to LA, and in five days had recorded five tracks, which included the three major singles from the album, 'Photograph', 'You're Sixteen' and 'Oh My My'."

While The Threetles were keeping busy in LA, McCartney and Wings were filming their television special for Lew Grade's ATV. The show was produced by Gary Smith and Dwight Hemion, who had been responsible for Elvis Presley's '68 Comeback Special. Presley's television show is widely regarded as reinvigorating his career. In many ways, it was the antithesis of the bland Hollywood fodder he'd been required to churn out year after year. It was a return to the Presley of old. Presley, the rocker and musician. This was precisely what McCartney needed. Wings hadn't exactly got off to a flying start but a well-produced prime-time television show had the potential to do just that. "[...] These people wanted us to do a TV show and they said they wanted a nice show and said you can do it anyway you want," McCartney recalled. "This seemed like a good opportunity, you know, to kinda get on the telly. So that one was just worked up that way. We met the guy when we went to Morocco. We were on holiday then and they came out and sat around the pool and talked about various ideas and came back to England and did it."

There was only one problem. As with *Magical Mystery Tour*, McCartney took control of the show's content and cobbled together a free-flowing, non-narrative programme that lacked any musical or visual consistency. It wobbled from live performances – the best part of the show – to kitsch pop promos and a Busby Berkeley-style dance routine. "We've got a script, but we are playing it by ear. We want it to be as spontaneous as possible. We've got a lot of original ideas, but if they don't come off as well as we hope they won't be used. Especially the comedy. We hope they'll be a lot of laughs," McCartney explained.

One of McCartney's more bizarre ideas was thankfully vetoed. McCartney thought it would be a wheeze to appear in drag as Diana Ross. This may have seemed like a giggle when stoned on Morocco's finest hashish. But not so in the cold light of an English March day. According to McCartney, it was the US sponsors who we have to thank for insisting that it was axed. "We had little things in there that would have been a bit mind-blowing. Like we were gonna do a drag scene. I do a song and dance thing and in the middle of it we were going to change all into drag and I was gonna come on and do like a big Diana Ross bit. And Linda was gonna be a fella and all the others were going to be girls. But Chevrolet sent a very heavy letter saying, 'Due to the sponsorship blah blah blah.' Chevrolet were the money behind it."

Because Wings were busy indulging McCartney's filmic fantasies, they had to reschedule their first UK tour of theatres. However, rather than say that the tour had been postponed, McCartney's manager, Vincent Romeo, decided that the best thing to do was say nothing and demanded that the booking agency, MAM, do likewise. A further sign of The Beatles' thawing relationship occurred around this time. McCartney contacted Mal Evans, The Beatles' road manager, amanuensis, and Apple executive and asked him to assemble a team of roadies for Wings' British tour. The last time Evans had worked for McCartney was in 1970, and all that involved was moving sound equipment to Morgan Studios. McCartney wanted nothing to do with Apple and consequently cut himself off from its day-to-day running and the people it employed. This included Evans. Now that The Beatles' managerial and business issues were moving closer to mutual resolution, McCartney once again called on the one person he knew to be the best person for the job.

One thing Romeo couldn't hide was McCartney's appearance in court, where, once again, he was facing charges of possession of cannabis. The difference this time was that he'd grown it himself. On 8th March, Paul and Linda McCartney flew by private jet to attend the hearing in Campbeltown, Scotland. McCartney was up before the beak for cultivating five cannabis plants in his greenhouse at High Park and two counts of possession of cannabis. McCartney's defence that fans sent the seeds and he had no idea what would come up when he planted them didn't convince the judge. Sheriff D. J. McDiarmid had none of it and fined McCartney £100, giving him 14 days to pay. McCartney shrugged off the fine; he'd spent £1000 on a private aeroplane to attend the hearing and made light of the ramifications his latest conviction may have had on his ability to enter the US. Talking to a reporter outside the courthouse, he said: "I understand that I might not get stopped from going into the States because it's a technical offence; I hope not anyway." Tell that to John and George. It did create problems, although they would be overcome. Meanwhile, the FBI and INS went about their business and added McCartney's name to their list of narcotics-using reprobates.

The following day, the McCartneys returned to Elstree to film a scene that featured Paul performing several songs, accompanying himself with acoustic guitar. The raw footage ran for over 40 minutes, but many performances were incomplete. McCartney's butterfly mind was racing from one song to another, pitching on one for a few bars before trying something else. The final scene showed McCartney performing 'Blackbird,' 'Bluebird,' 'Michelle' and 'Heart Of The Country'. ('Bluebird' was edited out of the US version of the show.)

Lennon, Harrison, Starr and Ono's contract with Klein had expired in February. But unsure of how to proceed, the contract had been renewed bi-weekly. With solo and Beatles releases in the pipeline, they had to work out something fast. Ono, who had attended the meetings to discuss their future, explained what they were looking for. "We really need someone who is an administrator, someone who can take care of our needs who also knows the legal side of things. In a way, Allen has a good head on his shoulders, but it fits his needs. It's not like The Beatles are just starting – John, George and Ringo are certainly established stars, they don't really need a manager; what they need are accountants, lawyers not someone who wants to be a pop star himself."

One of the many reasons The Beatles formed Apple Corps Ltd was to administer their many income streams, manage their accounts and minimise their tax liabilities. It was also there to represent them legally and protect their assets. Klein was hired to bring some order to the chaos they'd inadvertently created. He'd been mostly successful but had created a few problems that they could have done without. Perhaps it was because he had to represent four very different personalities while dealing with the legal consequences of a fifth who wanted to dissolve the partnership, rather than dealing with the group as a single entity, that stretched even his ability as a manager.

Two days after Starr appeared at the Grammys, work started on his album. The sessions were the very model of efficiency. Basic tracks for eight songs were recorded in ten days. Mal Evans was on hand to help organise the sessions, and one of the first songs Starr and the band rehearsed was Evans' 'You're Thinking Of Me'. On the first day of recording, they also tackled Randy Newman's 'Have You Seen My Baby' and the Sherman Brothers' 'You're Sixteen'. The album quickly began to resemble a Beatles reunion. Besides Evans, Harrison contributed 'Photograph,' 'Sunshine Life For Me (Sail Away Raymond)' and 'You And Me (Babe),' co-written with Mal Evans. Harrison had only been issued a visitor's visa, not a work visa, so he was breaking the conditions under which he'd been allowed to enter the US. But that was precisely the kind of devil-may-care attitude you could expect from someone with a reputation as a narcotics user.

Lennon contributed 'I'm The Greatest,' which was recorded on Tuesday 13th March. Richard Perry: "It was on that session that John came down, and it was the first time that I had met John. To say that it was an exciting experience to work with him would be a gross understatement because it was really quite unique and very special, and something I'll never forget, which goes without saying. The song wasn't quite complete, so we started to run it down, so there was also that very special thrill of experiencing a song being completed in the studio by John Lennon, and we all gathered round the piano and chipped in our ideas to help to complete it. Then the phone rang and it was George, who said, 'I hear there's a track going down. Is it OK if I come?', and I said, 'Hold on a minute, and I'll ask John if it's OK'. So here I am asking John if George can come down... And John said, 'Hell, yes, tell him to get down here and help me finish this bridge'. That was very much like John, and it was on that session that the three of them played for the first time, I believe, since the break-up of The Beatles."

It was like the old days, and to enhance the illusion, Mal Evans was on hand. Evans had moved to Los Angeles to rebuild his life and would hang out with group members when they hit town. Harrison and Evans even wrote a song together. They seemed to have been reminiscing about the good old days when they penned 'You And Me (Babe)' a romantic remake of 'With A Little Help From My Friends' for Starr. Looking back through rose-tinted spectacles to a time before the mania made their lives unbearable, it's a lyrical and musical snapshot of the band's golden era. Harrison perfectly tailored the song to Starr's friendly persona and vocal range. Perry's master-stroke was to programme it as the closing song on the album. Having Starr thank everybody involved brought the album to a perfect end. (It was a trick Lennon would borrow for his Rock 'n' Roll album.)

With three Beatles in town, rumours quickly spread about a reunion. The *Melody Maker* reported, "Rumours flashed through Los Angeles this week that three of The Beatles have again teamed up for recording purposes. John Lennon, George Harrison and Ringo Starr are all in Los Angeles with Klaus Voorman, the bassist rumoured to replace Paul McCartney after his departure from the group." The rumours persisted despite Capitol Record issuing a denial that a reunion was taking place. Lennon issued a typically humorous statement that had a dig at his ex-manager and ex-bandmate. "Although John and Yoko and George, and George and Ringo have played together often, it was the first time the three Beatles had played together since, well, since they last played together. As usual, an awful lot of rumours, if not downright lies, were going on, including the possibility of impresario Allen De Kline of ABKCO playing bass for the other three in an as yet untitled album called 'I Was A Teenage Fat Cat.' Producer, Richard Perry, who planned to take the tapes along to sell them to Paul McCartney, told a friend, 'I'll take the tapes to Paul McCartney.' The extreme humility that existed between John and Paul seems to have evaporated. They've spoken to each other on the telephone, and in English, that's a change, said a McCartney associate. 'If only everything were as simple and unaffected as McCartney's new single 'My Love' well then maybe Dean Martin and Jerry Lewis would be reunited with the Marx Bros., and Newsweek (sic) could get a job,' said an East African official - yours up to the teeth - John Lennon and Yoko Ono."

While Lennon, Harrison and Starr were having the time of their lives working together on a new song, McCartney's woes continued to dog him. On the same day as his ex-bandmates were recording 'I'm The Greatest' in LA, Henry McCullough and Denny Seiwell were having words with McCartney's manager. Neither were happy with the way the band was being run. When they joined Wings, they had been told they were joining what amounted to a workers' cooperative, each receiving a share of the income from concerts and recordings. This happened when they headed out on their first low-key tour of English universities. At the end of each gig, the band shared the door money. However, with little live work on the cards and a much more extensive UK tour having been postponed, they were still struggling to make ends meet on their weekly retainer of £70 (£724).

Whatever Vincent Romeo told them wasn't enough. On 14th March, Henry McCullough gave notice to quit. McCartney was in trouble. They were still working on the television special, and although the tour had been postponed, it hadn't been cancelled. McCartney needed McCullouch more than McCullouch needed him. An olive branch in the form of a £500 (£5,174.73) bonus for having to endure the recording of *Red Rose Speedway*, along with a further £1000 (£10,349.46) loyalty bonus was offered to McCullough and Seiwell and accepted. This brought their annual salary to £4,860 (£50,275), 30 times higher than the national average. Henry was content for the time being. Just as well, because Wings were scheduled to film the in-concert sequence of McCartney's television show four days later.

Members of the nascent Wings fan club were recruited to form the audience. They, at least, would be guaranteed to give Wings a good reception. Having shied away from associating Wings with The Beatles the previous year, as videotape rolled, McCartney opened the show with 'The Long And Winding Road'. It was Wings' first public performance of a Beatles song. It was a historic moment, but not one shared with a broader public because it was not included in the show's final cut. Wings followed this moment of fabness with 'Maybe I'm Amazed,' 'When The Night,' 'The Mess,' 'My Love,' 'Wild Life,' 'Go Now,' 'Hi, Hi, Hi,' and 'Long Tall Sally'. Having whipped the audience into a frenzy, the entire performance had to be repeated. The reasons for this are disputed. One source claimed it was because of technical problems. Another was that the audience hadn't been enthusiastic enough and needed to buck up their ideas.

Having played two short sets at Elstree Studios, Wings drove 15 miles down the A1 into London to perform at the Hard Rock Café. The unannounced show was to raise funds for Release, a UK agency that provides legal advice for people charged with the possession of drugs. Having had his collar felt by the cops in Sweden and Scotland for possession of cannabis, McCartney may well have benefited from the agency's advice. Tickets were priced at £5 (£51.69). The average weekly wage was £30, so if you could get a ticket, it would make a big hole in your pay packet. Not that many people could buy tickets. The Hard Rock Café had a 200 capacity, making it one of the most intimate gigs Wings had yet performed. However, you got to see Wings perform for roughly one hour in an intimate venue, and that alone would have justified the expense.

Besides sharing McCartney's enthusiasm for spliff, Brinsley Schwarz were booked as the support group. Brinsley Schwarz had no idea who the headline act was until they'd set up their equipment. "We opened at the Hard Rock Café and they said, 'Do you mind if the special guest uses your equipment' and we said, 'Well, who's that?', And they said, 'Paul McCartney,'" recalled keyboardist Bob Andrews. As McCartney explained, Brinsley Schwarz went down a storm, and they made him work a little bit harder. "Brinsley Schwarz were on before us and they kind of warmed it all up and they got a stand up," he said. "Once you've heard a band rock a bit you can't go on and not rock, you've got to play better. So we thought, 'Great', and we went on after Brinsley and that was the first night we thought we played at all well. We were all double made up with that night. We rocked a bit that night."

The following week was a busy one for Wings. On Monday, 20th March, they gathered at Hampstead Heath, London, to film the 'Mary Had A Little Lamb' scene. Neither McCullough nor Seiwell were happy. But they had taken the king's schilling and were duty-bound to appear before the cameras. Leaning against a tree with Denny Laine, McCullouch looked particularly detached and bored. On 22nd March, Wings travelled to Liverpool to record the public house scene. This was an excuse to gather the McCartney clan and get his aunties and uncles on the telly. While his relatives may have found the experience exciting, it did not translate well to the small screen. It was as visually exciting as a poorly directed episode of *Coronation Street*. This time, Denny Seiwell suffered for his art. "That was horrible. Everybody was drunk – we'd spent the whole day there, sitting around, singing old songs, and drinking, mainly – hanging out in a pub getting blotto. Henry, Denny [Laine] were in a limo, going back to London, and the limo driver drove about two blocks, opened the window and threw up. I said to him, 'Okay, you hop in the back here, I'm driving.' That night Denny [Laine] and Henry got into it, sitting in the back, putting out cigarette butts in each others faces. It was the longest night of my life."

Friday, 23rd March, was another big day for Paul McCartney and Wings. Their new single 'My Love' / 'The Mess' was released in the UK. Despite spending considerable time and money recording the song, McCartney wasn't convinced it represented the band. Another indication that, at this time, he had no clear idea where his career was heading. One assumes he had some say about what was released, although he had consented to EMI's request to release *Red Rose Speedway* as a single rather than a double album. 'My Love' was the standout track on the album. Very little else from the cut-down album would have made a solid single. One might have thought that he'd have more confidence in his song. It was the first to be issued under the revised terms and conditions of his new contract with ATV. "'My Love' was the first song I ever owned," he said. "Someone else had always owned everything else I had written. 'My Love' was my definitive one for Linda, written in the earlier days of our relationship, and that came easily." Reviews in the British press were mixed. Writing in the *Melody Maker*, Chris Welch suggested it was "A grand ballad from Paul, rather in the tradition of songs that turned out the troops in the days of the Cyprus crisis and other manifestations of the '50s. In away, it's appeal is timeless, and it certainly rates among his unstoppable flow of classics." *Record Mirror* thought that both sides: "have a strong ballad feel and the top-side highlights Paul's romantic vocal style, backed up with strings and at times a very Harrison-esque guitar style. It's bound to be a hit, and sounds like it could be one of those numbers that really seeps into your soul slowly. But, says one of our witty staffmen, the long and winding bore?!" Writing in *Sounds*, Penny Valentine said: "this is the first track Paul has put out that's likely to delight all his devotees of yesteryear. A tender, misty vocal with nice solid unobtrusive backing from Wings and a good guitar solo midway. Everything is tempered with the kind of professional touch that McCartney always used to show on his work – like it or not as the case may be – which he excels at." The *NME* disagreed and described 'My Love' as: "a piece of gush that's tailor-made for your most senile old aunt."

But what did the fan on the Clapham Omnibus think? Before social media and online forums, fans like Heather Hill of Kidderminster had to put pen to paper and write to the music paper of their choice to let the world know what they thought. Heather wasn't impressed with what she heard. "How does Paul McCartney get away with it? First it was 'Mary Had A Little Lamb', just a nursery rhyme, and now 'My Love', which is rubbish. 'My Love' consists of "my love does it good for me" and countless "woe, woe woes." Just because Paul made his name with The Beatles 10 years ago, he seems to think he can get away with anything. And what's more, the fans have put the disc on the charts. It is obvious, though, that they buy these records just because McCartney's name is connected with them. This was also true for Beatles records." It would be interesting to know what Heather was listening to. Pink Floyd? Led Zeppelin? King Crimson? Slade? T. Rex? Mud, perhaps? She certainly wasn't a Wings fan, and it didn't matter how hard McCartney tried; he would never win over people like Heather.

It was an equally momentous day for John Lennon. The Lennons and their lawyer, Leon Wildes, had been fighting a deportation battle with the INS for some considerable time. Now, it looked like time was up. Judge Fieldsteel had taken over a year to reach his verdict, finding that Lennon and Ono were 'deportable'. Ono, however, did have permanent resident alien status. Lennon did not. His application for permanent residency had been rejected because of his 1968 conviction for possession of cannabis. He was given 60 days to leave the country.

The Lennons had come to the US to gain custody of Ono's daughter, Kyoko. However, Judge Fieldsteel's lengthy decision suggested there was doubt as to whether or not Kyoko wanted to rejoin her mother. It was alleged that two years previously, Kyoko called her mother to complain that the private investigators sent to find her were harassing her. Friends of the Lennons replaced the investigators. "It would appear that if the child is able to telephone the respondents, and the detectives and their replacements are able to be close enough to the child so that she feels harassed, her whereabouts are not entirely unknown. In any event the human equities of the situation are apparent, they do not in any way alter the excludability of Mr. Lennon from the United States and his subsequent ineligibility for permanent residence," said Judge Fieldsteel.1 The decision meant that Ono had to decide between her child or husband. Lennon's battle wasn't over yet. He had ten days to appeal the decision, which is what his lawyer did.

On Saturday, 24th March, Wings were back in the film studio miming 'Big Barn Bed,' which saw them performing in front of a wall of television monitors showing images of an ecstatic audience. The following day, a Sunday, they mimed the unreleased theme to the next James Bond film, 'Live And Let Die'. This time, Wings were surrounded by the Jack Parnell Orchestra. The scene ended in typical Bond style, with the piano exploding. However, someone in the effects department was overly generous with the explosives. The resulting blast was such that it knocked McCullouch off his feet and frightened the bejesus out of the string section. Having successfully blown up a prop piano and half the string section, McCartney turned his attention to sweetening some of the audio Wings had explicitly recorded for television broadcast the previous month. Having completed most of Starr's album, Richard Perry took charge of the session. Perry wasted no time asking McCartney if he'd contribute to Starr's album. McCartney declined an offer to record backing vocals for 'I'm The Greatest' but promised to write a song for his old friend. Perry recalls: "He did not have any unused songs lying around that would suit Ringo, but he knew he could write one if he had a deadline. So I said 'Wednesday' and he came up with the tune 'Six O'Clock'."

On Wednesday, 28th March, Paul and Linda McCartney headed to Apple Studios in the basement of The Beatles' Savile Row HQ. With Klein out of the picture, there was no chance of bumping into his old nemesis, although there were plenty of ghosts to haunt McCartney as he made his way down to the state-of-the-art studio. McCartney kept his promise to Richard Perry and delivered a typically McCartney-esque melody tailored to Starr's vocal abilities. Today's recording session was considerably more productive than some of Wings' recent attempts. McCartney played piano to Starr's drumming. Take four was marked to receive overdubs, including the McCartneys' distinctive backing vocals and keyboards. McCartney's idea to give the song a lengthy reprise was edited from commercial copies of the LP. It did, however, sneak out on US promotional copies of the LP and, for some unknown reason, was available on original cassette copies of the album. With time to spare at the end of the session, McCartney added a 'mouth sax' solo to 'You're Sixteen'. "It's not a kazoo," he explained. "It sounds like a kazoo, but it's me doing an imitation. It was put through a fuzz thing. It's a bit daft, really, because it winds up sounding like a kazoo; I could have just done it on a kazoo. The idea was to make it sound like a great big funky sax."

The Beatles' two compilation albums, *1962 – 66* and *1967 – 70*, had been delayed again. *Billboard*, still referring to them by their working title "The History of The Beatles," claimed the: "two LP" set of two disks, each originally due out March 28th, is now set for release Monday 2nd April. Officials at Capitol Records and Apple Records said the reasons for the delay were "minor and would be cleared up soon." The reason for the delay was contractual. If the albums had been issued while Klein still managed Lennon, Harrison and Starr, he would have been entitled to a percentage of the money generated by the sale of the albums. By delaying the release date until after their contract with him had expired, Klein wouldn't receive a cent. Considering how much time and effort ABKCO had put into realizing the project, it said a great deal about how sullied their relationship had become that The Beatles should conspire to ensure he didn't profit from them. No love was lost between either party, and things would worsen before they got better.

WEEK ENDING 3 MARCH 1973
1. KILLING ME SOFTLY WITH HIS SONG: ROBERTA FLACK
2. DUELING BANJOS: DELIVERANCE
3. LAST SONG: EDWARD BEAR
4. COULD IT BE I'M FALLING IN LOVE: SPINNERS
5. CROCODILE ROCK: ELTON JOHN
6. YOU'RE SO VAIN: CARLY SIMON
7. LOVE TRAIN: O'JAYS
8. ALSO SPRACH ZARATHUSTRA: DEODATO
9. ROCKY MOUNTAIN HIGH: JOHN DENVER
10. DON'T EXPECT ME TO BE YOUR FRIEND: LOBO

WEEK ENDING 10 MARCH 1973
1. KILLING ME SOFTLY WITH HIS SONG: ROBERTA FLACK
2. DUELING BANJOS: DELIVERANCE
3. LAST SONG: EDWARD BEAR
4. COULD IT BE I'M FALLING IN LOVE: SPINNERS
5. LOVE TRAIN: O'JAYS
6. ALSO SPRACH ZARATHUSTRA: DEODATO
7. CROCODILE ROCK: ELTON JOHN
8. THE COVER OF ROLLING STONE: DR HOOK
9. ROCKY MOUNTAIN HIGH: JOHN DENVER
10. DADDY'S HOME: JERMAINE JACKSON

WEEK ENDING 17 MARCH 1973
1. KILLING ME SOFTLY WITH HIS SONG: ROBERTA FLACK
2. DUELING BANJOS: DELIVERANCE
3. LOVE TRAIN: O'JAYS
4. ALSO SPRACH ZARATHUSTRA: DEODATO
5. LAST SONG: EDWARD BEAR
6. THE COVER OF ROLLING STONE: DR HOOK
7. COULD IT BE I'M FALLING IN: LOVE SPINNERS
8. NEITHER ONE OF US (WANTS TO BE THE
9. FIRST TO SAY GOODBYE): GLADYS NIGHT & THE PIPS
10. DADDY'S HOME: JERMAINE JACKSON

WEEK ENDING 24 MARCH 1973
1. LOVE TRAIN: O'JAYS
2. KILLING ME SOFTLY WITH HIS SONG: ROBERTA FLACK
3. ALSO SPRACH ZARATHUSTRA: DEODATO
4. NEITHER ONE OF US (WANTS TO BE THE
5. LAST SONG: EDWARD BEAR
6. THE COVER OF ROLLING STONE: DR HOOK
7. DUELING BANJOS: DELIVERANCE
8. DADDY'S HOME: JERMAINE JACKSON
9. BREAK UP TO MAKE UP: THE STYLISTICS
10. AIN'T NO WOMAN (LIKE THE ONE I'VE GOT): FOUR TOPS

WEEK ENDING 31 MARCH 1973
1. KILLING ME SOFTLY WITH HIS SONG: ROBERTA FLACK
2. ALSO SPRACH ZARATHUSTRA: DEODATO
3. NEITHER ONE OF US (WANTS TO BE THE FIRST TO SAY GOODBYE):
   GLADYS NIGHT & THE PIPS
4. LOVE TRAIN: O'JAYS
5. AIN'T NO WOMAN (LIKE THE ONE I'VE GOT): FOUR TOPS
6. BREAK UP TO MAKE UP: THE STYLISTICS
7. LAST SONG: EDWARD BEAR
8. DANNY'S SONG: ANNE MURRAY

9. SING: THE CARPENTERS
10. THE NIGHT THE LIGHTS WENT OUT IN GEORGIA: VICKI LAWRENCE

UK

WEEK ENDING 4 MARCH 1973
1. CUM ON FEEL THE NOIZE: SLADE
2. CINDY INCIDENTALLY: THE FACES
3. 20TH CENTURY BOY: T. REX
4. PART OF THE UNION: STRAWBS
5. BLOCKBUSTER: THE SWEET
6. FEEL THE NEED IN ME: DETROIT EMERALDS
7. HELLO HURRAY: ALICE COOPER
8. KILLING ME SOFTLY WITH HIS SONG: ROBERTA FLACK
9. DOCTOR MY EYES: THE JACKSON 5
10. WHISKY IN THE JAR: THIN LIZZY

WEEK ENDING 11 MARCH 1973
1. CUM ON FEEL THE NOIZE: SLADE
2. THE TWELFTH OF NEVER: DONNY OSMOND
3. 20TH CENTURY BOY: T. REX
4. FEEL THE NEED IN ME: DETROIT EMERALDS
5. CINDY INCIDENTALLY: THE FACES
6. HELLO HURRAY: ALICE COOPER
7. KILLING ME SOFTLY WITH HIS SONG: ROBERTA FLACK
8. GONNA MAKE YOU AN OFFER YOU CAN'T REFUSE: JIMMY HELMS
9. SYLVIA: FOCUS
10. BABY I LOVE YOU: DAVE EDMUNDS

WEEK ENDING 18 MARCH 1973
1. CUM ON FEEL THE NOIZE: SLADE
2. THE TWELFTH OF NEVER: DONNY OSMOND
3. 20TH CENTURY BOY: T. REX
4. POWER TO ALL OUR FRIENDS: CLIFF RICHARD
5. FEEL THE NEED IN ME: DETROIT EMERALDS
6. KILLING ME SOFTLY WITH HIS SONG: ROBERTA FLACK
7. GET DOWN: GILBERT O'SULLIVAN
8. HELLO HURRAY: ALICE COOPER
9. CINDY INCIDENTALLY: THE FACES
10. GONNA MAKE YOU AN OFFER YOU CAN'T REFUSE: JIMMY HELMS

WEEK ENDING 25 MARCH 1973
1. THE TWELFTH OF NEVER: DONNY OSMOND
2. CUM ON FEEL THE NOIZE: SLADE
3. GET DOWN: GILBERT O'SULLIVAN
4. POWER TO ALL OUR FRIENDS: CLIFF RICHARD
5. 20TH CENTURY BOY: T. REX
6. FEEL THE NEED IN ME: DETROIT EMERALDS
7. TIE A YELLOW RIBBON ROUND THE OLD OAK TREE: DAWN
    FEATURING TONY ORLANDO
8. I'M A CLOWN/SOME KIND OF SUMMER: DAVID CASSIDY
9. KILLING ME SOFTLY WITH HIS SONG: ROBERTA FLACK
10. NEVER NEVER NEVER: SHIRLEY BASSEY

WEEK ENDING 31 MARCH 1973
1. THE TWELFTH OF NEVER: DONNY OSMOND
2. CUM ON FEEL THE NOIZE: SLADE
3. GET DOWN: GILBERT O'SULLIVAN
4. POWER TO ALL OUR FRIENDS: CLIFF RICHARD
5. 20TH CENTURY BOY: T. REX

6. FEEL THE NEED IN ME: DETROIT EMERALDS
7. TIE A YELLOW RIBBON ROUND THE OLD OAK TREE: DAWN
    FEATURING TONY ORLANDO
8. I'M A CLOWN/SOME KIND OF SUMMER: DAVID CASSIDY
9. KILLING ME SOFTLY WITH HIS SONG: ROBERTA FLACK
10. NEVER NEVER NEVER: SHIRLEY BASSEY

CHAPTER 4
APRIL: NOW IS THE TIME TO SAY GOODBYE (GOODBYE)

On Sunday, 1st April, John and Yoko took the redeye from Los Angeles to New York. The next day, they were due to give a press conference with their lawyer, Leon Wildes, at the offices of the Association of the Bar of the City of New York. Wildes suggested making public the invidious position the US government had placed Yoko in, having to choose between her husband or child. Journalists and camera crews were on hand to capture the occasion. Like many of the Lennons' public appearances, it turned into an event. Wildes opened by explaining the status of the legal proceedings against the Lennons, the situation they found themselves in, and how they would proceed. Next, John and Yoko were questioned by the assembled journalists. Lennon voiced his frustration when asked how he felt about the legal proceedings. "It seems Kafka-esque", he said. "It's bureaucracy and they get going and then what can they do, you know, they don't know where to turn, I suppose. The game's started, and we have to play it out." Yoko also refuted Judge Fieldsteel's statement that it wasn't clear whether Kyoko wanted to live with her mother. She made it clear that the child's father, Mr. Cox, was in contempt of a court order allowing her visitation rights and that the judge's statement was, in her opinion, unreasonable. "I'm very surprised. We're really trying to look for her, but it is a very complicated situation." Lennon also pointed out that the court case in Texas gave them joint custody of Kyoko and that it was irrelevant and inhumane for the judge to provide Yoko with permission to stay, not him.

Discussing legal proceedings wasn't the only game in town that day. Before taking more questions from the press, John and Yoko made a typical Fluxus-inspired announcement. Waving white handkerchiefs, which it transpired were, in fact, flags, Lennon read a statement declaring himself and Yoko ambassadors of a new country. "We announce the birth of a conceptual country, NUTOPIA. Citizenship of the country can be obtained by declaration of your awareness of Nutopia. Nutopia has no land, no boundaries, no passports, only people." Announcing the founding of a conceptual country focused attention on the ludicrous and cruel situation they found themselves in. As ambassadors of Nutopia, John and Yoko would have diplomatic immunity, in theory, anyway, if not in practice. As clever and theatrical as it was, it did little to stop the relentless State machine, which continued its legal proceeding to have Lennon deported.

Meanwhile, less than two miles away, Allen Klein's ABKCO Industries issued a statement confirming its management agreement with Apple Corps. Ltd., including Apple Records, had come to an end. The statement said that "no agreement was reached as to (ABKCO's) continued management of Apple Corps Ltd., its subsidiaries, and Messrs. (George) Harrison, (John) Lennon and (Ringo) Starr." There was some good news, but also a sting in the tail. ABKCO declared that it had terminated its efforts concerning the possible acquisition of Apple Corps Ltd. But claimed that it had a right to "continued commissions from revenues accruing out of agreements entered into during the currency of the ABKCO-Apple management agreements." Like Brian Epstein before him, Klein intended to keep a slice of the pie until The Beatles could find a way to stop him. However, he did conclude by taking the "opportunity to wish the Apple Group of Companies and Messrs. Harrison, Lennon and Starr continued success." In London, Leslie Perrin Associates, who handled Apple's press and publicity, said: "that for the present, Apple Corps will act as managers of these interests in place of ABKCO." Their statement added that Capitol Records, distributors of Apple Records, would handle the record company's affairs directly, out of Hollywood and that Yoko Ono and her publishing company, Ono Music, were no longer associated with ABKCO.

Publicly, Klien may have wished Messrs. Harrison, Lennon and Starr success, but privately, he wanted them gone. He wasted no time informing them that he wanted his offices cleared of their belongings. Allan Steckler recalled the urgency with which Klein wanted rid of them. "It all had to be out. They had a week to move out. When it was over, it was over." As Lennon lived just over a mile from ABKCO's offices, collecting four years of accumulated business clutter fell to him. Lennon asked his assistant, May Pang, to arrange to move everything into his new apartment. "We took out Apple and all the paperwork from the ABKCO offices and we brought it over to the Dakota and that's where we left it. We never set up another proper office until Tony King went out to LA," recalled Pang. It wasn't only paperwork; valuable master tapes that should have been in secure storage facilities were also included. The end of The Beatles' management contract with ABKCO marked the end of Apple Records. Without an office, it couldn't function properly, support what few artists it had on its books, or promote their records. It was the beginning of the end for the label.

One week after issuing his formal statement, Klein gave his reasons for the split with Lennon, Harrison, Starr and Ono. "There were a number of reasons why I didn't propose a renewal of the management contract," he said. "But one was just a gut reaction that it was time to let it stop; not so much that I quit. I was going to make a proposal for a continuation of the management contract. Then I decided not to. My position has always been that if things didn't work out for us, we should split. There's no question that the four of us were a great combination in so many ways. I said all along that if I was the one standing in the way I would get out. I said it to George only three weeks ago. Let's see if, with me not there now, they get back together. McCartney would certainly like to. But I would be surprised if the four worked together again as artists."

Klein was being disingenuous. His management agreement had been renewed, first monthly, then bi-weekly. By then, it must have been obvious that his role as their manager was over. Also, he must have known that there was little chance of achieving his goal of merging Apple Corps with ABKCO Industries. McCartney's lawyers were looking over his shoulder, which meant his hands were tied. Furthermore, Lennon, Harrison, Starr and Ono had good reasons not to renew the agreement. Speaking to ITN's *Weekend World*, two days before Klein made his statement, Lennon said: "There are many reasons why we finally gave him the push, although I don't want to go into the details of it. Let's say possibly Paul's suspicions were right... And the time was right. The contract expired I think in February, and we were extending it at first on a monthly basis and then finally on a two weekly basis, and then finally we pushed the boat out. […] My position has always been a 'Devil and the deep blue sea,' and at that time I do whatever I feel is right with the situation. Although I haven't been particularly happy personally for quite a long time with the situation, I didn't want to make any quick moves and I wanted to see if maybe something would work out."

Lennon was waiting in vain. No matter how long he waited, Klein was not going to change. The only way the present business situation would end was with the dissolution of The Beatles' partnership agreement. The stumbling block was how. Klein's departure did not make the problem any easier to solve. However, in the eyes of many, it made the possibility of a Beatles reunion more likely, and that included McCartney. "The Beatles could reform now that the manager Allen Klein is no longer involved. When Klein was there, the road was closed against the four of us ever working together. Now, as far as I am concerned, the road is open again," he said. "I saw Klein as a sharp operator who could only do harm with The Beatles. The others disagreed. Now they have come around to my way of thinking... There's no reason why we should not all work together again. Klein was one of my main worries. He promised The Beatles the earth but the only one to make any real profit was Klein. At last the others have decided that it was simply not in their best interest to have him as manager... Klein takes a percentage and if he could have had his way he would have owned The Beatles lock, stock and barrel. As it is, the money we earn goes into a central pot. Even some of the money I get with Wings goes into the pot. Every time we say we'd split the pot, Klein would say 'Think of poor old Ringo, he'll get far less than anyone. You'll have to give him some of your share.' Now I hope it's possible we can all own our own out of what we have earned and divide the pot between the four of us. We've all lived well but we have never touched a penny of the money we have earned as Beatles."

The problem remained: how to divide up the pot fairly. Speaking to David Wigg, Starr explained the situation they faced. "It's not fair that I should share in Paul's efforts or that he should share in mine because we don't work together. So we're trying to sort that out. But we did all sign those silly pieces of paper when we were lads, which keep us together until '76. Apple will have to go on forever because it has all The Beatles' stuff. I could just sit down for the next two years, do nothing, and collect, which is not fair. We're trying to stop that but it's very hard because once you sign your name on a piece of paper they try and make you stick by it, if it's fair or not. There's no way you can go and say 'Listen, it's not really fair we'd like to change it'. Oh, but you signed your name; we've got you by the balls."

As Ono noted, The Beatles needed an administrator. That task would fall to Apple Corps. It would become The Beatles' gatekeeper, control projects, and administrate the vast sums of money still pouring in. With Klein out of the way, Lennon, Harrison, and Starr would need personal managers, which could make the situation even more complicated. This was the last thing they needed. Klein wasn't an administrative genius. He was more interested in the deal than the details. One detail he overlooked was filing tax returns for his clients. Harrison's problems with the taxman still hadn't been resolved, and he blamed Klein for his woes. "When John, Ringo and myself got rid of Allen Klein, our notorious manager, I was five years behind with my taxes, and I needed someone to organise me out of all that mess," he explained. "I wanted someone to help me with my present and future, but unfortunately, he would have to get involved with my past." The past was always going to haunt The Beatles. It was something that all four would have to learn to deal with in their own ways.

Monday 2nd April saw two new albums by The Beatles and a new single by Wings released. Any pretence that Wings was anything other than McCartney's backing band vanished with the release of their new single. 'My Love' was credited to Paul McCartney and Wings. While few noticed or cared about the subtle change, it must have irked McCullough and Seiwell, who had already expressed dissatisfaction at the direction the band was taking and their roles. "We were still on this retainer, and we'd been told that as things progressed, we could contribute material, become part of a 'band' as such, but it never ever came to that. [...] I wanted to contribute, you know, 'Give me a chance – if it doesn't work out, we'll do it your way.' I felt it was time he allowed the musicians to have some of their own ideas used as part of this 'group' vibe. But all that was slowly being lost – the idea from the university tour, the van, the craic and all that started to go out the window. And I was trying desperately to hold onto it because I wanted it not just for the band but for him as well – for him to show people that he wasn't namby-pamby all the time, that he really had balls. And he does have an awful lot of balls; he just doesn't seem to get it down on record...," recalled McCullough.

McCullough was rightly proud of his guitar solo on 'My Love,' but if ever a song lacked 'balls' it was this. That is not to say it's a bad song, far from it. 'My Love' was McCartney at his melodic best. But McCullough's heart must have sunk even further when he read what McCartney told the *Liverpool Daily Post*. "I'm getting more into ballads, but I went off them I must say. I just wanted to play rock. Now I like a varied act? a couple of fast ones then a couple of slow ones." McCartney's desire to be all things to everyone threatened to turn Wings into a glorified upmarket Irish Showband, the last thing McCullough wanted.

US Radio stations had no reservations about Wings' new single; they loved it, and those who had received an advanced copy wasted no time adding it to their playlists. In the 7th April edition of *Record World*, Kal Rudman claimed: "As we go to press, most stations have not received it ('My Love'). Stations that jumped right on it include KJR, KHJ, KOL, WPGC, WRKO, WFIL, KLIF, WCAO, and KTAC. In my opinion, "Captain Crazy," Al Coury, Vice President in charge of promotion of Capitol Records, has done a remarkable job in turning the label around without the release of albums by his heavyweight artists. Those heavyweight releases are coming now. You should have the Paul McCartney album in about three weeks, and it will be followed by albums by George Harrison, Ringo Starr and the live Leon Russell album."

KLIF in Dallas added 'My Love' to a playlist that included the Jackson 5, Gilbert O'Sullivan, Neil Diamond, and Perry Como. Precisely the kind of varied acts McCartney liked. Back in Blighty, Slade topped the chart with 'Cum On Feel The Noize,' while Ringo's buddy Marc Bolan was at number 3 with '20th Century Boy'. The Glam Rockers didn't completely dominate the chart. There was room for everything from Alice Cooper to Dave Edmunds, Dawn to Focus. Perhaps McCartney's desire for Wings to be a varied act was right.

The UK charts varied because 3,000 singles were issued in 1973. There were roughly sixty singles to choose from every week. Of these, only a handful made it into the chart. Getting your record heard by as many people as possible was essential to its success. A record by an ex-Beatle was guaranteed radio airplay, but television also played its part.

On Wednesday 4th April, Wings headed to BBC Television Centre in White City, London, to videotape an appearance on *Top Of The Pops*. Despite the promise of bonus payments, McCartney was having trouble maintaining discipline. The band's core, the two Dennys and Henry, arrived an hour late, and McCullough was drunk again. He was so drunk that by the time they came to record their performance, he had to dive behind the scenery to throw up. McCartney took it in his stride. Yet, despite the good news that Klein no longer represented The Beatles, McCartney was in a black mood. He seemed full of self-doubt when talking to Steve Gaines and Andrew Tyler, journalists for rival music publications. Nothing he had written and recorded, including his latest song, seemed good enough. Speaking to John Halsall of the *Liverpool Daily Post*, McCartney claimed his crisis of confidence was because of the ongoing problems with The Beatles: "In the last couple of years, with all The Beatle problems, it's been a bit tough, you know. Because I don't think you do create as well if you've got a lot of problems, it hasn't been as good of late. But we've got some good ones coming now."

If McCartney had been inconsistent creatively, he had done nothing wrong commercially. Despite Wings' difficult start in life, the banned singles, the drug busts, and the mixed reviews, the hits kept coming. Rather than share his burden with other members of Wings, some of whom were more than willing to lend a hand, he shouldered it himself. He didn't have Lennon, Harrison, and Starr to help carry the weight. It was his and his alone, and he felt it now more than ever.

Another factor darkening McCartney's mood may have been competition. The four kings of EMI had been usurped by a younger generation of musicians who, in their own way, were shaking things up and making a big noise in much the same way as The Beatles had before them. The ex-Beatles were still part of an elite domain, but like a Shakespearean drama playing out in real-time before them, the musical sea surrounding them looked choppy, if not tempestuous. All four would have to redefine themselves against an ever-changing musical milieu that was shifting faster with every passing year. To make matters worse, Lennon, McCartney, Harrison, and Starr were in competition with themselves. As if to rub salt into McCartney's chronic wound, Capitol released two double albums by The Beatles on the same day it issued his new single.

McCartney had been here before. In 1970, he'd fought with the other Beatles over conflicting release dates for his debut album and The Beatles swansong *Let It Be*. On that occasion, he'd won. It must have seemed as if history was repeating itself. However, when he spoke to Paul Gambaccini, McCartney claimed that competition with his old band was good. "I thought it was good, rather than odd, because obviously the big hang up after The Beatles broke up was, and really still is, can any of them be as good as the unit? The answer in most people's minds, I think, is 'No, they can't.' Because the unit was so good."

After a slight delay, the albums *1962 – 66* and *1967 – 70* were issued in the US on 2nd April with a significant marketing campaign. Capitol placed full-page adverts in the music press and provided retailers with streamers emphasizing that both albums were "the only authorized collection of The Beatles on Apple Records and tapes." Capitol also worked closely with the Wherehouse chain of record retailers to launch a "Million Dollar Beatle Promotion" that featured all of The Beatles' LPs, tapes and singles, and solo releases. Taking a leaf from the pirates' book, the campaign involved local radio adverts tied into national print and television adverts. The retailer decorated its stores with Union Flags and banners, dressed its staff in Beatles tee-shirts and put The Beatles music into heavy rotation. It also gave away 25,000 John Lennon and 50,000 Beatles posters with the purchase of any Beatle product. Wherehouse was expecting to sell lots of Beatles products and stuffed each store with 60 stacks of Beatles records, two tape wall racks of tapes and a dump bin for singles. Pity the poor Rolling Stones and Led Zeppelin fans who worked on the shop floor day in and day out. They suffered for their pay-cheque and were undoubtedly as happy as Larry when the promotion ended.

The albums *1962 – 66* and *1967 – 70* had a retail price of $9.98 each ($69.32). The high price received more criticism than the music from some journalists, including Roy Carr, who dismissed the albums as cash grabs and complained about the cost – £ 3.99 (£41.41). "What do you receive for such expenditure? I'll tell you, a shoddy and overpriced package of most of The Beatles and our greatest moments... If this is supposedly a 'definitive' Beatles collection, then someone somewhere has blatantly sold the lads and the public short." Other reviews were considerably more optimistic. *Disc* saw them as essential totems that would continue to influence and incite youth culture in the decades to come: "[T]here will be the new generation, under 15, poised for the Seventies youth revolution who will be hearing some of these tracks in their original form for the first time - instead of the many hundreds of versions ranging from a murderous "Come Dancing" orchestra to tortuous

American vocalist versions of these classic songs. And classic, they were and are. They really were one of the things that brought about new clothes, hairstyles, concern and politics. They also brought about the "permissive society" and made dope-smoking into a problem. Ten years has not dulled their listenability." Another reviewer remarked upon the sheer scale of musical progression that the albums represent: "[I]f you're like me, they passed through a lot of lulls and hit some incredible highs and ultimate greatness but this compilation is a must for anyone who is remotely interested in the progression of music in the last decade and The Beatles influence on it - that's unless you're a Beatles' freak and by now the old 'uns will need replacing."

Although The Beatles had split up only three years earlier, there was already a generation for whom they were history. The *Red* and *Blue* albums were the gateway into a new musical world for this second generation of Beatles fans. A world that had been usurped by Slade, T. Rex, Mud, The Osmonds, The Jackson 5 and more. And yet, it was a world familiar to them through their parents' record collection or radio, which still played their records almost as frequently as the young Turks who'd replaced them in the pages of *Jackie* and *Fab 208*. Price was an issue for Carr, especially if you already owned the original albums. However, Carr overlooked the fact that retail stores, particularly in America, discounted the albums. British chain stores like HMV and Virgin would have discounted the albums, too. Those who shopped around could pick up the albums for less than the recommended price. In the UK, some retailers priced the albums from £3.39 (£31.30), saving 70p. For context, Pink Floyd's *Dark Side Of The Moon*, a single disc, retailed for £2.38 (£21.00).

American fans were better served because of greater competition. A report in *Record World* revealed precisely how competitive the retail environment in America was. A survey of the nation's leading record retailers - including independent stores, record chain stores, department stores and discount centres - revealed a widely varying pricing policy for the new Beatles albums. The two albums, listed at $9.98 ($69.32) each set, were selling at retail prices from $4.99 ($34.66) to $9.98. One-stops surveyed charged prices from $4.85 ($33.69) to $5.60 ($38.90). Most of the stores surveyed explained that they were treating the albums as any other with a similar list price of $9.98.

The recordings may have recouped their costs many times, but the albums were more expensive because of increased manufacturing costs. *Billboard* reported that spiralling costs such as lithography, paper, and jackets were causing record labels to increase the suggested list price. "Topping the list of increasing costs to the manufacturer are lithographs. Firms involved in their production have raised their price twice since the first of the year. At present, the increase represents a 15 percent hike, or $4 ($27.79) per thousand. Fabricating houses also have hiked their prices on jackets since the first of the year. The increase is now about 8 percent or $3 ($20.48) per thousand. Chipboard is in such short supply that many fabricating houses have been forced to resort to rationing and establishing a priority list based on the customer's needs."

Inflation may have been hitting the pockets of record labels and buyers alike, but some were better cushioned against the rising cost of living than others. After their press conference, the Lennons went house shopping. Strolling through Central Park towards the Dakota, they crossed Central Park West and entered the imposing building via the 72nd Street entrance. Having viewed the apartment, they headed back to their Bank Street address, where they gave an interview to *Rolling Stone* magazine. Later, they flew back to Los Angeles for more business meetings.

On 8th April, Wings gathered at a London studio to film a promotional video for 'My Love.' Directed by photographer Mick Rock, the film saw the band enveloped in smoke, intended to add atmosphere to this otherwise pedestrian performance video. Once again, Henry McCullough suffered for his art. Overcome by the oil-based stage smoke, he threw up during the song as he had earlier. A few days later, the first official Wings Fun Club newsletter was distributed to fans. As expected, it promoted the forthcoming James Paul McCartney show and the soon-to-be-released *Red Rose Speedway* album. Wings July UK tour also got a plug. Venues and dates were supplied; ticket prices were between 50p (£5.00) and £1.60 (£15.00).

McCartney's first solo TV special was receiving considerable publicity and was scheduled for broadcast on 16th April in the US and 22nd in the UK. Part of an intensive marketing campaign focused on promoting Wings' latest album, it ensured that McCartney and his music received maximum exposure to as wide an audience as possible. However, when the show aired, it received mixed reviews. The *Melody Maker* considered it "overblown and silly," while Derrik Hill's review for the *Liverpool Daily Post* didn't pull its punches. "Oh dear, to have to do this to one of our own. (Deep breath). *James Paul McCartney* (ITV) was a truly lousy show. For all of its 60 minutes, it strove mightily for mediocracy - and failed. What a gas! Someone must have thought to get Paul and let him do his own thing. So it was one of those anything goes happenings where the only thing that's positively not welcome is any sense of artistic self-criticism. So help me, we were subjected to the sight of

Paul and his group Wings singing 'Mary Had A Little Lamb' amidst a flock of sheep in the country; Paul and gang romping with a football; and Linda on a white horse in slow motion of course." Lennon was ambivalent: "I liked parts of Paul's TV special, especially the intro. The bit filmed in Liverpool made me squirm a bit. But Paul's a pro. He always has been." *Cash Box* closed its review by noting: "Those who disliked the special were obviously expecting something different from McCartney. Perhaps an entire concert with Wings. Or, maybe an intimate hour with Paul. But if we learn to take the best from what was given us, we will then be able to appreciate more of what we have." When asked how he reacted to the criticism, McCartney employed his usual trick of talking about the feedback he'd received from the man on the street. "You meet people on holiday, Americans, and they go (assuming southern accent), 'Hey, man, that was a real nice special ya did.'" He also blamed the show's sponsors, claiming they had tied his hands. "Let's face it, we were doing a special for Chevrolet, and you can't do an awful lot on a special for Chevrolet."

Six days after recording with McCartney, Ringo Starr passed through London Airport on his way to LA for more business meetings and to finish his album. Surrounded by a phalanx of journalists, he was asked the inevitable question about a Beatles reunion, to which he replied that there was "hardly any chance" of The Beatles appearing together again. "We are still good pals, but it's just not on." While McCartney's attempt at small-screen light entertainment had fallen on stony ground, Starr's performance on the silver screen was better received. Starring David Essex with Starr in a supporting role, *That'll Be The Day* premiered on 12th April at the ABC2 cinema in Shaftsbury Avenue, London. If the film's plot was criticised as being a little weak, reviewers from both national and local newspapers praised Starr's performance. The *Daily Mirror* said: "Brightest moments in the film are provided by Ringo Starr, as a sharp character, who teaches Jim how to chat up the girls and fiddle the fairground takings." The *Liverpool Echo* noted, "Ringo Starr in *That'll Be The Day* is a joy, projecting a sarcastic style which seems to fit him as perfectly as the carapace of the Beatle he once was." The *Harrow Observer & Gazette* claimed, "This part is a major breakthrough for Ringo, and is his best yet. His wit and sense of humour really come to the fore. He received good reviews from most national critics for this role, which regrettably doesn't take up much of the film." Ringo's star was rising, and now that they had put him in the movies, he lost no time attending Hollywood parties. Starr, accompanied by the Lennons, graced a party held by Universal Studios' Vice President Jennings Lang to raise money for the defence in the Pentagon Papers trial.

Starr could rub shoulders with some of Hollywood's biggest names, and the Lennons could donate money to a cause close to their hearts.

Nixon was hardly flavour of the month with the Lennons. But even they must have supported him when he asked the Senate to ratify the international anti-piracy treaty that called on each nation that signed it to protect record manufacturers against unlicensed duplication. It was estimated that over $100 million ($694,632,882) in pirated records and tapes were manufactured in the US yearly. Any legislation that would help combat this illegal multimillion-dollar business could only be applauded, even if it was Nixon who helped implement it. It would make life a little more bearable financially, but Lennon's woes were far from over. His dispute with Northern Songs and Maclen Music over Ono's claim to have co-written several of his more recent songs was still going through the courts. Lennon's lawyers had contended that the matter was a contract case, not a copyright case, and should be heard in another court. Judge Brieant thought otherwise and ruled that he would not dismiss the case because it involved copyrights, which would bring it under the purview of his court. So much for Lennon's letter to Jack Gill requesting they settle out of court.

Harrison was conspicuous by his absence. Unlike the other Beatles, he was keeping his head down. Nerry a mention of his name made it into the papers for months on end. That's not to say that he was idle, far from it. A new single was being prepared, his first since 'Banga-Desh,' released in July 1971. As well as attending business meetings with Lennon and Starr and helping Starr with his new album, Harrison was toiling over a hot mixing desk with his mentor and friend, Ravi Shankar. This odd couple were busying themselves at A&M Studios in Los Angeles recording what would become *Shankar Family and Friends*. Although he'd produced Shankar before, this was the first time they had collaborated on a studio album together. Shankar worked by improvising in the studio. "Ravi would tell everybody what their part was, and Indian musicians are very good at memorizing what they have to do," Harrison explained. "They would make some notation if they needed to remember something specific or especially difficult – and then he'd say, 'OK, ready?' He'd go to count them in, and I thought, 'This is going to be chaos.' But we'd start playing, and it would be magic."

The album was Shankar's first to fuse traditional Indian music with Western rock instrumentation—part of the album comprised music for a ballet to an un-staged performance. When asked about the album's making at the time of the original release, Shankar said: "I've written music for many ballets in India. But never, never in the West, with so many Western instruments. This one I did without trying to make it totally Indian at all. I thought of making something very international. That's why you hear all sorts of sound, starting from sitar or sarod to Moog synthesizer." The album was intended to be released by Apple Records. However, the Apple label was coming to an end, particularly now that ABKCO was no longer overseeing its day-to-day running. Harrison had been planning to start his own record company for some time. One idea was to buy out Apple Records from The Beatles partnership and run it with Starr. However, it proved too difficult to untangle all the legal knots and the idea was quietly dropped. Instead, he decided to form a record label of his own. He told Anne Nightingale, "Later down the line, someone needed a name for a company. Publishing it was. So I said: 'I can't think of any names.' I was sick of thinking of company names. So they said: 'How about one of your songs?' So I said: 'Okay, Dark Horse.' Then I thought, well, this period when Apple was getting swept under the carpet, and I still had a lot of things that I was working on, which were intended for Apple. So I decided: 'hell, I'll have a label too, and I shall call it Dark Horse.'"

While Harrison was working on Shankar's album, his rented house in Beverly Hills was burgled. The thieves took some of his possessions and a Gibson guitar that had been given to him by Eric Clapton. They left the master tapes of Shankar's album behind; perhaps they thought them worthless. Mal Evans' current squeeze was implicated in the robbery, which complicated matters. In short, Evans told a white lie when he reported the crime to LA's boys in blue to avoid incriminating the new love in his life. Evans used his showbiz connections and turned detective tracking down the stolen guitar to Whalin's Sound City. Unfortunately, the guitar had been sold less than half an hour before he phoned the store. The trail had gone as cold as last night's pizza. However, word of the burglary and the missing guitar had got around, and thanks to Canned Heat's road crew, Evans discovered the instrument's whereabouts. It had been bought in good faith by Miguel Ochoa, who had taken it back to Mexico. Negotiations ensued, and it was agreed that Harrison's guitar would be swapped for a similar instrument. Unsurprisingly, the price of a red Gibson Les Paul guitar tripled as soon as the news hit the street that Harrison was desperate to acquire one. Ochoa was no less mercenary. On learning that the guitar he'd bought belonged to Harrison, he insisted he wanted a replacement and a new bass guitar. Harrison wasn't going to quibble over the deal and was eventually reunited with his prized instrument. What's more, the LA police department managed to recover the other items stolen in the burglary. Evans was back in Harrison's good books; the guitar was safely under lock and key, and the tapes for Shankar's album were restored to A&M Studios.

With *Living In The Material World* finished, Mal Evans was tasked with arranging the photo shoot for the album's inner gatefold sleeve. Harrison, accompanied by Ringo Starr, Jim Horn, Klaus Voormann, Nicky Hopkins, Jim Keltner and Gary Wright, spent the day at the mock Tudor home of entertainment lawyer Abe Somer. Several set-ups were photographed that day by Ken Marcus and Barry Feinstein. Harrison used Ken Marcus's photo, which parodied da Vinci's 'The Last Supper'. Dressed in black and wearing a mitre, Harrison lampooned himself and aspects of the world he inhabited, poking fun at everything from Catholicism to conspicuous consumption. For the front cover, he went to UCLA's parapsychology department and was photographed using Kirlian photography holding a Hindu medallion in one hand and US coins in the other. The implication being that he was very much stuck in the middle.

WEEK ENDING 7 APRIL 1973
1. THE NIGHT THE LIGHTS WENT OUT IN GEORGIA: VICKI LAWRENCE
2. NEITHER ONE OF US (WANTS TO BE THE FIRST TO SAY GOODBYE):
   GLADYS KNIGHT AND THE PIPS
3. KILLING ME SOFTLY WITH HIS SONG: ROBERTA FLACK
4. AIN'T NO WOMAN (LIKE THE ONE I'VE GOT): FOUR TOPS
5. BREAK UP TO MAKE UP: THE STYLISTICS
6. TIE A YELLOW RIBBON ROUND THE OLE OAK TREE: DAWN
   FEATURING TONY ORLANDO
7. SING: CARPENTERS
8. DANNY'S SONG: ANNE MURRAY
9. ALSO SPRACH ZARATHUSTRA: DEODATO
10. THE CISCO KID: WAR

WEEK ENDING 14 APRIL 1973
1. THE NIGHT THE LIGHTS WENT OUT IN GEORGIA: VICKI LAWRENCE
2. NEITHER ONE OF US (WANTS TO BE THE FIRST TO SAY GOODBYE):
   GLADYS KNIGHT AND THE PIPS
3. TIE A YELLOW RIBBON ROUND THE OLE OAK TREE: DAWN
   FEATURING TONY ORLANDO
4. AIN'T NO WOMAN (LIKE THE ONE I'VE GOT): FOUR TOPS
5. SING: CARPENTERS
6. THE CISCO KID: WAR
7. DANNY'S SONG: ANNE MURRAY
8. BREAK UP TO MAKE UP: THE STYLISTICS
9. KILLING ME SOFTLY WITH HIS SONG: ROBERTA FLACK
10. CALL ME (COME BACK HOME): AL GREEN

WEEK ENDING 21 APRIL 1973
1. TIE A YELLOW RIBBON ROUND THE OLE OAK TREE: DAWN
   FEATURING TONY ORLANDO
2. THE NIGHT THE LIGHTS WENT OUT IN GEORGIA: VICKI LAWRENCE
3. SING: CARPENTERS
4. THE CISCO KID: WAR
5. AIN'T NO WOMAN (LIKE THE ONE I'VE GOT): FOUR TOPS
6. NEITHER ONE OF US (WANTS TO BE THE FIRST TO SAY GOODBYE):
   GLADYS KNIGHT AND THE PIPS
7. LITTLE WILLY: THE SWEET
8. MASTERPIECE: THE TEMPTATIONS
9. DANNY'S SONG: ANNE MURRAY
10. THE TWELFTH OF NEVER: DONNY OSMOND

WEEK ENDING 28 APRIL 1973
1. TIE A YELLOW RIBBON ROUND THE OLE OAK TREE: DAWN
   FEATURING TONY ORLANDO
2. THE CISCO KID: WAR
3. SING: CARPENTERS
4. THE NIGHT THE LIGHTS WENT OUT IN GEORGIA: VICKI LAWRENCE
5. LITTLE WILLY: THE SWEET
6. YOU ARE THE SUNSHINE OF MY LIFE: STEVIE WONDER
7. MASTERPIECE: THE TEMPTATIONS
8. THE TWELFTH OF NEVER: DONNY OSMOND
9. STUCK IN THE MIDDLE WITH YOU: STEALERS WHEEL
10. AIN'T NO WOMAN (LIKE THE ONE I'VE GOT): FOUR TOPS

WEEK ENDING 7 APRIL 1973
1. GET DOWN: GILBERT O'SULLIVAN
2. THE TWELFTH OF NEVER: DONNY OSMOND
3. TIE A YELLOW RIBBON ROUND THE OLD OAK TREE: DAWN FEATURING TONY ORLANDO
4. POWER TO ALL OUR FRIENDS: CLIFF RICHARD
5. I'M A CLOWN/SOME KIND OF SUMMER: DAVID CASSIDY
6. TWEEDLE DEE: LITTLE JIMMY OSMOND
7. CUM ON FEEL THE NOIZE: SLADE
8. NEVER NEVER NEVER: SHIRLEY BASSEY
9. LOVE TRAIN: THE O'JAYS
10. KILLING ME SOFTLY WITH HIS SONG: ROBERTA FLACK

WEEK ENDING 14 APRIL 1973
1. GET DOWN: GILBERT O'SULLIVAN
2. TIE A YELLOW RIBBON ROUND THE OLD OAK TREE: DAWN FEATURING TONY ORLANDO
3. I'M A CLOWN/SOME KIND OF SUMMER: DAVID CASSIDY
4. THE TWELFTH OF NEVER: DONNY OSMOND
5. HELLO! HELLO! I'M BACK AGAIN: GARY GLITTER
6. TWEEDLE DEE: LITTLE JIMMY OSMOND
7. POWER TO ALL OUR FRIENDS: CLIFF RICHARD
8. NEVER NEVER NEVER: SHIRLEY BASSEY
9. LOVE TRAIN: THE O'JAYS
10. PYJAMARAMA: ROXY MUSIC

WEEK ENDING 21 APRIL 1973
1. TIE A YELLOW RIBBON ROUND THE OLD OAK TREE: DAWN FEATURING TONY ORLANDO
2. HELLO! HELLO! I'M BACK AGAIN: GARY GLITTER
3. GET DOWN: GILBERT O'SULLIVAN
4. TWEEDLE DEE: LITTLE JIMMY OSMOND
5. I'M A CLOWN/SOME KIND OF SUMMER: DAVID CASSIDY
6. THE TWELFTH OF NEVER: DONNY OSMOND
7. POWER TO ALL OUR FRIENDS: CLIFF RICHARD
8. DRIVE-IN SATURDAY: DAVID BOWIE
9. NEVER NEVER NEVER: SHIRLEY BASSEY
10. PYJAMARAMA: ROXY MUSIC

WEEK ENDING 28 APRIL 1973
1. TIE A YELLOW RIBBON ROUND THE OLD OAK TREE: DAWN FEATURING TONY ORLANDO
2. HELLO! HELLO! I'M BACK AGAIN: GARY GLITTER
3. GET DOWN: GILBERT O'SULLIVAN
4. I'M A CLOWN/SOME KIND OF SUMMER: DAVID CASSIDY
5. TWEEDLE DEE: LITTLE JIMMY OSMOND
6. ALL BECAUSE OF YOU: GEORDIE
7. DRIVE-IN SATURDAY: DAVID BOWIE
8. THE TWELFTH OF NEVER: DONNY OSMOND
9. MY LOVE: WINGS
10. PYJAMARAMA: ROXY MUSIC

CHAPTER 5
MAY: THIS HEAVY LOAD

Wings' protracted and butchered album *Red Rose Speedway* was released in the US on 30th April and in the UK on 4th May. The planned two-record set had been condensed, against McCartney's wishes, to a single disc at the insistence of his manager. He might have got his way if he had a someone like Klein as a manager. If Yoko Ono, who Klein had managed until recently, could release two double albums on the trot, why not McCartney? However, for every action, there is an equal and opposite reaction, and for all the good Klein did, there was plenty of bad to balance it.

The cover showed what McCartney intended for the album before it was gelded. The single disc came wrapped in a gatefold sleeve, evidence that it was initially meant to be a two-record set. A glossy 12-page booklet featuring designs by Edwardo Palozzi and Allen Jones was sandwiched between the cover. It featured artwork for 'Seaside Woman,' a song written by Linda McCartney that was conspicuous by its absence. Despite the struggles McCartney and Wings endured while recording the album, despite the pressure McCartney was under from The Beatles' ongoing legal battle, and despite the stress of having his collar felt for growing cannabis on his Scottish farm, the album turned out well and received favourable reviews.

McCartney must have felt vindicated by the results of his efforts. *Billboard* considered the album to be the: "Best effort from McCartney since his break with The Beatles, featuring powerful rock material as well as the great ballads he was so well known for when the band was together." *Cash Box* claimed that: "*Red Rose Speedway* makes you smile, and that means a lot these days. Somewhere between quaint and romantic, Paul's new tunes grow on you with repeated listenings." *Rolling Stone* believed that the album was one of McCartney's best. "Still, despite expected hits and misses, I find *Red Rose Speedway* to be the most overall heartening McCartney product given us since the demise of The Beatles. After much experimentation with how best to present himself, Paul has apparently begun a process of settling down, of working within a band framework that looks to remain stable for at least the next vehicular period."

In the UK, *Record Mirror* was slightly more cautious in its assessment: "It's pretty difficult to come to terms with Paul McCartney's work, particularly as an immediate thing. There is a certain simplicity, naivete almost, in what he does, and that can be both enhancing and irritating. One thing is fairly certain, though, none of the material is instant. And that is generally the initial impression the album gives. Played more and more the songs could develop ... for McCartney's work seems to have that tendency." The review in *Disc* dismissed the album and lamented that McCartney's band hadn't been free to express themselves. "I just had the feeling, while I listened to the album, of those incredible musicians – the two Dennys and old Henry – and their capabilities and the things they've done and wondered if perhaps they weren't rather curbed. Bloody shackled, in fact. I would have thought they'd have been embarrassed doing an instrumental like 'Loup (1st Indian On The Moon)'. 'Hold Me Tight' is the only song that really let's go and rocks a little; and others on the Medley rip a bit more. Paul's voice stretches into its full heights only on 'Little Lamb,' where there's also some good guitar from Hugh McCracken. Technically, the album is good; everybody plays very nicely and sings very nicely, but for the first couple of hearings, it lacks light and shade, and the repetitive technique of the songs hits you between the eyes. Perhaps I will grow to love the album; perhaps it has hidden subtleties. I hope so." The *NME*'s Tony Tyler thought otherwise and, like his US counterparts, suggested that the album was one of McCartney's best: "Paul makes his stand here and, as far as I'm concerned, he's proved his point. And I also think that in the future, he's going to be able to look back on the last three years without cringing - which is more than Lennon will be able to do."

Perhaps one reason *Red Rose Speedway* was reduced to a single disc was cost and a shortage of materials. EMI had a reputation for penny-pinching. There were no picture sleeves for UK Beatles singles. When it did consent to The Beatles' request for a picture sleeve for 'Strawberry Fields Forever' b/w 'Penny Lane,' it insisted on limiting the production to a quarter of a million. It paid Klaus Voormann the standard flat rate of £50 for his artwork for *Revolver* and, to save money quibbled over the thickness of card stock for *The Beatles* (*White Album*). Even an act as big as The Beatles had to fight to get what they wanted. EMI would have been only too aware of the rising cost of materials. Not only was the cost of manufacturing and printing sleeves increasing, but the price of the vinyl used to manufacture records was growing, too. Inflation stood at around 9%, and there was a shortage of the raw materials used to manufacture long-playing gramophone records.

Although the vinyl shortage wouldn't hit the industry for another 12 months, there were already rumblings in the press. The UK music industry trade paper, *Music Week*, ran a feature about the shortage of vinyl and increased costs. "Concern is growing in the record industry over the world shortage of PVC/PVA, the raw material used to manufacture records, although the problem is not critical at the moment and production at record company and custom pressing plants has not yet been affected, there is a feeling that some firms might find themselves unable to maintain production later this year." The shortage was connected with the world energy crisis.

The material used to manufacture records, PVC/PVA, is derived from coal or oil, of which there was an international shortage. Marcel Rod, the managing director of Saga, told *Music Week*: "I use around 2000 tonnes of the compound per year, and at the moment, I am short by about 1000 tonnes. There just isn't enough available. My production has not been affected yet, but I am getting increasingly worried about what might happen later this year." The article went on to say that Decca's New Malden pressing plant used an average of 90 tonnes of PVC/PVA a week and that in the six months since December, the price of the vinyl compound had increased from around £140 (£1,448.92) a tonne to £160 (£1,655.91).

To make matters worse, 1973 was a big year for big-selling albums. Pink Floyd's *Dark Side Of The Moon*, Elton John's *Goodbye Yellow Brick Road*, Mike Oldfield's *Tubular Bells*, Led Zeppelin's *Houses Of The Holy*, Billy Joel's *Piano Man*, Rolling Stone's *Goat's Head Soup*, Stevie Wonder's *Talking Book* and David Bowie's *Aladdin Sane* to name a few. Besides having to meet demand for Pink Floyd's *Dark Side Of The Moon*, EMI had two double albums by The Beatles, two albums by Wings, and one album apiece from Lennon, Harrison, and Starr in the pipeline. All of which sold by the bucket load. And it wasn't just new albums that were selling. Lennon's *Imagine* album sold enough copies this month to keep it in the UK top 50 albums chart.

For a handful of independent record labels operating out of New Jersey, the vinyl shortage was the least of their worries. The lawsuit brought by George Harrison, Apple Records, Capitol Records, and Capitol Records Distributing Corp. against Audiotape Inc and various others had worked. State Supreme Court Judge Nathaniel Heiman handed down a preliminary injunction against the defendants, barring Audiotape Inc., Electro-Scanning Systems, Ltd., T. V. Products, Inc., and 100 John Does from manufacturing or distributing records and tapes by The Beatles. To give Klein and his lawyers credit, what they did was clever. Rather than base the complaint on copyright violations, they based it on unfair competition and invasion of privacy. Justice Nathaniel T. Heiman said, "Apple and Capitol have spent great sums of money and invested a great deal of time and effort to effectively manufacture and distribute records and tapes of Beatle works and performances. It appears that defendants will be and have been unjustly enriching themselves at plaintiffs' expense." He continued, "[...] they (the defendants) have effectively limited themselves to the final reproductive process. It would thus appear at this stage of the proceeding that Apple and Capitol are victims of unfair competition and should be afforded preliminary relief. [...] Accordingly, plaintiffs' motion for a preliminary injunction is granted to the extent of enjoining or restraining the defendants from manufacturing or distributing, either directly or indirectly, for sale in the State of New York, records or tapes of Beatle performances which are subject to the Apple and Capitol licensing agreements."

However, the case wasn't over yet. It still had to go to trial when the charge that the defendants copied and marketed Beatles recordings, taking them without authorization from Apple and Capitol Records, would be heard. Not that it mattered. The officially authorized albums *1962 – 66* and *1967 – 70* were heading for the top of the charts in the UK and US. The pirates may have stolen The Beatles' recordings, but it had provoked Apple and Capitol into action and provided them with a brace of hit albums.

Another double album with a Beatles connection was heading for the top of the charts, even though it didn't feature any material by The Beatles. The two-record soundtrack album of *That'll Be The Day* was released to tie in with the film, which went on general release in the UK on 13th May. Both the film and soundtrack did good business. Unfortunately, that couldn't be said for Starr's other film project, now titled *Son of Dracula*. Originally called Count Downe, the film starred Harry Nilsson and co-starred Starr as Merlin the Magician, who follows the birth and rise of young Count Downe. Unlike Starr's current blockbuster, *Son of Dracula* was an unmitigated flop. Filming was completed by November 1972, but shortly after, Starr called in Graham Chapman to re-write the script, which was dubbed over the film's uninspired dialogue. An alternative Pythonesque soundtrack was also recorded, which was rejected and shelved. *Born To Boogie* had been so successful that cinema showings had to be extended. It must have generated a sizeable amount of income for Apple Films, which the doomed *Son of Dracula* quickly lost. Ringo's folly was shown at a private screening for guests in the last week of April. Starr and his wife Maureen were joined by Harry Nilsson, George and Patti Harrison, David Geffen, and Richard Perry. All of whom no doubt said nice things about it.

While promoting *That'll Be The Day*, Starr claimed he was only offered roles that typecast him as the joker. "People offer me comedy film parts where I make everyone laugh but anyone can pull a funny face," he said. *Son of Dracula* was his chance to be funny and serious. Indeed, his description of his role in the film was blood chilling. "I get to rape a girl, stabbed her father, and beat up someone. It was a really great part for me." It was indeed a challenging role, but not one that found favour with the British Board of Censors. "Now they want to cut my best stuff before the film is shown in Britain," he explained. "It's tough, but most people up to the age of 35 would really dig it, I think. I won't let it come out in Britain unless they agree to leave in all my best scenes." The British public never did get to see Starr's best bits. Because of limited distribution, few Americans got to see them, either.

Before the film was shown inside commercial cinemas, Starr did his best to promote it. "*Son Of Dracula* has a great premise," he said, "which is that Drac takes the cure and marries the girl. I'm using all the elements: the Wolfman, Frankenstein, Merlin, and just the whole gang. It's like a non-musical, non-horror, non-comedy comedy... or it's a horror-horror, musical-musical, comedy-comedy." Despite the hype Starr tried to drum up, those who did see the film didn't think it was funny or horrific. Just horrible. It died a death worse than Dracula's.

The stress involved with movie making was getting to Starr, and he was starting to wonder if it was all worth it. "In the last two years," he said, "I produced two movies and directed one so that it was movie city for me. Out of it all, I think acting is the most comfortable deal. Directing I love to do but producing will drive you insane. Producers are worth their weight in gold for getting all those things together because it ain't easy." Starr was learning the hard way that being the boss was demanding. Acting naturally and letting the producer or director deal with the stress was less exacting. "With *Count Downe* I was there for the auditions for people who were doing small parts I was checking it out all the time. I realised the hassles that go on, but as an actor they tend to keep things away from you. They don't let you know someone's having a tantrum; they try and keep it really cool for you to do your part, but a lot of weird things go on." Work on the film would limp on for another year. It eventually received its premiere in Atlanta on 19th April 1974 before having a limited run in major cities across America and Canada.

A review in the *Miami Herald* praised the performances but complained about the lack of music. "*Son of Dracula* is a clever little movie that might have been a clever big movie if taken far enough. Producer Ringo Starr and director Freddie Francis manage the kind of eccentric, childlike but inventive humour we've come to expect in Beatles films, and the music." The reviewer also shared Starr's opinion that most people under 35 would dig it. "An engaging rock horror comedy because of the kinky, prankish, offbeat style, *Son of Dracula* offers good rock music (though I wish we could hear more of it), deadpan performances that are frequently funny, an affectionate little Valentine to ghoul movies in general, and the kind of feel and flavour audiences under 35 will find amusing." Reviews in other papers weren't as flattering. The *Boston Globe* called it "a bloodless bore." The *Austin American-Statesman* described the film as "mindless pop-schlock." The *Des Moines*

Tribune said, "Starr and Nilsson handle their wooden lines as though they are reading them from cue cards held up just off camera." The *Fort Lauderdale News* dammed the film with faint praise, "If *Son of Dracula* weren't so ungodly (pun intended) slow, it might have had a chance at being to horror what Zachariah was to the western."

Television commercials for the new Beatles compilation albums were somewhat more straightforward to produce and more successful. Capitol Records gave the job to Chiaramonte Films, which created 60-second and 30-second TV spots to promote the two new double albums. The commercials, combined with adverts in the print media and considerable support from radio stations playing Beatles oldies, ensured that both albums climbed steadily up the album chart. In the first week of May, the albums were at 6 (*1962 – 66*) and 7 (*1967 – 70*) on *Billboard's* album chart. The following week, they had climbed to numbers 4 and 5. A week later, they sat at numbers 2 (*1967 – 70*) and 3 (*1962 – 66*). Only Led Zeppelin's *Houses of the Holy* prevented The Beatles from topping the chart. But not even the mighty Zeppelin could keep The Beatles from the top spot. Even though Led Zeppelin had recently broken The Beatles' record for the largest paid concert attendance in US history, in the last week of May, The Beatles *1967 – 70* topped the US album chart.

George Harrison's new single, was released in the US on 7th May. (It wouldn't be released in the UK until the 27th.) Like the best of his work, 'Give Me Love (Give Me Peace On Earth)' is a song of hope and faith for all humanity, a beacon of light in a world overcast with doubt and despair. Like 'My Sweet Lord,' it was a cleverly disguised prayer. However, certain press sections were growing tired of Harrison's preaching, which meant he had to get his message across without alienating them. For many casual listeners, the message was irrelevant. It had a good tune and beat; that was all that mattered. The process of getting his new song heard started with radio airplay. Like Paul McCartney and Wings latest single, which was sitting at number 26 in the *Billboard* singles chart in the week that Harrison's single was released, 'Give Me Love (Give Me Peace On Earth)' was jumped on by US radio stations. Just five days after its release, 'Give Me Love (Give Me Peace On Earth)' had been added to playlists across the country and was listed in *Cash Box* as one of that week's top three additions to playlists, the other two being 'Shambala' by Three Dog Night and 'You'll Never Get To Heaven' by the Stylistics.

Like some of Harrison's recent projects, royalties from 'Give Me Love (Give Me Peace On Earth)' were donated to charity. Having had his fingers well and truly burnt with the *Concert For Bangla-Desh*, he wasn't about to make the same mistake twice. The second time around, he formed a charity in advance. The Material World Charitable Foundation was established to "encourage the exploration of alternate and diverse forms of artistic expression, life views, and philosophies as well as a way to support established charities and people with special needs."

Reviewers didn't miss Harrison's philanthropic nature, nor the fact that his latest song had a message. *Cash Box* said of the single: "Harrison is still well into the message song, and this time around, material possessions and the material world, in general, get the ax. Will rack up lots of material dollars on its way to achieving another Harrison material gold record." *Billboard* published a similar review, albeit one that paid more attention to his performance. "Harrison's voice and sweet, country-tinged guitar, each within a rippling but controlled rhythm base, lends itself to this plea for human understanding. His sincere sound engulfs the listener and brings him into the story." Writing in the *Los Angeles Times*, Robert Hilburn was unconvinced of Harrison's talents. "'Give Me Love (Give Me Peace On Earth)' is a reworking of Harrison's *All Things Must Pass* period that is pleasant enough to soar - with the help of his popularity - high into the national sales charts, but hardly the level of work we expect from a major artist. The obvious question, then, is whether Harrison is a major artist. I have my doubts."

One sign of a good song is how quickly other artists cover it. Some of The Beatles' songs were recorded by other acts within days of their release, hoping that The Beatles' magic would provide them with a hit. Little had changed in the nine years since Ella Fitzgerald recorded 'Can't Buy Me Love'. Singers were still looking for songs and hits. Tony Bennett knew a good song when he heard one. He knew two good songs when he heard them. Bennett wasted no time, and within weeks of Harrison's 'Give Me Love (Give Me Peace On Earth)' and McCartney's 'My Love' being issued, he'd recorded his interpretations of the songs. Recorded on 19th June with arrangements by Torrie Zito, who'd also written arrangements for Lennon's *Imagine* album, both songs were released on the album Tony Bennett's *Greatest Hits, Volume 7* and as a single in the UK. Back in the UK, Wings were preparing for their first proper tour of concert halls. It would be McCartney's first professionally promoted tour of the UK since The Beatles, and this time, Wings would have a support act to warm up the audience. Having seen Brinsley Schwarz in action at the Hard Rock Café, McCartney booked the band as a support act. "So he said will you come and do [the tour]," recalls Bob Andrews, "and we're not going to turn round and say no to him because there was a good feeling about it and that was always one of our things. If it felt right we'll do it."

Initially, McCartney's manager wanted the Brinsleys to pay to be on the tour. Most record companies would have fallen over themselves to get one of their acts onto a high-profile tour, even if it meant paying. But Brinsley Schwarz's manager, Dave Robinson, was adamant that they couldn't afford it. And anyway, why should they have to pay to play? Robinson pulled a few strings and got Wings' guitarist, Henry McCullough, who he'd managed when he was in Eire Apparent, to speak to McCartney about the group's predicament. McCullough talked to McCartney, who arranged to meet Robinson to discuss the proposed 'buy on'. "Henry McCullough got it for us, I think, because we'd known him for ages since he was in Eire Apparent, and he and Dave did some talking," explained Nick Lowe. Thanks to Robinson's tenacity, McCartney's manager agreed to book Brinsley Schwarz and pay them £125 a night. The irony was that Brinsley Schwarz were being paid more per man than were members of Wings. Brinsley Schwarz were being paid £25 each per gig, before deductions. McCullough, Laine, and Seiwell were still on a £70 weekly retainer. This meant that in the final week of gigs, each member of Brinsley Schwarz earned £175, while McCullough, Laine, and Seiwell earned £70. At least there was the promised loyalty bonus from McCartney for McCullough, Laine, and Seiwell to look forward to.

Wings rehearsed for the tour at the Manticore Theatre and Twickenham Film Studios, while Brinsley Schwarz rehearsed in the living room of their shared house. Not that they needed much rehearsing because, unlike Wings, Brinsley Schwarz played hundreds of gigs in Britain and Europe each year. While Wings were rehearsing at Twickenham, they also filmed more footage for the *Bruce McMouse Show*, a proposed film of their European tour.

Rehearsals over, Wings 1973 UK tour opened in Bristol at the Hippodrome on 11th May. Fans queued for hours to buy tickets from the box office and according to the *Bristol Evening Post*, some had travelled from the US to be there. Although Wings impressed James Belsey of the *Bristol Post*, he thought them good but not great. "The reception he and the group won was guaranteed from the start, because the audience was packed with McCartney fans from Devon to Texas USA, quite literally. But Bristol has seen louder welcomes since the days of The Beatles and Wings didn't really do enough to get all the audience on their feet. The music was beautifully balanced and centred largely on McCartney as an individual, a singer and a star." Although Belsey recognised McCartney was the star, it was one of his sidemen who impressed him most. "The man who tore the show apart was Denny Laine, one of the original members of The Moody Blues, a contemporary group of the early Beatles. McCartney made a really nice gesture by handing Laine the lead spot and he went on to play 'Go Now' and 'Say You Don't Mind' his two outstanding numbers. They were the best of the show."

On the 16th and 17th, Wings played Manchester's Hardrock Concert Theatre. Barry Coleman reviewed the first date for the *Guardian* and wasn't impressed. "[H]e treated us to a banal string of Beatles oldies, other people's oldies, and the odd Wings original, including their current top 20 ditty, 'My Love'. Were it not for its author, this would be just another bad song, oozing cheap sentimentality. As it is, it comes as a firm statement that McCartney has moved out of the area of worthwhile music. Given the scope of their material, the band, with the exception of one member, played well enough, but certainly no better than scores of others. They got a good reception from a full auditorium, but after their encore of 'Long Tall Sally' (their one impressive number) they admitted failure. Linda McCartney, photographer, sang in a painfully flat howl. Her piano playing was crudely inept and she was frequently defeated by the simple tambourine. No amount of kisses from the Prince will turn her into a musician, and her unnecessary and ungainly presence on the stage amounts almost to a contempt for the paying public. And you'd be lucky to get away with that for long, even in a fairy story."

Unlike Coleman, Brinsley Schwarz's manager, Dave Robinson, was impressed with Wings. McCartney considered soundchecks valuable rehearsal time, which he spent honing the band to perfection. It was an attitude Robinson admired, but one Brinsley Schwarz lacked. "I was frustrated not at the lack of success but at the lack of work," said Robinson. "They could have worked harder, and as a result, they would have got further. The Wings tour was where I realised that Paul McCartney, who didn't need to, was still working very hard, and at soundchecks trying to polish the music, trying to get it to be better, and my lot were in the pub."

Only Nick Lowe, lead singer and bassist with Brinsley Schwarz, was down the pub. His attitude was so laid back that Ian Gomm recalls starting their set without him. "I remember him walking on halfway through the set at a gig at the Liverpool Empire on the Wings tour," he says. Despite his lack of discipline, Lowe later suggested that the tour had been a real benefit in terms of learning: "They (Wings) had a kind of poppy show which is something we like, we're all pop fans really, and they had this feel of being a very high-class pop band."

The following day, Wings played Liverpool. It was a bittersweet homecoming. The last time McCartney played the Liverpool Empire was in 1965 when The Beatles played two shows as part of their UK winter tour. While the Empire Theatre had managed to keep its doors open, the the Cavern Club. had been struggling. The club's owner, Mr Roy Adams, said: "Today's customers are not interested in The Beatles or what has happened in the past. They are only interested in the present and the scene we give them now." Cavern customers weren't the only ones uninterested in the past. Neither was Liverpool Council, which, at the time, did little or nothing to preserve the historic site. The Cavern Club would eventually be bulldozed and replaced by a ventilation shaft for the city's underground rail loop.

Speaking to the *Liverpool Daily Post*, McCartney seemed ambivalent about the venue's fate: "It's a pity that Dingle and the Cavern were being knocked down, but what can anyone do? If I went it would be to play if they asked me." However, when he spoke to the rival newspaper, the *Liverpool Echo*, McCartney flipped his story. "If it had been physically possible, I would certainly have gone along to the old Cavern to kiss goodbye. When I heard the Cavern had to go in the near future, I wanted to take the group with me on a surprise farewell visit for an hour, after our Empire show. But there just wasn't the time available. I'd have loved to have done it. After all, The Beatles and a lot of other folk who eventually made it, the Cavern was where it all began." It wouldn't have required much effort from McCartney to take his band along for a late night visit. The Liverpool Empire is a ten-minute walk from the Cavern. A quick phone call by his manager to the owner of the Cavern would have facilitated a private view, and a brief visit would have shown support for local venues, musicians, and fans alike. If he could find time for the local press, he could have found time to visit the Cavern.

Perhaps he'd been upset by the Cavern's owner, Roy Adams, who claimed that people weren't interested in the past. Cavern dwellers may not have been interested, but when it came time to review Wings concert, the *Liverpool Daily Post* couldn't help but mention McCartney's former band. "A touch of Beatlemania magic returned to Liverpool last night as more than 5000 fans sang, stomped, and clapped their way through the music of Paul McCartney and Wings in the cavernous Empire Theatre. The first house show started quietly enough as Wings launched into 'Big Barn Bed' and 'When The Night' from their latest album, *Red Rose Speedway*. But by the time they were into 'Maybe I'm Amazed,' 'Go Now,' and 'Hi, Hi, Hi,' few people were still in their seats, and downstairs, most were leaping about in the aisles." It wasn't quite like the old days; times had changed, and so had McCartney's audience. Girls still screamed at their heroes. They screamed at The Osmonds, T. Rex and the Partridge Family. They didn't scream at McCartney and Wings for the simple reason that they had grown up.

The first half of Wings' tour ended at the Hammersmith Odeon. An extra date was added because the Birmingham date had to be cancelled. *Record Mirror* reported that: "It will be the band's final appearance of their first British tour and takes the place of a scheduled gig at Birmingham." It was, in fact, the last night of the first leg of the tour. More dates would be forthcoming. *Record Mirror* continued: "A spokesman for the group said the concert at the Birmingham Theatre had to be cancelled because of electrical danger from a water-tank. It was particularly disappointing since Birmingham is Denny Laine's hometown but the band hope to play there later in the year."

Living near one of the country's busiest music venues must have been trying for residents, particularly as many shows continued late into the evening. It had become such an issue for residents living near the Hammersmith Odeon that the local newspaper, the *Shepard's Bush Gazette*, reported that the three days passed peacefully without neighbours complaining about noisy concert goers. The venue employed extra staff to control fans, but at least one managed to break through the security to plant a smacker on Macca. The first leg of the tour having ended, a party was thrown that ended with an all-star jam session. "By the end, we had Elton John on the piano, Denny Laine on the bass, Henry McCullough on the guitar, and Keith Moon on the drums. Bob Andrews – our keyboard player – was on guitar," recalled Ian Gomm.

While McCartney was basking in the warm glow of a successful UK tour, there was more bad news for Lennon, Harrison, and Starr. On 26th May, Klein made public his intention to reclaim money he'd lent the Fab Three while he was their manager. Klein claimed Lennon Harrison and Starr owed him £2,000,000 (£20,698,921.06). "That's the money they owe me and is still outstanding. I just hope they pay up like the good honest fellas they are. Oh God, it will be sad if that doesn't happen, and I have to fight them for the cash. Naturally I'm disappointed my association with the three boys is over. I had enormous personal feeling for them and this overruled the money aspects involved." Klein wasn't about to write off the loans. But the fact that he went to the press to embarrass them rather than approach them privately says much about how his relationship with them had changed.

On the same day, *Cash Box* published an article about the ATV Music Group and Sir Lew Grade's ambitions for America. Although McCartney had resolved his dispute with ATV, Lennon's was ongoing. However, Lennon and McCartney had significant leverage because ATV planned to focus on exploiting its major song copyrights, a catalogue built on Lennon's and McCartney's compositions. McCartney was a hot asset because of his current single, 'My Love,' and the forthcoming theme song for the next James Bond film, *Live and Let Die*. Lennon, less so. But even he was still writing and recording songs to help fill ATV Music Group's coffers. Not the least of which was 'Happy Xmas (War Is Over),' which, among several other compositions, was currently the cause of the dispute.

While Lennon was battling Northern Songs and Maclen Music, there was good news from the courts. On the 14th May, Judge Peter Solito had awarded Yoko permanent custody of her daughter, Kyoko. It was, however, a hollow victory because Ono's former husband had taken Kyoko and was in hiding. Lennon's fight with the INS was still being dragged through the courts, and now Allen Klein was threatening further legal action if the money he'd loaned him wasn't repaid. Worse still, Klein's very public announcement in the *Daily Mirror* may have alerted Bank of England officials who began an investigation into how Lennon and Harrison had moved large sums of money in and out of the UK, which at the time was tightly controlled. The Bank of England noted that Lennon had been "advanced various sums by non-resident companies," which had not been disclosed to the Bank. It wanted "full details of these transactions" and started to keep a file on the offenders. The job of investigating the transactions was given to Mr. A.M. Willson-White, who wanted to know more about payments to Harrison of £300,387 (£3,108,843.40) and loans of £30,000 (£310,483.82) and $10,000 ($69,463.29) to both Lennon and Harrison. As ever, the world of Beatles finances was complicated and convoluted.

The follow-up to Harrison's colossal *All Things Must Pass* was scheduled for release in the US on 28th May. *Melody Maker* reported that the album's British release date was planned for 21st May but was delayed. One reason for its delayed UK release may have been that EMI struggled to meet demand. Singles by T. Rex and Geordie had to be subcontracted to pressing plants in Holland. Even then, only a few record shops managed to get copies. Harrison's album was eventually released in the UK on 22nd June.

A confessional and cathartic exploration of personal doubt and spiritual crisis affecting him, some took exception to what they viewed as the album's "preachy overtones" and "relentlessly pious nature." *Rolling Stone*, however, thought it "the most concise, universally conceived work by a former Beatle since *John Lennon/Plastic Ono Band*." *Cash Box* was equally fulsome in its praise. "This is the long overdue collection from George that most folks have been anxiously awaiting since his *All Things Must Pass* grouping of a couple of years back. Naturally, the wait was well worth it and this brilliant collection of ballads, rock and rollers and pure, heartfelt sentiments should be readily accepted with open arms by the masses." Not everyone was as impressed. The *Los Angeles Times* found the album disappointing. "Harrison's chief strength should be his sincerity. Several of the songs on the new album reflect a spirit of altruism and spiritual concern that should earn the album a place in the rock music as a philosophy of life shelf next to Peter Townshend's *Who Came First*. [...] If Harrison is serious about the message in his music, he has got to be more careful with the music. At present he seems more concerned with the commercial nature of the song than the philosophical overtones."

British reviews were equally mixed, although one reviewer echoed the view espoused by *Rolling Stone*. "Musically, there are no radical departures from what I suppose has to be called the style of *All Things Must Pass*, it's more a case of the basic George Harrison music stripped down a bit and refined. This album is Harrison's *Imagine*, if only because it seems equally crafted in its form and acute in its self-assessment. But whatever neat phrases you can dig up to apply to *Living In The Material World* (and doubtless many will find many) the album is there for you to respond to as you-will. Unlike Lennon, Harrison hasn't come to you demanding confrontation - merely that you listen." Writing in the *NME*, Tony Tyler bemoaned the deification of The Beatles: "First, we all suffer from a collective blind spot when it comes to criticising ex-Beatles work. Because many of us found, in The Beatles, a complete raison d'etre for getting into music in the first place, we tend to venerate them beyond considerable limits (except Paul McCartney, who, for some obscure reason, has been required by a heartless public to make it all over again.) Result? John Lennon and George Harrison have suffered from an almost total absence of reasoned criticism concerning their post-Beatles product."

Tyler was right. The Beatles had been placed on a pedestal. That pedestal got higher with each passing decade. However, his last comment is disingenuous. Tyler and his fellow music journalists had all scorned the ex-Beatles solo releases. He also makes inflated claims about critics' influence on their music: "This has affected their music," he claimed. "*Living In The Material World* is George's second solo album. It's an improvement on *All Things Must Pass* – pleasant, competent, vaguely dull and inoffensive. It's also breathtakingly unoriginal and lyrically – at least – turgid, repetitive and so damn holy I could scream." It was the message rather than the medium that Tyler objected to. He wasn't alone. However, whereas the *Los Angeles Times* thought the music was too commercial, too polished, and sophisticated, Tyler thought it was the opposite. Whatever critics thought didn't stop the album from reaching number 1 in the US and 2 in the UK.

WEEK ENDING 5 MAY 1973
1. TIE A YELLOW RIBBON ROUND THE OLE OAK TREE: DAWN
   FEATURING TONY ORLANDO
2. THE CISCO KID: WAR
3. LITTLE WILLY: THE SWEET
4. YOU ARE THE SUNSHINE OF MY LIFE: STEVIE WONDER
5. THE NIGHT THE LIGHTS WENT OUT IN GEORGIA: VICKI LAWRENCE
6. DRIFT AWAY: DOBIE GRAY
7. STUCK IN THE MIDDLE WITH YOU: STEALERS WHEEL
8. THE TWELFTH OF NEVER: DONNY OSMOND
9. SING: CARPENTERS
10. FRANKENSTEIN: EDGAR WINTER GROUP

WEEK ENDING 12 MAY 1973
1. TIE A YELLOW RIBBON ROUND THE OLE OAK TREE: DAWN
   FEATURING TONY ORLANDO
2. YOU ARE THE SUNSHINE OF MY LIFE: STEVIE WONDER
3. LITTLE WILLY: THE SWEET
4. THE CISCO KID: WAR
5. DRIFT AWAY: DOBIE GRAY
6. STUCK IN THE MIDDLE WITH YOU: STEALERS WHEEL
7. FRANKENSTEIN: EDGAR WINTER GROUP
8. THE NIGHT THE LIGHTS WENT OUT IN GEORGIA: VICKI LAWRENCE
9. DANIEL: ELTON JOHN
10. THE TWELFTH OF NEVER: DONNY OSMOND

WEEK ENDING 19 MAY 1973
1. YOU ARE THE SUNSHINE OF MY LIFE: STEVIE WONDER
2. TIE A YELLOW RIBBON ROUND THE OLE OAK TREE: DAWN
   FEATURING TONY ORLANDO
3. LITTLE WILLY: THE SWEET
4. FRANKENSTEIN: EDGAR WINTER GROUP
5. DANIEL: ELTON JOHN
6. MY LOVE: PAUL MCCARTNEY AND WINGS
7. DRIFT AWAY: DOBIE GRAY
8. STUCK IN THE MIDDLE WITH YOU: STEALERS WHEEL
9. PILLOW TALK: SYLVIA
10. WILDFLOWER: SKYLARK

WEEK ENDING 26 MAY 1973
1. FRANKENSTEIN: EDGAR WINTER GROUP
2. MY LOVE: PAUL MCCARTNEY AND WINGS
3. DANIEL: ELTON JOHN
4. TIE A YELLOW RIBBON ROUND THE OLE OAK TREE: DAWN
   FEATURING TONY ORLANDO
5. YOU ARE THE SUNSHINE OF MY LIFE: STEVIE WONDER
6. PILLOW TALK: SYLVIA
7. LITTLE WILLY: THE SWEET
8. DRIFT AWAY: DOBIE GRAY
9. WILDFLOWER: SKYLARK
10. HOCUS POCUS: FOCUS

WEEK ENDING 5 MAY 1973
1. TIE A YELLOW RIBBON ROUND THE OLD OAK TREE: DAWN FEATURING TONY ORLANDO
2. HELLO! HELLO! I'M BACK AGAIN: GARY GLITTER
3. DRIVE-IN SATURDAY: DAVID BOWIE
4. HELL RAISER: THE SWEET
5. TWEEDLE DEE: LITTLE JIMMY OSMOND
6. SEE MY BABY JIVE: WIZZARD
7. ALL BECAUSE OF YOU: GEORDIE
8. GET DOWN: GILBERT O'SULLIVAN
9. BROTHER LOUIE: HOT CHOCOLATE
10. I'M A CLOWN/SOME KIND OF SUMMER: DAVID CASSIDY

WEEK ENDING 12 MAY 1973
1. TIE A YELLOW RIBBON ROUND THE OLD OAK TREE: DAWN FEATURING TONY ORLANDO
2. HELL RAISER: THE SWEET
3. HELLO! HELLO! I'M BACK AGAIN: GARY GLITTER
4. SEE MY BABY JIVE: WIZZARD
5. GIVING IT ALL AWAY: ROGER DALTREY
6. AND I LOVE YOU SO: PERRY COMO
7. BROTHER LOUIE: HOT CHOCOLATE
8. DRIVE-IN SATURDAY: DAVID BOWIE
9. MY LOVE: WINGS
10. NO MORE MR. NICE GUY: ALICE COOPER

WEEK ENDING 19 MAY 1973
1. SEE MY BABY JIVE: WIZZARD
2. HELL RAISER: THE SWEET
3. TIE A YELLOW RIBBON ROUND THE OLD OAK TREE: DAWN FEATURING TONY ORLANDO
4. HELLO! HELLO! I'M BACK AGAIN: GARY GLITTER
5. AND I LOVE YOU SO: PERRY COMO
6. DRIVE-IN SATURDAY: DAVID BOWIE
7. GIVING IT ALL AWAY: ROGER DALTREY
8. BROTHER LOUIE: HOT CHOCOLATE
9. ALSO SPRACH ZARATHUSTRA: DEODATO
10. NO MORE MR. NICE GUY: ALICE COOPER

WEEK ENDING 26 MAY 1973
1. SEE MY BABY JIVE: WIZZARD
2. HELL RAISER: THE SWEET
3. AND I LOVE YOU SO: PERRY COMO
4. TIE A YELLOW RIBBON ROUND THE OLD OAK TREE: DAWN FEATURING TONY ORLANDO
5. CAN THE CAN: SUZI QUATRO
6. ONE AND ONE IS ONE: MEDICINE HEAD
7. ALSO SPRACH ZARATHUSTRA: DEODATO
8. HELLO! HELLO! I'M BACK AGAIN: GARY GLITTER
9. BROTHER LOUIE: HOT CHOCOLATE
10. GIVING IT ALL AWAY: ROGER DALTREY

CHAPTER 6
JUNE: AN OPEN BOOK

On Friday, 1st June, Wings released a new single. The band's name, now minus 'Paul McCartney,' had reverted to Wings. However, the change didn't last long. By the time their next single was released, it had reverted back to Paul McCartney and Wings. 'Live And Let Die' was issued by Apple Records with an Apple label. Gone were the custom designs employed for previous Wings releases. With Klein out of the picture, McCartney was happy to be associated with the record company he co-founded. Ron Kass, who'd previously worked for Apple, asked McCartney if he'd be interested in writing the theme song for the next James Bond film. McCartney jumped at the chance.

This significant commission would reinforce his reputation as a composer outside The Beatles. He'd previously written theme songs for film and television, but nothing as high profile as this. It would also generate significant income to bolster the McCartney coffers. Besides the $15,000 ($102,939.86) fee he'd receive for writing the song, there would also be mechanical and Performing Right Society (PRS) royalties from the sale of records and airplay. Not only would Wings get to release the song as a single, but it would also feature on the film soundtrack LP. And for those who didn't care for Wings' recording of the song, RCA issued 'Live And Let Die' as a single by B.J. Arnau, whose version was used in the film. Wings recorded 'Live And Let Die' on Thursday, 19th October, at AIR studios, London. McCartney left nothing to chance. Unlike some of Wings' recent recording sessions, which had seen them aimlessly jamming for hours, 'Live And Let Die' was refined before they entered the studio. "The band had been rehearsing it and when we got it as near perfection as possible we took it to the studio," recalled McCartney. George Martin was asked to produce the session to ensure everything went smoothly. The plan was to record 'Live And Let Die' as they had recorded 'My Love'. Wings would set up in the studio along with the orchestra and record everything live. Having done something similar with The Beatles when they performed 'All You Need Is Love' live on the global television broadcast *Our World* in 1967, Martin insisted they have a back-up plan.

First, Wings were recorded live in the studio without the orchestra, just in case the band and orchestra didn't coalesce when they recorded together. Wings captured the song in ten takes, which, for the moment, were put to one side. Later that evening, they started afresh with the orchestra, and as Martin suspected, they encountered problems. The string section was too loud and was bleeding into McCartney's microphone. The solution was to put the orchestra in a separate studio and record Wings and orchestra together but in different rooms. With the technical problems resolved, Wings recorded three takes with the orchestra, which satisfied Martin that they had everything they needed.

Demand for the single was strong, but Wings' latest single suffered distribution problems like other EMI acts. EMI couldn't meet demand, with *Record Mirror* reporting: "Demand for their new single could not be met. This has stopped them from having a notable first-week entry place." Despite this, 'Live And Let Die' entered the UK chart at 37, climbing to number 15 the following week. In the same week, 'My Love' was at number 50, and George Harrison's 'Give Me Love (Give Me Peace On Earth)' at number 11.

Reviews for McCartney's Bond theme were favourable. Bond themes had become significant in the public imagination, akin to the annual competition to be number one at Christmas. Releasing a new Bond theme was a big event for the music and film industry. Theme song and film had a symbiotic relationship; the song promoted the film, and the film promoted the song. A poor theme song would harm the film. A bad film wouldn't attract audiences; fewer people would hear the song and want to buy it. The power of a strong soundtrack was significant. One of the biggest-selling albums of the 1960s was *The Sound Of Music*, which sold more than 20 million copies worldwide. That was more than The Beatles' *Abbey Road* album. *Disc* compared both recordings of 'Live And Let Die' and decided that Wings came out on top. "On balance, this version is slightly better than the B.J. Arnau version, which is used for the film. The group take it at a slower pace than Miss Arnau, which seems to suit the song better. They also include a dramatic instrumental sequence, which is an important feature of their version, and does not appear on the other. This composition compares favourably with other Bond themes and illustrates the extraordinary versatility of McCartney's songwriting talent." Reviewing the single for the *NME*, Ian MacDonald was indifferent. "It's not intrinsically very interesting, but the film will help to sell it and vice versa."

If British reviewers were full of reserve, their American counterparts were full of praise. *Billboard* thought it was the best thing since the British invasion. "A bit of distinctively sweet McCartney melody, a sudden booming uproar of massed symphony orchestra, a snatch of reggae and some more bombast a la 1812 Overture. The best 007 movie theme of all and one of McCartney's two or three most satisfying records ever." *Cash Box* was equally impressed: "From the motion picture of the same name comes the title track as well as Wings' second number-one single. This is absolutely magnificent in every respect. More gold for McCartney and friends!"

Wings were constantly doing better in America than in Britain. Unfortunately, McCartney was struggling to obtain a work visa because of his recent convictions for possession of cannabis and was unable to exploit his success other than through TV shows and airplay. In the first week of June, Wings occupied the number one spot in the *Billboard* singles and albums charts, preventing Elton John and Led Zeppelin from topping the charts. *Billboard* reported McCartney's remarkable achievement and predicted similar success for Harrison. "Ex-Beatle Paul McCartney has done something in the United States which no other Beatle has accomplished - he has the number one single and number one album in the nation concurrently this week. In the wings (pardon the term) is George Harrison's own single, 'Give Me Love (Give Me Peace On Earth)' which is in its third week on the survey, with his LP *Living In The Material World* due out shortly. So George may be able to follow Paul in heading the list on both our surveys. Paul's accomplishment is only the fourth occurrence during the past two years."

All these solo Beatles records were good for business. Even rival record companies claimed that they stimulated sales. Vince Cosgrove, vice president and director of sales at MCA, said: "I'm delighted when a new George Harrison album comes out. It brings people into the stores and they might also buy my goods when they're buying Harrison's album." Harrison's new album sold well enough to enter the *Billboard* chart at number 11 on the week ending 16th June. In the same week, Paul McCartney and Wings were at number 1, The Beatles *1967 – 70* at number 2, The Beatles *1962 – 66* at number 5, Led Zeppelin at number 3, Paul Simon at number 7 and Pink Floyd at number 8.

Led Zeppelin had recently broken The Beatles' record for the largest paid concert attendance. They had reached the top and were well-placed to indulge their rock 'n' roll fantasies. As members of elite rock royalty, they had so much cash they could have bought the hotels they trashed. Once again, *Billboard* was on hand to report what some in the industry considered normal rock star behaviour. "Led Zeppelin was in good destructive form during their LA stay last week, a stay extended when Jimmy Page sprained a picking finger when he stumbled against a fence at San Diego Airport which postponed to Sunday. The boys reportedly threw a table out of their ninth-floor party suite at the Continental Hyatt House after their disappointment at not being able to toss liquor glasses into an open Lincoln convertible parked below. They also smashed up the lobby paintings and restrooms at a film theatre where a late-night party was being thrown by Atlantic for Jo Jo Gunne. For a grand finale, they spread a four-foot cake around the house and swimming pool." Harrison was on hand to witness this wanton destruction and took it in his stride. "George Harrison and wife Patti received no peace on earth when Zeppelin drummer John Bonham threw them both, fully clothed, into the swimming pool in celebration of his 25th birthday," the paper claimed. "Their respective hosts felt it was all in fun, and the Zep always pay for their damages. They can afford to, having cleared over $300,000 from their California concerts."

Like Led Zeppelin, Harrison wasn't short of a few bob. No matter how hard he tried to give it away, his new album would generate a sizable chunk of money. Writing in *Record World*, Kal Rudman reported that Capitol Records projected sales of 1,600,000 in the first two months in North America. "Since the United States represents 60 percent of the world market, Al 'Captain Crazy' Coury of Capitol calculates that the album will sell approximately three million worldwide in the first two months. Based on the fact that The Beatles album *Abbey Road* has done nine million in the United States, Coury estimates that this album will sell thirteen million and will garner approximately $20,000,000 ($138,926,576.58) worldwide in albums and tapes." This may have been hyperbole on the part of Al Coury. It was undoubtedly speculation. We know that Living In The Material World was selling fast. *Cash Box* reported that the LP received RIAA certification as a million-dollar seller within two days of release. His single was climbing the charts, and two albums by The Beatles were in the top ten. A lot of records were being sold, and a lot of money was being made. Sales in the UK may not have been as large as those in the US, but they were still significant. *Record Mirror* reported, "The current success of the two Beatles double-album sets has meant a sale to date in excess of 105,000 copies."

Some of the money from Harrison's album went to his recently formed charity. The publishing royalties from *Living In The Material World* were going to his Material World Charitable Foundation. Publishers receive two types of royalty payments: mechanical and performance. The income from both varies from territory to territory. In the US, the mechanical royalty rate payable was 2 cents, which means that for *Living In The Material World*, which has eleven songs, Capitol paid 22 cents per album to the publisher. If Captain Crazy was correct and the album sold 1.6 million copies in its first two months, the amount it raised for charity, based on the US royalty rate, was $32,000 ($221,829). Royalty rates were significantly higher in the UK, where the mechanical royalty was 6.25% of the retail price. This had been set in 1956 but was due to expire in July 1973. Now that the UK had joined the EEC, publishers believed the time was right to harmonise rates across Europe and were lobbying for a 10% royalty rate. (MCPS charge a royalty rate of 8.5% (excl. VAT) of Published

Dealer Price or, if unavailable – 6.5% (excl. VAT) of the retail price.) With different rates applicable in other countries and without precise sales figures, it isn't easy to calculate how much *Living In The Material World* raised for charity. It was indeed a considerable amount.

While record companies were dealing with increasing costs and shortages of materials, the US government did its bit to make it even more difficult for record companies and retailers to balance their books. On 13th June, President Nixon addressed the nation. While many were hoping he'd announce his resignation, he called for a price freeze, imposing a 90-day freeze on wages and prices to counter inflation. The US government enacting wage and price controls for the first time since World War II. This is rarely good news and a sign that a government has lost control of the economy. The freeze was the fourth phase of an Economic Stabilization Plan, which was designed to see a return of more mandatory price controls. Nixon needed to curb the country's galloping inflation but stressed that controls would be "temporary" and would "not put the American economy in a straitjacket." Nixon had failed to keep inflation at no more than 2.5%. Indeed, the annual increase in retail prices soared to over 9%, and some wholesale rates soared to a wallet-sapping 23%. While a price freeze may have been good for the consumer, it was matched by a wage freeze, and it came at a time of upheaval in the record industry. All this had little effect on record sales, with several large retailers claiming they had seen no change in sales patterns.

The Lennons continued to pursue their political interests and, on 1st June, travelled to Cambridge, Massachusetts, to attend the first International Feminist Planning Conference. The Lennons would spend a week attending events and giving interviews to the press and radio. Talking to Loraine Alterman of the *Melody Maker*, Ono explained how she'd helped Lennon become a feminist: "He was a male chauvinist when I met him, and I think he was rather surprised. He didn't expect that he'd have to change so much but it wasn't like I tried to sort of force him into it. He's a sensitive character, and he sort of immediately picked up, so he started to get aware of what was going on. I think the fact that I was working in society helped because I think he had never really lived with somebody who was actually working in society. He said he started to compare me with him, and of course, I had more difficulty than he had. He began to see what kind of handicap all women have."

For his part, Lennon wasn't embarrassed to speak about their temporary role reversal. Speaking to Betty Danfield of The *Detroit Herald*, Lennon suggested that because of The Beatles' ongoing legal struggles to dissolve their partnership, he was being supported financially by Ono. "I've been living off my wife because I can't get my money out of England." Lennon couldn't access his money held in the UK for two reasons. Firstly, it was being held by the official receiver until The Beatles could resolve their partnership agreement. Secondly, the Bank of England had strict controls on how much money could leave the UK, and Lennon was already under investigation by the Bank because it suspected him of moving large sums of money offshore. His only other option had been to borrow money from his manager, or his wife.

On Saturday 2nd June, Ono performed at the old Cambridge Baptist Church. Backed by Lennon on guitar, Ono performed eight songs drawn from her most recent album, along with songs from *Some Time In New York City* and new songs that had yet to be recorded. Photos taken at the concert show someone documenting the event with a video camera, although only stills of the event surfaced. Lennon's presence at the conference may have upset some of the attendees. It was reported that much debate concerned whether men could be feminists and whether they should be allowed to attend. Delegates held a vote, and it was decided that in the future, men would not be allowed to participate in the conference.

While John and Yoko discussed feminism in Massachusetts, McCartney kept busy writing new songs for Wings, Rod Stewart, and his brother, Mike McGear. Having recently left GRIMMS, McGear was considering his options but was persuaded to go solo by his brother. The brothers collaborated on a brace of new songs designed to get McGear a new recording contract. They co-wrote 'Sweet Baby' and worked on a new McCartney composition, 'Leave It'. The basic track for 'Sweet Baby' was recorded on a Revox tape machine at McGear's house, with overdubs added by Paul and Mike at Island Studios in London. 'Leave It' was recorded at EMI Studios Abbey Road with Denny Seiwell on drums, Tony Coe on saxophone and McCartney on bass. 'Sweet Baby' and 'Leave It' were cut to acetate and sent to the Eastmans in New York, tasked with securing McGear a new recording contract.

At around this time, Paul and Linda chanced upon the village of Peasmarsh in Sussex. Driving along its leafy country roads, they spotted a house for sale. Just off Starvecrow Lane, down a short track, was a circular house set in woodland with a nearby stream. The McCartneys fell in love with the property and bought it as a weekend retreat for a reported £42,000 (£437,054.36). As with his Scottish farm, McCartney bought several additional tracts of land to expand his property and maintain his privacy. The Waterfall Estate (Woodlands Farm) would become McCartney's primary residence when not in London. It would eventually be complemented with the addition of a state-of-the-art recording studio – Hogg Hill Mill – in nearby Icklesham.

Meanwhile, McCartney's London office announced the second leg of Wings' UK tour. Five more dates were scheduled for England in early July. The additional dates were Sheffield City Hall, Stoke Tranton Gardens, Birmingham Odeon, Leicester Odeon, and Newcastle City Hall. The spokesperson for MPL said that the extra dates were added because of "overwhelming demand for more appearances. They can now play venues which had to be dropped from the early part of the tour, which means, in the case of Birmingham Odeon, that the group will fulfil their promise to return after their originally set gig at the Hippodrome had to be cancelled." As with the tour's first leg, Wings were supported by Brinsley Schwarz. McCartney was also scheduled to give an interview to David Symonds on Radio Luxembourg on 30th June, which he would no doubt use to publicize Wings forthcoming mini-tour.

If The Beatles thought they were free of Klein, they were wrong. On 6th June, ABKCO began legal proceedings in New York against Apple Films and Apple Records, seeking repayment of loans. The loans had been paid to Lennon, Harrison, and Starr. Although the official receiver paid them a monthly wage, they would still have to approach him to pay specific bills, which they were unwilling to do. These bills were considerable. Producing films and records does not come cheap; they all need financing. Klein had loaned each of the three Beatles £13,666 (£141,990), based on an average of the previous year's expenditure. However, the loan to Starr came with a caveat. Klein had persuaded Starr to confirm in writing that the loan could be treated "as a payment against any part" in Starr's interest in Apple to ABKCO. This would have helped facilitate ABKCO's acquisition of Apple, which had failed. This was followed on the 16th by further legal proceedings in Los Angeles against George Harrison for repayment of a $270,350 loan ($1,874,116.13). Klein filed a similar claim in New York on 6th July against Lennon. Lennon had borrowed as heavily as Harrison, if not more so. Klein claimed that since 1971, Lennon had borrowed £50,000 (£519,503), plus $34,000 ($235,694.28) to cover expenses incurred in the search of Ono's daughter, Kyoko and $48,000 ($332,744.86) to fund Bag Productions. On 28th June, the *Liverpool Echo* reported that Klein separately sued Lennon and two associated firms for a total of £195,000 (£2,026,065). It also said, "The one against Lennon says ABKCO made payments on his behalf to various persons, corporations and governmental bodies totalling £48,800 (£507,035.77), which had not been repaid."

Not only did Klein want his loans repaid, now they were no longer represented by him, the Lennons access to ready cash stopped. Their expenses far outweighed their income. It was time to liquidate some of their assets and start slashing costs. To pay for their apartment in the Dakota building, they put Tittenhurst Park on the market for £500,000 (£5,195,038.61). It was bought by Ringo Starr. Elephant's Memory were on a monthly retainer of $200 ($1,386.44). The Lennons were paying the going rate for sidemen, but it was considerably less than McCartney was paying Wings, who were paid the equivalent of $719 monthly. Nevertheless, it was an expense that the Lennons couldn't afford. Consequently, Lennon wrote to each band member, stating that he could no longer justify employing them and terminated their contract. "Dear Elephants, It's costing too much bread to keep you 'on a retainer' – and I/we have no plans to tour or anything 'money making'." The easiest way for Lennon to make money had been denied him. A concert tour of the US would have generated much-needed income. Thus far, he'd only been able to perform in the US because he did so free of charge. If he'd wanted to go on tour to make money, he'd have needed a work visa. That he was in dispute with the INS meant this couldn't happen. Further cuts followed when Ono withdrew funding for a film, Cain's Book, by Dan Richter, that was being made for Joko Films.

Although the Lennons cut back on their expenditure, Ono's expenses continued to mount up. It has been alleged that her monthly telephone bill averaged $3,000 ($20,796.55). She was also planning another new album. While her husband seemed to suffer from writer's block, she could barely contain her creative impulses. The time had come to record her second album in twelve months. Studio time was booked at the Record Plant, and a group of session musicians was hired to help record the album.

The hourly rate charged by the Record Plant was $110 ($762.54) on weekdays or $140 ($970.51) at weekends. The amount charged by session musicians is harder to come by but varied from $200 – $400 for live performances for a six day week by band leaders. Sidemen were paid roughly half that. Session rates for studio performances ranged from $25 – $37.50 an hour for demo recordings. According to May Pang, whose job was keeping track of who played on what session so they could be paid, session musicians were paid $90.00 ($625.17) for a three-hour session. It would have been far more cost-effective to use Elephant's Memory, whose members were paid $50 a week. If only they hadn't terminated their agreement with the band. The session musicians were costing almost as much an hour as each member of Elephant's Memory had been paid a week. Sacking them had been a false economy. However, whether they would have been suitable for Ono's or Lennon's albums is debatable. Elephant's Memory had an edgy, hard rock sound and attitude that would not have suited the Lennons' new approach to their music.

Recording Ono's album wasn't going to be cheap either. An eight-hour session at the Record Plant would cost $880 ($6,112), plus somewhere in the region of $1,200 ($8,335) for the musicians, taking the total for an eight-hour recording session to $2,080 ($14,457). The cost of five days recording was roughly $10,400 ($74,867). With little money coming in, no plans to tour or do anything 'money-making', ongoing legal fees to pay, and loans to be repaid, that was a lot of money to find. It wasn't that Lennon didn't have the money; it was just that he couldn't access it. He was caught between a rock and a hard place. He could do little about it until the dispute over The Beatles' partnership was resolved.

Sessions began on Friday, 22ⁿᵈ June, at the Record Plant, New York, with a group of crack session musicians that included David Spinozza, Jim Keltner, Ken Asher, and Gordon Edwards. Although Ono was the producer, Lennon attended several sessions, which ran until the first week in July. Speaking to Loraine Alterman of the *Melody Maker*, Ono explained how she approached her latest album: "This time what I really wanted to do was to produce it in a way I wanted, which means I'm not just particularly keen on having rock. I wanted each song to have a different style and I needed people who are versatile enough. I called up Jim Keltner first and he introduced me to David Spinozza, who got most of the musicians. They all have production ability as well, so they really understood the full sort of feeling of the pieces. Also the sensitivity level was the same." Ono's sessions were as productive as her husband's. Most days, the band cut the basic tracks for two songs, and on one particularly productive day, they cut the basic tracks for four songs.

Running concurrently with these sessions, the Lennons' immigration lawyer, Leon Wildes, was busying himself with filing applications to the INS on behalf of the Lennons. The Lennons' very public battle with the Nixon administration, and their continued activism, only fuelled its intent to have them deported. Besides supporting women's rights, and the American Indian Movement, the Lennons were actively advocating on behalf of Michael X, the leader of the UK Black Panthers, who, having been found guilty of murder, was awaiting execution. All of the causes they supported were feminist consciousness, minority consciousness, grassroots, anti-establishment movements that opposed and objected to the Nixon administration.

The Lennons were still very much a thorn in the side of the Establishment, and someone in power was applying pressure to high-ranking officials within the INS to obstruct Wilde and hinder the Lennons' case. The case had become a priority for the Nixon administration, but Wildes' requests for documents to show which cases had been declared 'non-priority' were being stonewalled. Eventually, Wildes was forced to use the Freedom of Information Act to obtain documents that revealed the FBI's involvement, interest and purpose in investigating the Lennons. It became clear that the government had a political, rather than a legal, reason for wanting them deported .

Lennon wasn't the only Beatle with a gripe against the INS. Earlier in the year, Harrison had been stopped upon entering the US and denied an extension to his visa. When George and Pattie returned to the UK, around 28th June, he fired off a telegram in the heat of the moment to President Nixon, complaining, in terms not dissimilar to those used by Lennon when he returned his MBE, about how he'd been treated. "Sir, how can you bomb Cambonian (sic) citizens and worry about kicking me out of the country for smoking marijuana at the [same] time. Your repressive emperaour (sic) war monger ways stop before too piece luv. We will run the world Harry Krisher, Hare Hara Krishne (sic) Hare Hara Hare Hara Krishner (sic). George Harrison." An INS official, James Greene, replied in typical bureaucratic fashion: "I am informed that in denying your application for an extension of stay in May 1973 the district director of our service office in Los Angeles advised you of the reasons for this denial."

If he didn't get any joy from the INS, he could at least console himself with the fact that *Living In The Material World* had been released in the UK on 22nd June and, in the same week, rocketed to the number one slot on the *Billboard* album chart in the US. According to *Record World*, the album was "often outselling Paul Simon and Yes by three and four to one." Wings were at number 2 on the album charts, The Beatles *1967 – 70* at number 5 and *1962 – 66* at number 11. Wings were also at number 1 in the US singles chart with 'My Love,' while 'Give Me Love (Give Me Peace On Earth) was four places below at number 5.

Harrison's current single received a boost in the UK when the BBC broadcast an alternative version that Harrison had prepared for them. *Radio One Club* and the *David Hamilton Show* broadcast the exclusive recording on the 18th, 19th, 20th and 21st. *Radio One Club* was not broadcast on the 22nd, it was replaced by *Round Table*, but it was played on the *David Hamilton Show* on Friday 22th . On the day that *Living In The Material World* was issued in the UK, The Beatles *1967 – 70* was at number 5, *1962 – 66* at number 8, and Wings at number 16 in the album chart. The following week, Lennon's *Imagine* album re-entered the UK album chart at number 42.

There was more good news. Harrison's legal proceedings to prevent Audiotape Inc. marketing and selling the *Alpha Omega* album succeeded. Although it had stopped *Alpha Omega* in its tracks, the case rumbled on until 1978. The 28th January 1978 edition of *Billboard* printed the news: "Capitol Records has succeeded in getting a permanent injunction against the manufacture and sale of recordings purporting to be performances by The Beatles on a mail-order label. The injunction, handed down here by the US District Court, was granted in response to a civil suit brought by the label over a radio and television campaign for the sale of albums and tapes under the name "Beatles *Alpha Omega*."

However, it was the landmark case of Goldstein vs. California that eventually led to a change in copyright law. The case had gone all the way to the Supreme Court, which affirmed the right of individual states to enact anti-piracy laws against unauthorized duplicators of unprotected recordings by federal statute. This made it more difficult for the likes of Audiotape Inc. to manufacture and sell pirate records. Unless Congress took further action on unprotected recordings, individual states had the right to enforce laws against record piracy. The Supreme Court rejected the claim that federal copyright law was pre-emptive over all state law about copyright and held that the unlimited duration of state copyright protection was too "narrow" a scale to collide seriously with the constitutional and congressional limiting of copyright duration in federal law.

A day or two before the Harrisons flew back to England, the Lennons visited Washington, D.C.. Lennon, his hair recently shorn, accompanied by Ono, joined a small group of protesters outside the Vietnamese embassy. Here they donned coolie hats and mingled with the protesters calling for the release of Mrs. Ngo Ba Thanh, who, they claimed, was being held as a political prisoner. Next, they made their way to the United States Senate to attend the Watergate hearings. Sitting in the spectator section of the Senate Caucus Room, they watched John W Dean III and his wife Maureen give evidence. As part of his evidence, Dean brought a copy of Nixon's 'Enemies List', a long list of individuals considered dangerous to the administration. As well as political opponents, senators and members of Congress, it listed several celebrities, including Gregory Peck, Barbra Streisand, and Dick Gregory, who had interviewed the Lennons for the 26th October 1972 edition of *Jet*, which featured them on the front cover.

When asked by the press for his opinion, Lennon sat firmly on the fence. "We're somewhere in the middle," he claimed. He wasn't. He'd spent part of 1971 and much of '72 campaigning against Nixon and his administration. He was still advocating for minority groups, albeit in a less visible way. He was willing to lend his name to causes he felt passionate about, but he nevertheless distanced himself from activism because of his immigration case, which the Nixon administration had already politicized. Whenever he spoke to the press, radio, or television, he was always cautious not to give the Nixon administration anything it could use against him. He clarified his non-partisan position by stating that nobody had asked him to take sides with Mr. Dean or Mr. Nixon. He also said that he didn't think President Nixon would have to resign because he was a lawyer and hid the real reason for his being there by saying: "Since we saw the Watergate hearings on TV, we thought we'd take them in. But I don't know what to make of Dean." Ono was less reticent and suggested that the select committee investigation was helping their immigration battle."[T]he Watergate scene is helping a little. I think maybe it's slow going because it's summer. We're just sort of crossing our fingers and waiting for the good news." Unlike her husband, who claimed to be of two minds about the proceedings, Ono found them inspirational. "The Watergate hearing we went to was very exciting. In fact, I wrote 'Men, Men, Men' when I was in that courtroom. I got inspired."

Lennon found the reality of the hearings disappointing. He preferred it when the proceedings were mediated through a television screen. Speaking to Chris Charlesworth, he said: "I thought it was better on TV anyway because I could see more. When it first came on I watched it live all day, so I just had the urge to actually go. I had other business in Washington anyway. The public was there and most Senators have children, so every time there was a break in the proceedings I had to sign autographs. I was looking like a Buddhist monk at the time with all my hair chopped off, and I thought nobody would spot me. They spotted Yoko before me, and assumed – rightly – that I must be with her. It was quite a trip."

WEEK ENDING 2 JUNE 1973
1. MY LOVE: PAUL McCARTNEY AND WINGS
2. DANIEL: ELTON JOHN
3. FRANKENSTEIN: EDGAR WINTER GROUP
4. PILLOW TALK: SYLVIA
5. TIE A YELLOW RIBBON ROUND THE OLE OAK TREE: DAWN
   FEATURING TONY ORLANDO
6. YOU ARE THE SUNSHINE OF MY LIFE: STEVIE WONDER
7. I'M GONNA LOVE YOU JUST A LITTLE MORE BABY: BARRY WHITE
8. LITTLE WILLY: THE SWEET
9. HOCUS POCUS: FOCUS
10. PLAYGROUND IN MY MIND: CLINT HOLMES

WEEK ENDING 9 JUNE 1973
1. MY LOVE: PAUL McCARTNEY AND WINGS
2. FRANKENSTEIN: EDGAR WINTER GROUP
3. PILLOW TALK: SYLVIA
4. DANIEL: ELTON JOHN
5. PLAYGROUND IN MY MIND: CLINT HOLMES
6. I'M GONNA LOVE YOU JUST A LITTLE MORE BABY: BARRY WHITE
7. TIE A YELLOW RIBBON ROUND THE OLE OAK TREE: DAWN
   FEATURING TONY ORLANDO
8. YOU ARE THE SUNSHINE OF MY LIFE: STEVIE WONDER
9. HOCUS POCUS: FOCUS
10. LONG TRAIN RUNNIN': THE DOOBIE BROTHERS

WEEK ENDING 16 JUNE 1973
1. MY LOVE: PAUL McCARTNEY AND WINGS
2. PLAYGROUND IN MY MIND: CLINT HOLMES
3. PILLOW TALK: SYLVIA
4. I'M GONNA LOVE YOU JUST A LITTLE MORE BABY: BARRY WHITE
5. DANIEL: ELTON JOHN
6. FRANKENSTEIN: EDGAR WINTER GROUP
7. WILL IT GO ROUND IN CIRCLES: BILLY PRESTON
8. GIVE ME LOVE (GIVE ME PEACE ON EARTH): GEORGE HARRISON
9. KODACHROME: PAUL SIMON
10. TIE A YELLOW RIBBON ROUND THE OLE OAK TREE: DAWN
    FEATURING TONY ORLANDO

WEEK ENDING 23 JUNE 1973
1. MY LOVE: PAUL McCARTNEY AND WINGS
2. PLAYGROUND IN MY MIND: CLINT HOLMES
3. I'M GONNA LOVE YOU JUST A LITTLE MORE BABY: BARRY WHITE
4. WILL IT GO ROUND IN CIRCLES: BILLY PRESTON
5. GIVE ME LOVE (GIVE ME PEACE ON EARTH): GEORGE HARRISON
6. PILLOW TALK: SYLVIA
7. KODACHROME: PAUL SIMON
8. DANIEL: ELTON JOHN
9. LONG TRAIN RUNNIN': THE DOOBIE BROTHERS
10. RIGHT PLACE WRONG TIME: DR. JOHN

WEEK ENDING 30 JUNE 1973
1. GIVE ME LOVE (GIVE ME PEACE ON EARTH): GEORGE HARRISON
2. MY LOVE: PAUL McCARTNEY AND WINGS
3. WILL IT GO ROUND IN CIRCLES: BILLY PRESTON
4. I'M GONNA LOVE YOU JUST A LITTLE MORE BABY: BARRY WHITE
5. KODACHROME: PAUL SIMON

6. PILLOW TALK: SYLVIA
7. PLAYGROUND IN MY MIND: CLINT HOLMES
8. LONG TRAIN RUNNIN': THE DOOBIE BROTHERS
9. RIGHT PLACE WRONG TIME: DR. JOHN
10. SHAMBALA: THREE DOG NIGHT

UK

WEEK ENDING 2 JUNE 1973
1. SEE MY BABY JIVE: WIZZARD
2. CAN THE CAN: SUZI QUATRO
3. AND I LOVE YOU SO: PERRY COMO
4. ONE AND ONE IS ONE: MEDICINE HEAD
5. HELL RAISER: THE SWEET
6. TIE A YELLOW RIBBON ROUND THE OLE OAK TREE: DAWN
   FEATURING TONY ORLANDO
7. YOU ARE THE SUNSHINE OF MY LIFE: STEVIE WONDE
8. ALSO SPRACH ZARATHUSTRA: DEODATO
9. BROKEN DOWN ANGEL: NAZARETH
10. WALK ON THE WILD SIDE: LOU REED

WEEK ENDING 9 JUNE 1973
1. SEE MY BABY JIVE: WIZZARD
2. CAN THE CAN: SUZI QUATRO
3. ONE AND ONE IS ONE: MEDICINE HEAD
4. AND I LOVE YOU SO: PERRY COMO
5. RUBBER BULLETS: 10CC
6. ALBATROSS: FLEETWOOD MAC
7. YOU ARE THE SUNSHINE OF MY LIFE: STEVIE WONDER
8. HELL RAISER: THE SWEET
9. TIE A YELLOW RIBBON ROUND THE OLE OAK TREE: DAWN
   FEATURING TONY ORLANDO
10. WALKING IN THE RAIN: THE PARTRIDGE FAMILY

WEEK ENDING 16 JUNE 1973
1. CAN THE CAN: SUZI QUATRO
2. RUBBER BULLETS: 10CC
3. SEE MY BABY JIVE: WIZZARD
4. ONE AND ONE IS ONE: MEDICINE HEAD
5. ALBATROSS: FLEETWOOD MAC
6. GROOVER: T.REX
7. AND I LOVE YOU SO: PERRY COMO
8. STUCK IN THE MIDDLE WITH YOU: STEALERS WHEEL
9. YOU ARE THE SUNSHINE OF MY LIFE: STEVIE WONDER
10. WALKING IN THE RAIN: THE PARTRIDGE FAMILY

WEEK ENDING 23 JUNE 1973
1. RUBBER BULLETS: 10CC
2. ALBATROSS: FLEETWOOD MAC
3. CAN THE CAN: SUZI QUATRO
4. GROOVER: T.REX
5. WELCOME HOME: PETERS AND LEE
6. SEE MY BABY JIVE: WIZZARD
7. SNOOPY VERSUS THE RED BARON: HOTSHOTS
8. STUCK IN THE MIDDLE WITH YOU: STEALERS WHEEL
9. ONE AND ONE IS ONE: MEDICINE HEAD
10. GIVE ME LOVE (GIVE ME PEACE ON EARTH): GEORGE HARRISON

WEEK ENDING 30 JUNE 1973
1. SKWEEZE ME PLEEZE ME: SLADE
2. RUBBER BULLETS: 10CC
3. ALBATROSS: FLEETWOOD MAC
4. WELCOME HOME: PETERS AND LEE
5. GROOVER: T.REX
6. SNOOPY VERSUS THE RED BARON: HOTSHOTS
7. CAN THE CAN: SUZI QUATRO
8. GIVE ME LOVE (GIVE ME PEACE ON EARTH): GEORGE HARRISON
9. LIVE AND LET DIE: PAUL MCCARTNEY AND WINGS
10. STUCK IN THE MIDDLE WITH YOU: STEALERS WHEEL

CHAPTER 7
JULY: ON THE ROAD, AGAIN

Back in Britain and locked safely behind the ornate iron gates of Friar Park, George Harrison had something to celebrate. It wasn't his wedding anniversary, it wasn't his birthday, it was the success of 'Give Me Love (Give Me Peace On Earth)' and *Living In The Material World*, both of which were sitting on top of the US charts, depending on which chart you looked at. In the last week of June, Harrison topped both the *Billboard* singles and albums charts, replicating McCartney's earlier achievement. Harrison was knocked off the top of the singles chart the following week by his friend Billy Preston, who was at number 1 with 'Will It Go Round In Circles'. McCartney was at number 3, having dropped one place from the previous week. However, according to the *Cash Box* chart for the week ending 7th July, Harrison was still at number 1 on the albums and singles charts. *Cash Box* put Preston at number 2 and McCartney at number 6. Harrison was still slowly climbing the singles chart in the UK, up one place to number 9.

Like his fellow former bandmates, Harrison faced far greater competition at home than abroad. Or rather, he faced a different kind of competition. The British music scene was changing fast. A new cadre of musicians, not all of whom were as young as they claimed, had stormed the charts. Glam Rock was at the height of its popularity, with the likes of Slade, Gary Glitter, David Bowie, Suzi Quatro, Wizzard, Sweet, Mott The Hoople, and T. Rex all fighting for space in the singles and albums charts alongside more established acts like Perry Como, Stevie Wonder, and Paul Simon.

Slade were enjoying their fifteen minutes of Slademania and had gone straight to number 1 with their single 'Skweeze Me Pleeze Me,' which topped the chart for three weeks before being ousted by folk/pop duo Peters and Lee. Ever watchful of what was happening in Britain, Lennon had his eye on Slade. Talking to Chris Charlesworth, he said: "I like some of their records. They get it off. I saw them on TV here, and it was all right. It must be so hard for them when they come here and they're used to be treated like God in England, but I think they'll survive they're a good band. They're a singles band am I'm a singles man." Some British journalists may have likened Slade to The Beatles, but they were no substitute for the real thing. A Beatle was still a Beatle, even if they were now officially an ex-Beatle.

Living In The Material World entered the UK album chart at number 9. It did much better in the *Record Mirror/BBC* album chart, where it entered at number 2. The same chart put The Beatles at number 7 (*1967 – 70*) and 8 (*1962 – 66*). Although it didn't feature music by The Beatles, a Beatles-related album, the soundtrack to *That'll Be The Day* topped the album chart in July.

McCartney continued to rack up chart entries with 'Live And Let Die,' which entered the *Billboard* singles chart at number 69 before jumping to number 44 the following week. McCartney couldn't have asked for better publicity than having the single open the latest James Bond film. Besides the film, there was also a soundtrack album, which was issued in the US on 2nd July. *Billboard* asked its readers: "Can Martin's music and Paul McCartney and Wings' presence singing the title tune turn this LP into a hotshot package? The odds seem to say so, for in the world of name power, these two associations are first-rate." The *Cash Box* review was equally optimistic: "Featuring Paul McCartney and Wings on the title tune, the film music is as exciting as the flick itself. Album is a spectacular walk down Bond Street." The soundtrack album was a hotshot package, although perhaps not as hot as some expected. It sold well, reaching a chart high of number 17 on the *Billboard* chart. But unlike some other soundtrack albums, it failed to top the chart. McCartney also continued to accumulate gold records when 'My Love' received RIAA certification as a million seller on 5th July.

The day before Wings were awarded their latest gold disc; they played the first of four dates in the north of England, again with Brinsley Schwarz supporting. The tour opened on 4th July in Sheffield, where Wings played the 2,300-seat City Hall. This was a big step up for Brinsley Schwarz, who were more used to playing at the smaller Black Swan pub, a short walk from the venue. Wings played their usual set, opening with the unreleased 'Soily' and continuing with material from their recently released album. Recent hits 'My Love,' 'Live And Let Die,' and 'Hi, Hi, Hi' followed along with a few deep dives into McCartney and Wings' back catalogue. But still no Beatles songs.

The following day, Wings were back in London to attend the premiere of the latest James Bond blockbuster. The soundtrack album, already available in the US, would be released in the UK on Friday 6th July, the same day they played the Odeon Cinema in Birmingham. Three days later, they were in Leicester, where they played another Odeon Cinema. *Record Mirror* was on hand to review both shows, which couldn't have been more different. Birmingham was reckoned to be the better of the two shows. "Wings took to the stage after a nice warm up from Brinsley Schwartz, a tight country rock outfit (writes John Clegg). Inevitably, there was an immediate impact as soon as McCartney came on stage. I went to this concert to see a childhood hero in the flesh; to see how a myth would shape up live. I wasn't disappointed and neither was the mainly young audience who started to bop as soon as the band came on and didn't stop until they were ready to collapse." The

Leicester gig suffered from amplification problems and a sedate audience who "showed very much a start-of-the-week attitude (it was Monday night) and didn't start bopping until the last few numbers."

Nicholas Owen, writing for the *Birmingham Post*, mirrored Clegg's review. "The reception was greatly reminiscent of the old Beatles days, with security police dragging desperate teenagers from the stage and the stalls and the circle behaving more like the terraces at a football match." While the fans were going wild, Owen was there to listen and review, and according to him, it took Wings a while to warm up. "Last night's performance started in undistinguished manner with some very ordinary songs, but the McCartney quality broke through in style, especially in the film theme song 'Live And Let Die' with no little help from Birmingham's talented Denny Laine."

Being a Beatle had its advantages but solo success had to be earned. Something McCartney knew only too well. He told *Record Mirror*: "The gig for us is to play to people, you know. Some nights you don't get good audiences. But on the nights you do, I mean most nights we have had like a fair audience and there's nothing to match that. When you've got a good audience. It's very, you know, if you're a performer it's in your blood. I still think stage acts are like the fairground or the circus coming to town. You've got to have things they know. I mean people go to the circus to see a lion, but if you put like a ballet on, just a ballet, they would say 'Ugh whatdye mean' it wouldn't work."

McCartney knew what audiences wanted and worked hard to give it to them. He was an old-fashioned showman who worked hard to avoid accusations of trading on nostalgia. Although he was keen to give audiences the songs they wanted, he claimed he didn't include any Beatles songs because he didn't want to come across as an indifferent tribute act. "But it's a good thing we didn't because you've got the danger then of developing a second-rate Beatles and you can get left in the lurch. You could develop the most incredible Beatles or McCartney act and blow it by not keeping up with the times. Then it's going to be 'Oh they're a very nice nostalgic group' and I don't want that, I'll leave it to all the bands playing down in Benidorm."

McCartney was walking a tightrope. How to appear la mode while avoiding associations with the past would always be a hard act to pull off. Although he'd developed quite the mullet, and Linda sported a Bowie-esque hairstyle, he wisely avoided donning make-up and going down the Glam route. Others, Roy Wood, Garry Glitter, and Alvin Stardust, all McCartney's contemporaries, didn't. If he wanted to be seen as relevant, the only way to do that, for the time being, was to avoid any reference to his recent past and ignore the elephant in the room. That would never be easy with two Beatles albums in the top ten.

The tour ended on 10th July in Newcastle, where Brinsley Schwarz joined Wings for a blistering version of 'Long Tall Sally'. A week after the gig, the Newcastle upon Tyne *Evening Chronicle* published a review that focused as much on the audience as the concert. It compared the band's reception to Beatlemania, claiming that the audience comprised a lot of "second time rounders" who were now young married women. The audience also comprised young girls who were there to scream and swoon at McCartney. If McCartney wanted to distance himself from his Beatles past, the local press wasn't helping. The unnamed reporter closed with a somewhat confusing statement that suggested that the only reason people paid to see Wings was because the singer and bassist happened to be an ex-Beatle: "As it happened Wings gave a good concert in Newcastle. But they didn't have to. They just had to be Paul McCartney."

No matter how hard he tried, McCartney would never escape the long shadow cast by The Beatles. As for Wings being a band of equals, forget it. McCullough and Seiwell were already unhappy with how their boss was sidelining them. Each had musical ideas that they were keen to contribute to the band, which, with one or two exceptions, were ignored by McCartney. Speaking to James Johnson of the *NME*, McCullough said: "Perhaps I would like the band to be a little freer. It's just been kept that way so far. But I could never be just Paul McCartney's backing guitarist. I'd leave if it was like that. I want to contribute as well." McCullough was thinking about his future with McCartney and was far from happy with how things were shaping up. There were tensions within the band, which even McCartney had to admit. "Once or twice, you know we had a few kinda arguments and stuff like 'I don't like the way you do that' and oogh friction."

McCartney was no stranger to inter-band fighting. But this time, it was different. He was the band leader now, and what he said was law. The Beatles were different. They were friends, bandmates, business partners, and, importantly, equals. Even so, they were still arguing and hadn't played a note of music together for the best part of three years. Reading between the lines, there was a split within Wings that saw the McCartneys and Laine on one side and McCullough and Seiwell on the other. Speaking to *Beat Instrumental*, Laine suggested that McCartney encouraged everyone to contribute to the band and that it would improve. "He (Paul) has been trying to bring it [songwriting] out in all of us. Henry is going to have to write some songs. Well, he does write songs, but he's not confident enough of his songs to push them on the band yet. When he does it will be a better band. This is all to strengthen the band, really."

Having previously implied that the band constrained him and that he'd prefer more freedom, McCullough toed the line and changed tack, claiming that everyone in the band contributed equally. "Now I think Wings have reached the point where music is really starting to come out of the band. Everybody's contributing and the results are a five-piece product. That's what it's getting to and it's great. Obviously it'll always be Paul McCartney's group, but we've worked out of this system where it was just 'Paul McCartney and his group Wings.'"

However, reviews like the one published by the Newcastle upon Tyne *Evening Chronicle* didn't see it that way. As far as the *Evening Chronicle's* reporter was concerned, it was McCartney that people went to see, not Wings. According to them, all McCartney had to do was stand on stage to be worshiped like some secular saint. The review was published under the byline 'Paul and his apostles' to drive the point home. The truth was somewhat more nuanced. There were different levels of fandom, from the superfan to the casual music fan. Some people went to worship at the feet of their idol; others went to listen to the music and be entertained. As McCartney explained to John Mitchell of the BBC: "We've got a lot of fans from what we've been doing now, who've written afterwards and said, 'When I came to see you, I thought it really would just be a kind of sentimental evening where I'd think, "Ah! I wish I'd been with The Beatles.' But they write and say, 'It's amazing, I'm really happy. When are Wings coming back to town, as we're really interested?'" Perhaps McCartney was being economical with the truth? Maybe he was trying to big up Wings to distance himself from The Beatles? Possibly McCullough and Seiwell had got it wrong? Perhaps sections of the audience thought of Wings as a band rather than a backing band? Maybe it was a combination of different factors? Looking out from the inside is very different from being outside looking in.

Times had changed, and so had audiences. When Wings played Oxford the previous month, the audience reaction was typical; among the cheers and applause, there were moments of silence between songs. Audiences didn't go to scream; they went to listen. They could appear subdued because Wings were playing a lot of unfamiliar material from their latest album. As McCartney acknowledged: "I mean at the moment we are playing quite a few songs that either they don't know, or they don't know so well, but eventually I think it will get so that it will be numbers they know."

The fact that audiences were less noisy than they had been a decade earlier made no difference as far as McCartney was concerned. According to him, the kind of reception they got didn't matter. What was important was that the audience enjoyed the show. Talking to John Mitchell, McCartney said: "We played Glasgow and got a ridiculous welcome there, and it was really a bit like The Beatles, you know? It was ridiculous, there were police outside and crowds and stuff, the whole bit – in some places you go, it really is like that. But we're just as pleased if the audience in the hall that night just enjoyed it. If they don't enjoy it then we'll be disappointed. But if they like it, it doesn't really matter if it's a pub in the King's Road or Madison Square Gardens to us, you know."

It wasn't only the lack of musical freedom creating tension within Wings. Money, or the lack of it, was adding to inter-group stresses. McCullough, Seiwell, and Laine were still on their £70 weekly retainer. They had also been paid their £500 (£5,195.31) bonus for *Red Rose Speedway*. But that was peanuts compared to what McCartney was earning, even if the official receiver held onto some of his money. "And so the money was real tight in the band. It was very tight. Needlessly so, I think," recalled Seiwell. "And it was wearing on us, the situations that were occurring, when we were doing so well, yet we were living like a garage band. I mean, I was making one-tenth of the money I used to make in New York doing sessions. And living that way, too! It was wearing on us, and it's one of my only regrets in life, actually, is that I didn't sit Paul down and talk to him about that particular thing, to see if we could work out some sort of agreement."

McCartney didn't have an endless supply of money. But he was making enough to cover his costs and give his band a pay rise. Wings had just been awarded a gold disc for selling one million copies of 'My Love.' In America, the mechanical royalty rate was two cents. With two McCartney compositions on the record, the publisher made four cents on each disc. That's $40,000 ($277,181.08). 'My Love' was published by McCartney Music Inc. and Maclen Music Inc. The publishing royalty split was 55/45 in McCartney's favour. Wings current single, 'Live And Let Die,' would also be awarded a gold disc for sales of one million copies. That's another $40,000 split 55/45. Then there were the mechanical royalties from the sale of Wings' number one album, *Red Rose Speedway*, another gold record awarded for sales of 500,000 copies. The album contained 12 McCartney compositions, which would have generated a mechanical royalty rate of 24 cents per album, earning another $120,000 ($833,559.46) that was split 55/45. And this was only for sales in America. Mechanical royalties would have been coming in from around the world. Add on performing rights royalties for radio and television airplay, and the total income from copyrights would have been more than enough to keep a band happy.

The official receiver was holding money from other income streams. Accessing this money could only be achieved by all four Beatles working together and compromising. The money would start flowing once they'd agreed on dividing the pot. Like the other Beatles, McCartney may have been experiencing cashflow problems, but he was far from broke. However, the rest of Wings did not benefit from the millions of records they sold. They were little more than hired hands who received a weekly wage. Nor was the band a functioning democracy. McCartney admitted as much when he spoke with *Beat International*. When asked if the band was a democratic one or not, McCartney replied: "Well, it's a bit democratic, but if the band is looking for a decision, I make it." In other words, no. Wings was not democratic. The matter of pay was such that the Eastmans met with Wings to discuss the issue and explain the situation to them. There was little they could do. Even if the three engaged in collective bargaining, McCartney had the leverage. McCullough, Seiwell, and Laine had little or nothing that would change their bargaining position. Brinsley Schwarz's manager, Dave Robinson, once said: "Musicians are like pebbles on a beach." McCartney had his pick of the pebbles, and they knew it.

When Denny Laine spoke to *Disc* a few days after the tour finished, he made light of the group's financial woes. "There's a lot of freedom in the band, some people have called it lethargic," he claimed. "I can see what they mean but the other side is that there's nobody uptight and nobody broke! That's the trouble with most groups – they're all broke. No one's particularly rich either, not even Paul. He has to wait and wait for his money. It's a good set up and I don't care what anyone says. I'm in it, I know!" It wasn't a good setup. When they joined Wings, they were told they were joining a band. In reality, they were nothing more than sidemen.

Perhaps McCartney was wary of entering into any binding legal agreement with McCullough, Seiwell, and Laine because of what had happened with The Beatles' partnership agreement. Laine's existing contract with Tony Secunda complicated matters. But if these issues concerned McCartney, he should have told them. McCartney may not have been wealthy; but it was obvious that Wings was generating a lot of money. He may have paid them a bonus to keep them sweet; but the chances of them sharing in the profit they were helping to generate were slim. Although it wouldn't have resolved McCullough's dissatisfaction with his role in the band, it might have helped oil the wheels. Laine may have been content to live in a caravan, but the others expected something better, particularly as they played in packed venues and had the number-one single and album in America.

McCullough, Seiwell, and Laine weren't the only ones with money on their mind. The renewed interest in The Beatles meant that entrepreneurs were keen to cash in, just as they had at the height of Beatlemania. One businessman eager to grab a slice of The Beatles was Robert Stigwood. The Australian impresario had links to The Beatles, stretching back to 1967 when he merged his agency with Epstein's NEMS Organization. Having wheedled his way into NEMS with the death of Brian Epstein in August 1967, Stigwood attempted to position himself as a potential candidate to become The Beatles' new manager. However, The Beatles were having none of it and refused anything to do with him. Like several other business people within their circle, he was disliked and considered treacherous. But while they tolerated some, they detested him so much that, according to McCartney, they were prepared to sabotage their career rather than have him manage them. Speaking to Greil Marcus, McCartney said: "We said, 'In fact, if you do, if you somehow manage to pull this off, we can promise you one thing. We will record 'God Save the Queen' for every single record we make from now on and we'll sing out of tune. That's a promise. So if this guy buys us, that's what he's buying."

Stigwood may have failed to become The Beatles' manager, but that didn't stop him from trying to make money from them. He planned to produce a new theatrical show based on *Sgt. Pepper's* and *Abbey Road* called 'Sgt. Pepper's Lonely Hearts Club Band With the One and Only Billy Shears'. He planned to tour it in the US, starting at the Auditorium Theater in Chicago on 17th August, before moving to Minneapolis, Milwaukee, Detroit, Philadelphia, and New York. Understandably, McCartney wouldn't allow someone else, let alone someone like Stigwood, to exploit The Beatles' name and music. He instructed his attorneys to take "all necessary steps" to prevent the proposed stage presentation. McCartney's initial statement denied that Stigwood had secured authorization for the proposed show from himself, Lennon, or The Beatles. Peter Brown, who'd previously served as a board member of Apple Corps, was now working for Stigwood and claimed that the rights to the songs had been purchased by the Stigwood Organization from Northern Songs, publishers of the original material. He also asserted that the problem stemmed from "a lack of communication between Northern Songs and McCartney's representatives."

Eastman & Eastman countered this claim, rejecting Brown's comment, arguing that McCartney retained legal control over the material. They also said that although no further action had been taken against the production, legal actions against the proposed show would be taken if necessary.

While McCartney was busying his in-law attorneys, two former associates of The Beatles were hatching their plan to become millionaires on the back of the group. Ted Kingsize Taylor and Alan Williams had recently rediscovered a quarter- inch reel of tape of The Beatles performing at the Star Club in Hamburg, Germany. In the early 1960s, Taylor led the Liverpool beat combo Kingsize Taylor and the Dominoes. Like The Beatles, Taylor and his group played the clubs in Hamburg. The king size singer bought a Phillips tape recorder to check his band's sound balance. Any band playing at the club was free to use the machine, and Taylor had, he claimed, two hours of live Beatles recordings. Although he now asserted the tape could be worth millions of pounds, he hadn't taken much care of it. "I was playing it in a studio in Liverpool, which my friend owned, and it just got left there for about five or six years. In fact, it never even crossed my mind until I mentioned it to Alan Williams," he said. The tapes were in a building in Hackins Hey, Liverpool that was due to be demolished. Speaking to the BBC, Williams said he had to break into the building to access the studio, where he found the tape covered in five years of dust.

As to its value, Williams suggested that: "If this goes out as a Beatles album, it could be worth anything, 8 million, 10 million, 20 million pounds." There was only one problem. Who was the legal owner of the tape and the recordings? According to Taylor, he was. Speaking to the *Daily Mirror*, he said he'd bought the rights to the recordings from The Beatles for a few drinks. With nothing more than his boozy recollection and nothing in writing to say that he was the lawful owner, Tayor was finding it difficult to get a record label to take it on. Williams confirmed that it was fear of being sued by The Beatles that had prevented any record label from releasing the recordings. "The major difficulty, it appeared, was that record companies were afraid to touch it because of the legal aspects of it. Copyrights, and whether we were legally involved to be able to do this." Having knocked on the door of every record company he could think of, the only option left to Williams was to approach The Beatles directly.

Having managed The Beatles, Williams was well placed to use his contacts and arrange a meeting. He approached Neil Aspinall and secured a meeting on 15th August with Harrison and Starr at Apple's London HQ. Williams asked for an advance of £100,000 (£1,034,946.05) and royalties from sales. The meeting went well, with Harrison and Starr making all the right noises. "They liked the idea of it, and they said sure, somewhere along the line, they felt that it could be used," Williams said. "But they want four copies, one for each, and they will sort of dress it up and present it to Paul and John. At the moment, they're going through difficulties of their own, and as soon as this is sorted out then we hope to have this out."

Things were looking up for Taylor and Williams. They were receiving plenty of national coverage, they'd secured a meeting with two of The Beatles that had gone well, and The Beatles were keen to take control of their recordings to prevent them from getting into the hands of bootleggers. Lennon was an avid collector of Beatles bootlegs and had recently added a copy of The Beatles' Decca audition to his collection. He told Chris Charlesworth about his collecting habit: "Did you know that there's a bootleg out now of The Beatles Decca audition, which The Beatles did? I have a copy of it, but I'm trying to find the tape. It's beautiful. There's us singing 'To Know Her Is To Love Her' and a whole pile of tracks, mostly other people's but some of our own. It's pretty good, better than that Tony Sheridan thing on Polydor. […] I got copies made from this Decca audition and sent it to them all. I wouldn't mind releasing it." If Lennon were keen to release The Beatles' Decca audition, surely he'd be happy to release Taylor and Williams's historic live recording? If they could persuade Lennon, all they had to do was sway McCartney, sort out legal ownership of the tape, clean up the recordings to make them good enough to release commercially and find a record label to release the album. What could go wrong? What went wrong was that Apple wasn't interested. According to Tom Dooley's column in the British trade magazine *Music Week*, "Apple is not interested in purchasing King Size Taylor's tapes of early Beatles live recordings in Hamburg." It was back to the drawing board for Taylor and Williams.

In New York, Yoko Ono continued to work on her album, recording new songs and mixing those she'd finished. While Ono was putting the finishing touches to her new album, Lennon was readying himself to start recording his latest batch of songs. Lennon had not been nearly as prolific as his wife but he had managed to gather enough material for a new album. At least one of the songs he'd record dated back three years, albeit with newly written lyrics; others were more recent.

No sooner had Harrison returned home than he was off again. George and Pattie returned to America to attend Ken Mansfield's wedding. The American producer had been appointed manager of Apple Records for the US. He helped set up and launch Apple Records and guided the careers of Apple artists such as James Taylor, Mary Hopkin, Badfinger, and Jackie Lomax. It says a great deal about Harrison that he found time to fly 3000 miles to attend his wedding. Mansfield had wisely moved to MGM Records when Klein took control. Although he was no longer in charge of Apple

Records, he may have talked with Harrison about the label's future. It wasn't looking good. From July, Capitol Records was no longer distributing any of the Apple catalogue, except titles released by the ex-Beatles. Consequently, back catalogue albums and singles by Badfinger, Elephant's Memory, James Taylor and Yoko Ono would no longer be distributed. On the bright side, none of the albums would revert to Allen Klein. New albums by the ex-Beatles, Yoko Ono and Badfinger would continue to be distributed by Capitol. But most of the unsold albums were destined to sit in warehouses collecting dust until being sold off cheap as deletions. It wouldn't be long before the back pages of the British music weeklies were full of adverts for cheap American pressings of Apple Records.

Returning to Britain, Harrison spent several days in meetings with his spiritual master A.C. Bhaktivedanta Swami Prabhupadaat. Harrison was still at a crossroads. It's not every day you get to speak with a Divine Master, and Harrison used his meeting with Swami Prabhupadaat to unburden himself. "I go around in circles," he said. "Maybe it's something to do with me being, you know, the Pisces. They show one fish going this way and one fish going that way. And periods when I just can't stop chanting, and then other periods where, you know, I turn into a demon again and then forget to..."

Harrison had found to his cost that the road to enlightenment was paved with disillusionment. The further he went on his spiritual quest, the more troubling he found it. For him, the process was uncomfortably alienating. "There is one sort of problem in a way, that I found when chanting all the time, and that was that I start being able to relate less and less to all the people I know. I mean, then it's... There's only times when I see people like Syamasundara or just a few people, then, that's okay, but most of the other people... You know, I suddenly found myself on such a different level that it's hard to relate, and then it's like it feels as though it's a point where I have a decision of either slowing down and pulling back towards those people in order to try and pull them with me, or maybe if, because I'm not ready to go, or just cutting the thing off and just going completely."

Harrison didn't spend all this time oming and ahing, he still had several projects to keep him busy. Besides Ravi Shankar's album, there was a feature film, *Little Malcolm And His Struggle Against The Eunuchs*, to finish. *Little Malcom* was filmed by Suba Films Limited, produced by Apple Films, currently being sued by Klein, and was one of Harrison's pet projects. He'd been taken to see the original stage play by Brian Epstein when it opened at the Garrick Theatre, London, in 1966. The original production wasn't a success, opening on 3rd February and closing on 19th February.

The short-lived play featured John Hurt, who reprised his role in the film production. Hurt suggested that the film's screenwriter, Derek Woodward, contact Harrison about financing the film. Harrison agreed to back the production, and filming took place in Oldham.

Little Malcolm And His Struggle Against The Eunuchs deals with sex, power, and alienation. Themes that must have resonated with Harrison. Its release was delayed because of financial problems. When released in 1975, its gritty realism was out of fashion. Had it been made ten years earlier and shot in black and white, it would have sat comfortably alongside other Northern Realist films of the period. Like several projects associated with The Beatles, the fates and lawyers intervened. Harrison's role was minimal; as executive producer, he was in charge of supervision, and as such, he employed Stuart Cooper to direct the film, and helped with some of the soundtrack music. He also had to persuade the official receiver to release the film for screening. He was only partially successful. The film received a limited screening at the Berlin Film Festival in 1974 but didn't receive its official premiere until the following year. Even then, it was hardly a box office smash and did little better than Ringo's *Son of Dracula*. It is, however, a much better film. Cooper began his career as an actor and met Harrison through Derek Woodward. Harrison had also seen 'A Test of Violence,' a short film Cooper made about the work of Spanish artist Juan Genovés, which he'd liked. "He was an absolute delight, totally committed to the project," recalled Cooper. "George was a kind of 'spiritual' leader. He had this lovely quality about him; unpretentious, very passionate, and very genuine. It wasn't only that George liked the play; I think it dovetailed with his kind of humour. Think about the films that he made later with HandMade Films such as the Monty Python films. George had a great sense of humour, he loved comedy. There was a link, although *Little Malcolm* is such a subversive piece, such a black comedy. He was also a big fan of John Hurt and his performance in the play, so George stepped up to get the film made."

Cooper asked Harrison if he'd provide the film's music, but he couldn't due to other commitments. The film score was composed by Stanley Myers, but Harrison did contribute to the soundtrack by producing 'Lonely Man' by Splinter. Mal Evans had been working with Bobby Purvis and Bill Elliot for some time. Evans had been touting a tape of their band, Half Breed, around Apple's offices, which may have led to Elliot singing lead vocals on the Lennon penned 'God Save Us,' a song intended to raise funds for the *Oz* magazine obscenity trial. However, the band broke up before recording a single note for Apple; at this point, Evans signed Purvis to a management and publishing contract. With Elliot still in the picture, they formed a duo, Splinter. Purvis was couch surfing at Evans' house, and together they wrote 'Lonely Man'. Using his connections, Evans had managed to get Splinter cast to perform in a nightclub scene in Little Malcolm. The song they performed was the Purvis/Evans original 'Lonely Man,' and when Harrison heard it, he loved it. Harrison was so taken with Splinter he volunteered to produce the song for them and release it to tie in with the film. However, as the film was delayed, work on Splinter's debut single was put on hold. This may have disappointed them, but it would lead to bigger and better things. Harrison was planning a new record label, and Splinter and Ravi Shankar would be the first to be signed up.

With the basic tracks for his latest album finished, Starr began mixing the multi-tracks down to a stereo master. Working closely with his producer, Richard Perry, Starr spent hours refining the mix of each song until both he and the producer were happy. This was a laborious process, with some songs requiring up to sixteen attempts before a satisfactory mix was completed. In some cases, edit pieces were made along with mono mixes used for promotional records issued to US radio stations. Once the master had been completed, all that remained was design work for the album sleeve. Ringo would be a lavishly packaged record. The LP came in a gatefold sleeve designed by Barry Feinstein, with the cover painted by Tim Bruckner. Starr also commissioned Klaus Voormann to produce ten drawings illustrating each song to be reproduced as a 12x12 inch booklet included with the album. It may have been Voormann's low productivity that contributed to the album's delayed release. According to *Billboard* magazine, "Artwork still holding up the release of Ringo Starr's next solo effort featuring his three famous friends, among others."

For reasons unknown, Capitol was struggling to coordinate the release of Starr's new album. Tony King joined Apple as general manager in 1970 and was called in to help organise the project. "I had gone over to America in the spring of 1973 to help Capitol put the art together for the Ringo album," he recalled. "Capitol was having a lot of problems with getting the artwork together, so they asked if someone from Apple could come out to California to help, so I went out." Capitol wasn't the only record label having problems. Major record labels had finally had enough of the bootleggers and pirates and had taken a stand. As in America, changes were taking place in Britain to stop the trade in illegal recordings and records. A firm trading as Marble Arch Motor Supplies, Ltd., an odd name for a record label if ever there was one, was convicted of the illegal copying of pre-recorded tapes in the

High Court and fined £885 (£9,267.18), ordered to turn over 1228 pirate tapes and to hand over accounts of all its sales and profits. The lawsuit had been brought by several major labels that included WEA, Decca, EMI, CBS and A&M. Among the tapes that Marble Arch Motor Supplies was accused of duplicating without authorization were albums by Carole King, The Carpenters, Blood, Sweat and Tears, Santana, The Moody Blues, The Beatles, Elvis Presley, The Jefferson Airplane, Tony Bennett, Barbra Streisand and Frank Sinatra. These lawsuits would never stop the trade in pirate and bootleg records, but they did force them underground or under the counter. They would no longer be available in high street shops, where they were sold alongside legitimate releases. Instead, they had to be hunted down from back street independents, market stalls, or through mail-order outlets. Nevertheless, the net was tightening, and time was running out for the big-time bootleggers.

WEEK ENDING 7 JULY 1973
1. WILL IT GO ROUND IN CIRCLES: BILLY PRESTON
2. KODACHROME: PAUL SIMON
3. MY LOVE: PAUL MCCARTNEY AND WINGS
4. GIVE ME LOVE (GIVE ME PEACE ON EARTH): GEORGE HARRISON
5. BAD, BAD LEROY BROWN: JIM CROCE
6. PLAYGROUND IN MY MIND: CLINT HOLMES
7. SHAMBALA: THREE DOG NIGHT
8. YESTERDAY ONCE MORE: CARPENTERS
9. RIGHT PLACE WRONG TIME: DR. JOHN
10. I'M GONNA LOVE YOU JUST A LITTLE MORE BABY: BARRY WHITE

WEEK ENDING 14 JULY 1973
1. WILL IT GO ROUND IN CIRCLES: BILLY PRESTON
2. KODACHROME: PAUL SIMON
3. BAD, BAD LEROY BROWN: JIM CROCE
4. SHAMBALA: THREE DOG NIGHT
5. GIVE ME LOVE (GIVE ME PEACE ON EARTH): GEORGE HARRISON
6. YESTERDAY ONCE MORE: CARPENTERS
7. PLAYGROUND IN MY MIND: CLINT HOLMES
8. SMOKE ON THE WATER: DEEP PURPLE
9. MY LOVE: PAUL MCCARTNEY AND WINGS
10. RIGHT PLACE WRONG TIME: DR. JOHN

WEEK ENDING 21 JULY 1973
1. BAD, BAD LEROY BROWN: JIM CROCE
2. WILL IT GO ROUND IN CIRCLES: BILLY PRESTON
3. YESTERDAY ONCE MORE: CARPENTERS
4. SHAMBALA: THREE DOG NIGHT
5. KODACHROME: PAUL SIMON
6. GIVE ME LOVE (GIVE ME PEACE ON EARTH): GEORGE HARRISON
7. SMOKE ON THE WATER: DEEP PURPLE
8. BOOGIE WOOGIE BUGLE BOY: BETTE MIDLER:
9. PLAYGROUND IN MY MIND: CLINT HOLMES
10. NATURAL HIGH: BLOODSTONE

WEEK ENDING 28 JULY 1973
1. BAD, BAD LEROY BROWN: JIM CROCE
2. YESTERDAY ONCE MORE: CARPENTERS
3. SHAMBALA: THREE DOG NIGHT
4. SMOKE ON THE WATER: DEEP PURPLE
5. WILL IT GO ROUND IN CIRCLES: BILLY PRESTON
6. DIAMOND GIRL: SEALS & CROFTS
7. KODACHROME: PAUL SIMON
8. BOOGIE WOOGIE BUGLE BOY: BETTE MIDLER:
9. THE MORNING AFTER: MAUREEN MCGOVERN
10. GIVE ME LOVE (GIVE ME PEACE ON EARTH): GEORGE HARRISON

WEEK ENDING 7 JULY 1973
1. SKWEEZE ME PLEEZE ME: SLADE
2. WELCOME HOME: PETERS AND LEE
3. RUBBER BULLETS: 10CC
4. LIFE ON MARS: DAVID BOWIE
5. ALBATROSS: FLEETWOOD MAC
6. SNOOPY VERSUS THE RED BARON: HOTSHOTS
7. BORN TO BE WITH YOU: DAVE EDMUNDS
8. GROOVER: T.REX
9. TAKE ME TO THE MARDI GRAS: PAUL SIMON
10. GIVE ME LOVE (GIVE ME PEACE ON EARTH): GEORGE HARRISON

WEEK ENDING 14 JULY 1973
1. SKWEEZE ME PLEEZE ME: SLADE
2. WELCOME HOME: PETERS AND LEE
3. LIFE ON MARS: DAVID BOWIE
4. SNOOPY VERSUS THE RED BARON: HOTSHOTS
5. BORN TO BE WITH YOU: DAVE EDMUNDS
6. RUBBER BULLETS: 10CC
7. TAKE ME TO THE MARDI GRAS: PAUL SIMON
8. ALBATROSS: FLEETWOOD MAC
9. SATURDAY NIGHT'S ALRIGHT FOR FIGHTING: ELTON JOHN
10. GIVE ME LOVE (GIVE ME PEACE ON EARTH): GEORGE HARRISON

WEEK ENDING 21 JULY 1973
1. WELCOME HOME: PETERS AND LEE
2. I'M THE LEADER OF THE GANG (I AM!): GARY GLITTER
3. LIFE ON MARS: DAVID BOWIE
4. SKWEEZE ME PLEEZE ME: SLADE
5. ALRIGHT, ALRIGHT, ALRIGHT: MUNGO JERRY
6. GOING HOME: THE OSMONDS
7. SATURDAY NIGHT'S ALRIGHT FOR FIGHTING: ELTON JOHN
8. BORN TO BE WITH YOU: DAVE EDMUNDS
9. TAKE ME TO THE MARDI GRAS: PAUL SIMON
10. SNOOPY VERSUS THE RED BARON: HOTSHOTS

WEEK ENDING 28 JULY 1973
1. I'M THE LEADER OF THE GANG (I AM!): GARY GLITTER
2. WELCOME HOME: PETERS AND LEE
3. LIFE ON MARS: DAVID BOWIE
4. ALRIGHT, ALRIGHT, ALRIGHT: MUNGO JERRY
5. GOING HOME: THE OSMONDS
6. SKWEEZE ME PLEEZE ME: SLADE
7. SATURDAY NIGHT'S ALRIGHT FOR FIGHTING: ELTON JOHN
8. GAYE: CLIFFORD T. WARD
9. RANDY: BLUE MINK
10. BORN TO BE WITH YOU: DAVE EDMUNDS

John Lennon, Allen
Klein and Yoko Ono at
the BMI banquet for top
performed songs 1971.

Mr & Mrs McCartney at the launch of Wings'
'Hi, Hi, Hi' single, held at the Village
Restaurant, London.

Klein Replies To Retailer Charges On 'Bangla' Album

NEW YORK—Five Dollars from each of the "Concert For Bangla Desh" LP's will be going to the people of Bangla Desh through UNICEF, Allen Klein, president of Abkco Industries, rep for Apple Records which produced the album, revealed last week.

"This is an unheard of sum for a charity from any single album," said Klein. "Have you ever heard of any album giving off more than $5 a package?" he asked the people at a press conference originally designed to announce the news that Abkco Industries would distribute Abkco Records through indie distribs (the first item being the Rolling Stones "Hot Rocks" tapes; see separate story.)

But the conference had to touch on the "Bangla Desh" LP as well because of the huge success of the LP and the tremendous publicity it has received.

Answers Charges

Klein was actually rebutting the criticism on the part of some rack jobbers that distribution could have been handled in a manner more advantageous to the retailers so that more LP's could be sold. Klein suggested that if he had listened to the requests of various interests who were looking for a standard margin of profit, the charity wouldn't have gotten more than $1.20 a package. "And," he continued, "if we had committee meetings about the LP on how it would best be sold, we still wouldn't have the LP out on the market."

Klein said he set a fair price of $8.13 per album to Capitol and advised it should be sold at retail for $12.98. "Since Apple is the manufacturer," Klein went on, "and is taking all the risk, and had printed up over 1,000,000 booklets and boxes, we felt

(Cont'd on p. 28)

ALBUM OF THE YEAR

HARE KRSNA

APPLE

THE CONCERT FOR BANGLA DESH

Sales and Cost Comparison
on
3,000,000 Units

	Apple Records' Costs		Costs Per New York Magazine		Difference
Apple Sales Price Per L.P. To Capital		$ 8.135		$ 8.135	
Costs:					
Pressing Costs	$ 865		$ 865		0
Book, Box, Cover, Sleeves, Lables	731		.500		$ 231
Inventory On Hand	110		0		.110
Publishers Royalties	705		.500		205
A.F.M.	165		.130		035
Unicef Royalties	5.000		5.000		0
Returns, Studio, Artwork, Freight and other Overhead Costs	523		0		523
Cost of Concert	067		0		067
Total Costs Per Apple		8.166			
Total Costs Per N.Y. Magazine				6.995	
Loss Per Album To Apple		($ .031)			
N.Y. Magazine Charge of Difference Not Accounted For				$ 1.140	
NEW YORK MAGAZINE OMISSION AND ERRORS.					$1.171

Allen Klein presents the new Beatles album at a trade show for the first time.

THE BEATLES 1962-1966

THE BEATLES 1967-1970

Trade advertisements for The Beatles 1962 - 66 and 1967 - 70.

BEATLES TO GET BACK TOGETHER?

APPLE CORPS LTD, representing John Lennon, George Harrison and Ringo Starr, announced at the beginning of the week that Allen Klein's ABKCO Industries are no longer managing the Beatles and allied interests, and for the time being, Apple Corps will manage the Beatles' interests. Yoko Ono, too is no longer managed by Klein. This move opens the way for the group to reform if they wish.

Klein for his part issued an announcement to the effect that ABKCO "has terminated its efforts with respect to its possible acquisition of Apple Corps Ltd." and he took the opportunity "to wish the Apple group of companies and Messrs. Harrison, Lennon and Starr continued success."

Rumours concerning the reformation of the Beatles have been circulating recently with more than usual frequency, following announcements that John, George and Ringo had been working with Klaus Voorman, on an album for Ringo in Los Angeles, and the present announcement that Allen Klein has relinquished his control seems that legally, at least, the way is clear for all of the group to reform.

Lee Eastman, who is Paul McCartney's business manager as well as his legal adviser and father-in-law, said, after Klein's announcement, that "the four of them used to work together."

"We have always had the bond on film and now I think we can put the plan together. They have all agreed in principle to the outline of the plan and there is no reason why they can't work together."

Much has been made of the feuding between the various

Alan Klein

Beatles in the past, but it seems that the rifts have been healed. Paul, who refused for a year to step inside the Apple offices, is now a frequent visitor.

Now the Beatles ballyhoo is a thing of the past and all legal obstacles to their reunion have been removed; the one remaining puzzle concerns Paul. Will he leave Wings at a point when their popularity is growing?

★ American Beatle rumours: See page 8.

John Lennon, Yoko Ono and Ringo Starr
attend Barbara Streisand's fundraiser.

George and Patti Harrison attend the
marriage of Mr and Mrs Ken Mansfield.

Billboard TOP LP's & TAPE

Wings bring romance

PAUL McCARTNEY AND WINGS: "MY LOVE" (RED ROSE SPEEDWAY). As my tears veritably soak into this paper — my last week at SOUNDS drawing to its end — my only small consolation is that no tongue will I have to suffer the tirade of the P.O. postal system. Without cited for its lack of efficiency throughout the British Isles. Because of it this record now arrives on my desk nearly two weeks late for review. My apologies to all concerned. Understand by bittersweetness write on . . . to say that this is the first track Paul has put out that's likely to delight all its devotees of yesteryear. A tender, misty vocal with nice solid unobtrusive backing from Wings and a good guitar solo midway. Everything is tempered with the kind of professional touch that McCartney always used to show on his work — but it is not as the case may be, which he excels at. Lovely and romantic it is, too.

● PAUL McCARTNEY: misty vocal

SINGLES

REVIEWER:
PENNY VALENTINE

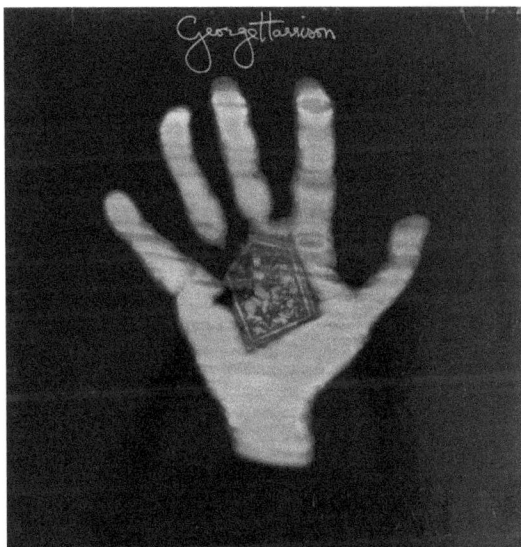

Billboard TOP LP's & TAPE

★ STAR PERFORMER—LP's registering greatest proportionate upward progress this week.

GEORGE HARRISON
Living In The Material World
Apple SMAS 3410

PAUL McCARTNEY & WINGS
Red Rose Speedway
Apple SMAL 3409

TEMPTATIONS
Masterpiece
Gordy G 965 L (Motown)

DAWN featuring Tony Orlando
Tuneweaving
Bell 6 1112

AL GREEN
I'm Still In Love With You
Hi XSHL 32074 (London)

SLADE
Slayed?
Polydor PD 5524

BETTE MIDLER
The Divine Miss M
Atlantic SD 7238

LOU REED
Transformer
RCA LSP 4807

RECORD MIRROR, JUNE 2, 1973

MIRRORPICK

PETER JONES on the new singles

George to slide up with love

GEORGE HARRISON: Give Me Love (Give Me Peace On Earth) (Apple R 5988). With an instantly catching slide-guitar opening, this is George on his semi-preaching, firmly-demanding kick. Certain mates didn't like this at all: but I've a feeling that familiarity could put it up there in the Sweet Lord category. A pleading vocal performance that gets the message across with intensity. Everything fits; nothing is overdone. Specially the guitar and piano segments. CHART CERT.

SHOW SOUVENIR

THIS BOOK IS DESIGNED FOR YOUR FURTHER ENJOYMENT OF THE SHOW

WINGS

PAUL McCARTNEY &
WINGS
ON TOUR

ODEON NEW STREET ON THE STAGE
BIRMINGHAM 021 643 0615/6

FRIDAY, JULY 6th, at 8 p.m.
MPL and HAM presents

PAUL McCARTNEY
AND WINGS

TICKETS £1.65, £1.35, £1.00, 80p, 60p.

BOOKING MONDAY, JUNE 18th at 10.30 a.m. Tickets are limited to FOUR
PER PERSON, obtainable by PERSONAL APPLICATION ONLY from Theatre
Booking Office.

PAUL FINED OVER POT FROM A FAN

Paul McCartney had five cannabis plants at farm

Paul McCartney, the former Beatle, was fined £100 at Campbeltown, Argyll, yesterday for cultivating five cannabis plants in a greenhouse at High Park Farm, Campbeltown last September 19.

He pleaded guilty, but denied two charges of having cannabis in his possession and under his control at High Park and Low Ranachan farms, Campbeltown, the same day, and these charges were dropped by the prosecution.

Sheriff D. J. McDiarmid told Mr McCartney, who was allowed 14 days to pay the fine: "I take into account the fact that these seeds were given to you in a gift, but I also take into account the fact that you are a considerable figure of public interest, particularly among young people, and you must be dealt with accordingly."

Mr Ian Stewart, prosecuting, who said a crime prevention officer spotted the plants while visiting High Park, had submitted that the penalty should be related not only to the crime but also the ex-Beatle's means. "If your Lordship believes, as I do, that monetary penalty is appropriate in this case, I suggest it should be a severe one," he added.

Mr John McCluskey, QC, for Mr McCartney, said: "These seeds, which, in fact, were planted and grown in the greenhouse, were a gift from a fan received through the post. I want to emphasise that they were grown absolutely openly."

No attempt was made at concealment, said Mr McCluskey. When the complaint was made, a layman could not tell by looking at the plants that they were of the genus cannabis. The plants were not then capable of being made into cannabis resin, to which the regulations applied. He submitted that the offence was a technical one, and that the quantity of cannabis obtainable from the five plants would be extremely small.

Mr McCartney, who had flown from London for the hearing, said afterwards that he was "very pleased" with the way his case had gone, and added: "I must admit I did expect it to be worse. As it was, I was planning on writing a few songs in gaol. It would not be too bad, as long as you had a guitar."

The control room, EMI Studios, Wharf Road, Apapa, Lagos.

Fela Kuti and Paul McCartney make peace at The Shrine, Lagos.

John and Yoko at a New York press conference on April 2nd, 1973 where they would announce the conceptual country of Nutopia.

John Lennon, Anne Murray, Harry Nilsson, Alice Cooper and Mickey Dolenz at the Troubadour in Los Angeles.

MIND GAMES
JOHN LENNON

Billboard TOP LP's & TAPE
JOHN LENNON
MIND GAMES

RINGO

CashBox Top 100 Albums
1 RINGO
2 GOODBYE YELLOW BRICK ROAD
3 QUADROPHENIA
35 LONG HARD CLIMB
36 PAPER ROSES
37 AMERICAN GRAFITTI/SOUNDTRACK
38 MARSHALL TUCKER BAND
HAT TRICK
67 HEAD TO THE SKY
BARBRA STREISAND . . . AND OTHER MUSICAL INSTRUMENTS
UNDER THE INFLUENCE OF
70 BIG BAMBU
YOU'RE SIXTEEN
RINGO

CHAPTER 8
AUGUST: OUT THE BLUE

August was a busy month for John Lennon. On 1st August, he entered the Record Plant studios in New York to record his first album of new 'pop' songs since *Imagine*. (*Some Time In New York City* is a JohnandYoko album rather than a solo Lennon effort.) Since the release of Imagine two years earlier, he had written little of merit. The only song of note was 'Happy Xmas (War Is Over),' which was only a partial success. Its American release was bungled, it was released too late and to an indifferent audience which resulted in its failure to chart. Released in Britain the following year, it achieved the success it deserved. Since then, he'd managed to scrape together enough material for a new album, re-writing songs he'd held back and composing a slack handful of new ones. Considering the legal, financial and personal pressures he was under, it's remarkable that he wrote anything.

Yoko Ono finished recording her second album of the year on 31st July, but mixing and editing would continue throughout August. (Final mixes were completed on 21st August and readied for the next stage in production, cutting the lacquers from which the records would be manufactured.) The following day – 1st August – Lennon occupied the studio using the same group of session musicians and began work on three songs, 'I Know,' 'Tight A$' and 'Rock 'n' Roll People'. Speaking to the *Melody Maker* the following month, Ono said: "John has just recorded with the same people. After I used them, he heard what they were playing and liked it."

A few weeks earlier, Lennon made a rough home demo recording of 'I Know' and an early version of 'Steel And Glass'. Lennon recorded several takes of his demo recording of 'I Know,' even going to the trouble of double-tracking his vocals. 'Rock 'n' Roll People' dated from late 1970 and had been initially demoed, along with several other songs, including what became the album's title song. He returned to 'Rock 'n' Roll People' sometime later and recorded a second demo using electric guitar rather than piano, which he had used the first time. When he entered the recording studio, he recorded several takes on successive nights with different levels of success. Lennon must have known it wasn't up to scratch because he left it off the album and couldn't even be bothered to issue it as the B-side to his next single.

Unlike his old, estranged fiancé, Paul, Lennon's sessions were the very model of efficiency. It would be unfair to claim that he didn't indulge in jamming, but it tended to be at the end of the session once the day's work had been done. There would be no getting stoned, no wasting studio time, and no squandering valuable recording tape. Lennon was on a mission and wouldn't let anything stop him from recording what he had as quickly as possible. Although Lennon sounded confident during the recording sessions,

Ono claimed he was nervous about returning to the studio after such a long break. Although he'd seen his new session musicians at work on Ono's album, they were new to him. A self-conscious guitarist and singer, he would have been anxious about working with a group of relative strangers, all of whom were better musicians than he was.

On the second night of sessions, Lennon recorded 'Intuition' and 'Bring Back The Lucy'. He'd previously recorded piano demos of 'Intuition,' which slightly differ in the melody and lyrics. When he entered the studio to record the song, he took lyric sheets and, if the musicians were lucky, chord sheets to help them routine the song. If he hadn't prepared chord sheets, it was a case of playing the song to the musicians until they had learned it. As can be seen by the rate at which they were racing through Lennon's songs, it was an efficient process. Lennon was working with seasoned professionals, several of whom had backgrounds in jazz and could pick up a song at the drop of a hat. 'Bring On The Lucy' had been written and demoed the previous year when it was titled 'Free The People'. The original demo, recorded with a dobro steel guitar, has more than a hint of 'John Sinclair'. When recording the demo, Lennon was still very much in agitprop mode. Consequently, he re-wrote the lyrics but kept the melody.

On 3rd August, Lennon recorded the basic tracks for another three songs, 'You Are Here,' 'Meat City' and 'Only People'. Lennon liked to work fast. He'd started his career in the days when bands were expected to record two or three songs in one session. For the most part, but not exclusively, he continued working in the same fashion. Backing tracks were recorded live with a band and overdubbed later. David Spinozza explained: "When I worked with John Lennon, he seemed like he wanted it done quickly. He went in and would show you the songs, but he wanted to do a take and get out of there. Then he probably came in later and overdubbed guitar parts himself and took time with that and vocals. But the basic tracks were done really fast with John."

The musicians Lennon hired to help record his songs wouldn't have found 'Meat City' a challenge. It is a simple rock 'n' roll song, simplified as the composition developed. Lennon made home demo recordings of the song on two occasions. The earliest home recording dates from 1971. It features Lennon playing an acoustic guitar and singing a nostalgic lyric about the rock 'n' roll of his youth. Lennon felt most comfortable jamming on this kind of material and was captured playing some of his favourite rock 'n' roll songs when the Lennons made their film *Clock* at the St. Regis Hotel in September 1971. Lennon took these early influences, added a pinch of Chuck Berry, and wrote a song with the working title

'Just Gotta Get Me Some Rock And Roll' or alternately 'Shoeshine'. It remained unfinished until 1973, when he returned to the song, possibly because he hadn't written anything new and was raiding his notebooks and cassette tapes to find something to record. His rewrite was, if anything, even more straightforward than his earlier demo recording.

'You Are Here' was more melodically sophisticated than 'Meat City' but used only four chords. Combining two themes close to his heart – love and peace – Lennon imagines a world without differences, modelled on his idealised relationship with Ono. The image he paints is far from the truth. The song is graceful and joyful, while their marriage was troubled and fractious. Although he'd said in private that JohnandYoko was finished, publicly, he maintained the illusion.

It was around this time that Lennon started his affair with May Pang. It was an open secret that the Lennons' marriage was on the rocks. They had done an excellent job building and maintaining their fairytale romance. But that was all it was. A fairytale. Lennon had been openly unfaithful to Ono on more than one occasion. It says a lot about their relationship that it didn't fall apart much sooner. Few marriages could withstand such egregious behaviour, and the Lennons were no exception. Despite this, Ono also maintained the illusion. Speaking to Andrew Tyler of the *NME*, she said: "I don't know what the impression is outside, but we manage as people." However, she suggested that their relationship could be changeable and that Lennon found it difficult to accept her divergence from what were then rigidly defined gendered roles. "I don't know who is dominant and not dominant. It depends on the day, I suppose. I felt that, in the beginning, it was hard for John, too, though I didn't feel it would be hard for me because I didn't know any other way. And I didn't really understand the male chauvinism problem. I had always worked, so I didn't think there was any problem. Whereas John, I think, wasn't prepared to meet someone who was always working." Lennon had expected his previous wife, Cynthia, to be a mother and housewife. She was not expected to have a career outside of the house. In this respect, Lennon was as conformist as any other middle-class man of his generation. Ono was growing creatively and was far more productive than her spouse. She was more socially engaged and artistically progressive. She wanted to develop her career as a songwriter and performer and had already made inroads into the live circuit. Performing was something her husband showed little or no interest in. Ono needed more space to be herself. Her latest album provided a clue to her current state of mind. It was a tentative step away from being the wife of John Lennon.

The Lennons were also under immense pressure. They had recently split with their manager, their income had been reduced, they had a new and expensive apartment to pay for, their publishers were suing them, and Lennon was facing deportation. On top of this, the reason they went to America in the first place, to gain custody of Ono's daughter, Kyoko, had evaporated. Although they had won the battle, they had lost the war. Talking to Loraine Alterman of the *Melody Maker*, Ono appeared wearied and broken by her failure to reunite with her daughter. "She's ten now and when I saw her last she was five," she said. "I don't even know how she looks now. It's like five years is a long time. So I more or less have started to think that instead of pushing and trying to chase after her, I'll wait and she'll come around because she's getting old enough." Speaking publicly about how their custody case had changed, Ono may have inadvertently created serious ramifications for Lennon's deportation case. His defence had rested, in part, on their attempt to gain custody of Kyoko. This kind of talk wouldn't help his deportation case, and they knew it.

The stress they were experiencing must have played a part in the breakdown of their marriage. According to Ono, it was partly to blame for their inability to have children. Under the headline "Tensions stifle John and Yoko's family plans," the *Evening Standard* reported that Ono had visited London to see doctors about their inability to have a child. Stress undoubtedly contributed to Ono's 1969 miscarriage, which occurred only weeks after her husband was arrested for possession of cannabis. The ongoing tensions the Lennons were experiencing would have only made things worse. "At one time, we thought there might be a problem, but now we have both been told that there is nothing wrong with either of us," she said. "I have always been a nervous sort of person, and John and I have had a lot of problems which have caused tensions. The doctors have told me that too much worry and tension could easily affect me. We have reached a time in our lives where we would like to have a family."

If Ono did want to have a family with Lennon, her next move made it almost an impossibility. Rather than drawing her husband closer, she pushed him away. She was used to managing every aspect of his life and saw a way to establish the space she needed while maintaining control over him. With all the subtlety of a flying mallet, Ono manipulated the situation, telling her assistant, May Pang, that she wanted her to have an affair with her husband. Pang was shocked that either of them thought it was a good idea. However, Ono knew precisely what she was doing. Speaking to David Marsh about how men controlled women, she said: "In 2,000 years they carefully cultivated women who would be favourable to them – like a domesticated animal. They would select women who are not threatening: women who are smaller and not that intelligent... and the very intelligent, radical women just didn't get married. This has gone on for 2,000 years until finally we became what we are. Women are capable of this sort of thing too, but of course that's not the final answer. We fall in love. And we appreciate men as human, too."

Ono was undoubtedly capable of this sort of thing. She carefully selected her husband's lover, not from peers but from someone who could be easily influenced. Pang was that unwitting ingenue and was aware that Lennon could be equally manipulative. Recalling her time working for Lennon, she said: "He seemed fully aware that he need only raise his voice or change the expression on his face and people would become hurt and frightened. That's how much we loved and wanted to please him." Pang may have been shocked by the indecent proposal, but she also wanted to please her employers. Ono knew this only too well. Not only was Pang no real threat to her, but she could be relied on to keep Lennon out of trouble. She was more than capable of managing his day-to-day affairs and lacked the ambition to steal him from her permanently. It was a dangerous game, but Ono held all the cards.

On 4th August, Lennon recorded three more songs; 'Mind Games,' 'You Came To Me' (re-titled 'Intuition'), and a remake of 'Rock 'n' Roll People'. Further evidence that Lennon had been struggling to write new material came in the form of 'Mind Games'. The song dated from 1970 and began life as 'Make Love Not War'. The slogan was associated with the American counterculture of the 1960s and was used to oppose the Vietnam War. Lennon had already coined his anti-war slogan, 'Give Peace A Chance,' and quickly abandoned the idea, possibly because even he knew that recycling an already cliched slogan was beneath him. Next, he reworked the song, keeping much of the melody but re-writing the words to form a more generic love song called 'I Promise'. This version featured the chorus 'Love is the answer, and you know that it's true' that he'd keep for the third and final re-write. But it too was abandoned because it borrowed a little too heavily from 'Bring It On Home To Me' and, as Lennon noted at the end of his home recording, "I keep using the same middle eight for every song." Lennon eventually rewrote the lyric after reading the book *Mind Games: The Guide to Inner Space* by Robert Masters and Jean Houston. Whether inner or creative, space was obviously on Lennon's and Ono's minds. Each was playing mind games with the other and the public. The backing track for 'Mind Games' was recorded this evening, but adding numerous guitar overdubs would transform it into something magical.

'Intuition' was one of the newer songs that Lennon had written for the album. He recorded a home demo on the piano that segued into 'How' and 'God'. At this early stage, neither melody nor lyrics were finished, hence his drifting into these earlier songs. Unhappy with his first attempt at 'Rock 'n' Roll People,' Lennon led the band through a much tighter remake. Having played it a few nights earlier, the band powered through the song, giving a confident, upbeat performance. However, at the end of take five, Lennon said: "It sounded suspiciously like the other night to me." Although tonight's re-make was an improvement, he still wasn't happy with the song and decided to leave it in the can.

Also on this day, *Cash Box* revealed that Elephant's Memory, who had been let go by the Lennons, had been busy recording with Chuck Berry. The band had briefly worked with Berry the previous year when JohnandYoko appeared with the rocker on the *Mike Douglas Show*. On 27th January 1972, Lennon finally met and played with one of his heroes. Backed by Elephant's Memory, Lennon and Berry performed two songs, 'Memphis' and 'Johnny B. Goode'. "I had a call from the *Mike Douglas Show*, and they mentioned that John Lennon would be there. They asked me what we were going to do, so I said 'Let's do 'Memphis' and 'Johnny B. Goode'. I know he sings and I invited him to the microphone, and we did 'Memphis' in two part harmony. It was almost like a gig," Berry recalled. Lennon was considerably more starstruck than Chuck, who seemed to take meeting a Beatle in his stride. Lennon's nervousness at playing with one of his heroes was all too visible; although he managed to get through it without messing up, he later explained exactly how nervy he was. "When Berry said to take it, I nearly fell over. I couldn't play I was so scared. I thought. 'What's he telling me to take it for? He's supposed to take it.' I just go bumdebumdebumdebum."

Elephant's Memory cut four tracks with Berry for the album *Bio*. Tony Glover reviewed the album for Rolling Stone magazine and wasn't impressed. But he did have something positive to say about Elephant's Memory: "On all but two numbers, Chuck is accompanied by members of Elephant's Memory, and they add a nice solid backup, working well within the limits Chuck sets — he don't like anybody getting too fancy, you understand."

The final day of recording backing tracks showed the urgency with which Lennon was working. Another four songs were recorded today. New songs 'One Day At A Time' and 'Aisumasen' were recorded along with re-makes of 'Bring Back The Lucy' and 'Tight A$'. 'One Day At A Time' paints a rosy picture of the Lennons' relationship. Lennon may have been sincere when he wrote the song, but by the time he recorded it, he must have been embarrassed by the hypocrisy. It was all part of the myth of JohnandYoko, intended to maintain a public narrative that the Lennons had fostered since 1968. As he was short of material, he had little choice but to record it. As was his habit, Lennon recorded a vocal with each take, which he sang in his usual register. However, when he overdubbed his vocal a few days later, he sang it in a falsetto, which, it is alleged, was Ono's suggestion.

Another song about the Lennons' relationship, 'Aisumasen,' was recorded today. This was at least a more honest appraisal of their marriage. However, it was another 'old' song that Lennon began writing in September 1971 and was more evidence that their marriage had been troubled for some time. It was initially titled 'Call My Name'. Two years later, Lennon rewrote the lyric and changed the title to 'Aisumasen' — Japanese for I'm sorry. The re-make of 'Tight A$' improved on the earlier recording and was selected for additional overdubs. Similarly, 'Bring Back The Lucy' was improved and given a more urgent treatment than the early attempt. It also has a similar arrangement to 'Mind Games'; both songs relied on a slide guitar part to provide a hypnotic sonic wash of sound. With these four songs finished to Lennon's satisfaction, all the backing tracks for the album had been completed in just five days. Lennon returned to the Record Plant the following day to make rough mixes of the songs he'd recorded the previous week. He then took a short break from the studio, perhaps to review his work at home, before returning to start adding overdubs on Friday, 10th August.

Some recording artists can take five days to get a drum sound. Lennon had recorded the basic tracks for an entire album in a working week. The speed at which he worked came in for criticism from Richard Perry, who suggested that Lennon wasn't meticulous enough. Lennon recorded backing tracks quickly, but Perry overlooked Lennon's attention to detail during post-production. He would spend much longer overdubbing and mixing than recording. Responding to Perry's criticism, Lennon said: "If there's a quality that occasionally gets in the way of my talent, it's that I get bored quick unless it's done quick. [...] But I do them as quick as I possibly can, without losing (a) the feel and (b) where I'm going. But I don't want to make myself so painstaking that it's boring. But I should (pause) maybe think a little more. Maybe. It gets too slick and somewhere in between that is where I'd like to go."

While Lennon was trying to figure out where to go musically, his lawyers were busy working out where The Beatles partnership was heading legally. On Saturday 11th, *Billboard* published an article about a possible settlement of the various disputes between the four individual Beatles and Apple. It was reported that recent meetings between lawyers representing John Lennon, George Harrison, Paul McCartney, and Ringo Starr had taken place at the Apple offices in London. These involved McCartney and Lee Eastman, Starr, and David Braun representing Harrison. It was reported that the meetings had resulted in the possibility of McCartney breaking away from Apple and switching back to the EMI label.

By now, the amount of money held by the official receiver must have been considerable. Except for Starr, each Beatle had scored number one albums, and now there was income from the two Beatles' compilation albums to be added. The Beatles' success, as a group and as solo performers, was such that their American record label, Capitol Records, reported healthy profits. *Billboard* reported that: "All divisions and subsidiaries of the company contributed to the higher earnings. Improvement can be attributed, among other reasons, to new releases of The Beatles, as well as successes of both new artists and established acts." For the first time in two years, Capitol Records paid a 25-cent dividend to shareholders. With new albums from Lennon and Starr just around the corner, the future looked very bright for Capitol Records, its artists, and its shareholders.

While Lennon was busying himself in the studio, his immigration lawyer was busy filing Freedom Of Information Act requests with the courts. Leon Wildes had been making slow but steady progress on Lennon's behalf. Wildes knew how to work the system and had been making Freedom Of Information Act requests that uncovered a two-tier immigration system of 'non-priority' and 'priority' cases. Although the government denied the practice, Wildes tenacity paid dividends and he eventually accumulated enough correspondence with government officials to prove that Lennon's case had been made a priority. What he hadn't been able to demonstrate was that the two-tier immigration process was official government policy with written regulations. However, by the end of the year, Wildes had a 'non-priority case summary' form that proved him right.

Speaking on the *Tomorrow Show*, Wildes outlined the case against Lennon. "John was charged with being deportable in the United States for being an overstay. By a very interesting turn of events, the district director of the New York Immigration Service charged him with being an overstay after he gave him a two-week extension of his time. He had originally come in as a visitor and he had a number of extensions and then finally the Immigration Service gave him a two week extension. Right in the midst of that two week final extension they revoked the period that they had given him and they declared that he had been here as an overstay for the week that he had been here with their authorisation. And thus the Immigration Service created the very status that they charged him with being deportable for. We fought that deportation case and a decision was finally rendered after about a year that he was in fact an overstay. Now the essential problem in a deportation case, what lies beneath the surface, is that the only way one can get out of it is either to ask for permission to leave this country voluntarily, and get out, which John was not prepared to do. Or to apply for permanent residence status, and the law prescribes that any person who had ever been convinced of any offence, no matter how small, relating to the possession of marijuana, at any time in his lifetime and under any circumstances, cannot obtain residence. And so what was happening when the government did this little routine of revoking his stay and charging him with being an overstay, they were locking him into a position where the only application he could make was one which they were pretty sure he could never succeed in – for permanent residence."

The INS case against Lennon was beginning to look very suspect. The government had maintained that its case against Lennon was based on a 1968 British conviction for possession of marijuana. However, Wildes Freedom Of Information Act requests uncovered 118 cases of individuals who were allowed resident status in America "even though they have convictions at least as serious as my client's." Indeed, some of those given permanent residence included a convicted murderer and one individual "with six convictions including rape, burglary and impairing the morals of children." Lennon joked: "Murderers, rapists, multiple convictions for dope, heroin, cocaine. What the hell? I'll fit right in."

Wildes also filed Freedom Of Information Act requests with the FBI. This provided vital evidence that the purpose of the investigation was political. The FBI had made it evident that it was surveilling the Lennons. It used a surveillance technique called 'tailgating' or 'an open tail' to intimidate the person under investigation. It also tapped the Lennons' phone. The FBI's tactics worked in as much as they affected Lennon's mental health. But it didn't stop him from telling the world what was happening to him. Lennon said about the situation: "Not only was I physically having to appear in court cases, it just seemed like a toothache that wouldn't go away. But there was just a period where I just couldn't function, you know? I was so paranoid from them tappin' the phone and following me. ... How could I prove that they were tappin' my phone? There was no way. And when they were following me, I went on 'Dick Cavett' and said they were following me, and they stopped. But when they were following me, they wanted me to see they were following me. I was so damn paranoid." Wildes filed a lawsuit against the attorney general, claiming illegal wiretapping.

Lennon was wise to the government's tactics. He explained the government's duplicitousness on the *Tomorrow Show*: "One interesting point was that when they started the initial case, they claimed it was a local New York problem. And they also started the proceedings against John and Yoko. Well, halfway, or a third of the way through, the proceedings they discovered that actually Yoko did not have any record in England and also she had a green card by a previous American husband. So this local case that was just another case like any other alien, which is what they kept claiming, was not one of those cases. So then they had to suddenly find something else which was this overstay business, which they pulled a fast one. And so they had to give Yoko the green card. Now one of them, I think his name is Green, keeps writing to the papers saying they're still treating me like a normal alien only on overstay. They no longer mention about marijuana and the original normal reason I was being thrown out. And it's just interesting that the case keeps changing to suit them."

It was around this time that the FBI started to play dirty. If the government couldn't deport Lennon because of his conviction for possession of marijuana, and if it couldn't deport him for being an overstay, it needed another reason. It planned to use the Lennons' custody case against them by claiming Lennon had committed perjury. L. Patrick Gray, acting director of the FBI, argued that the Lennons had Kyoko hidden in Houston. He wrote: "Actual location of Ono's child and subsequent prosecution for perjury in this instance is responsibility of INS and Houston being instructed to disregard lead except for contact with established sources only. In view of possible court proceedings, active investigation by FBI in this area could result in FBI agents testifying which would not be in bureau's best interest and could result in considerable adverse publicity."

It will come as no surprise that the FBI was lying. The Lennons did not have access to Kyoko. They did not have Kyoko hidden at a secret address. Nor had they committed perjury. The Lennons were very concerned for Kyoko. John wrote a letter to Kyoko the previous year, addressing their concerns. "No Police. No FBI No Detectives on our authority, although there is pressure from many sources for us to act unwisely against Kyoko's interests in the long term. We understand the problems. Please get in touch with us thru anyone at group media you trust. We are making no moves. We wait for your call/letter." Sadly, the call/letter never came. But as Lennon said in his letter, they knew what the authorities were doing.

On 16th August, Wildes filed a "Brief on Behalf of Respondent" for consideration by the Board of Immigration Appeals. It stated that the service violated its invariable agency practice regarding the commencement of proceedings in cases with compelling humanitarian aspects and those involving approved third-preference petitioners. It called for the decision making Lennon deportable to be reversed because the government had no sustainable burden of proof that the facts alleged were actual. It also stated that Lennon's conviction for possession of cannabis was not a bar for permanent residence.

Lennon began phase two of his album on Friday, 10th August. He would spend the next week adding overdubs to the backing tracks. Michael Brecker, 'Sneaky' Pete Kleinnow, and Something Different all added extra instrumentation and backing vocals. May Pang attended these sessions and recalled Lennon's technique: "Whenever John had a guitar solo he would play it a number of different times, inventing a different phrasing each time he did so. He'd do a clean version, then a spacy version, then a raunchy version of the same solo. Each of these was recorded on a different track, and later John would select the performance he liked best to include on the album. Even though he did not feel confident about his guitar playing, the grittiness of his work that night made it apparent that he was a consummate rock and roller."

The overdub sessions were completed as quickly and efficiently as the previous week's work and were followed by mixing sessions starting Tuesday, 21st August. Although Lennon and Ono were drifting apart, they continued working together. Work on Ono's album was completed earlier in the day with the creation of the cutting master for side one of her album. She continued to attend mixing sessions for Lennon's album until it was completed in early September.

However, separation, both physically and creatively, was now a reality. Speaking to Loraine Alterman of the *Melody Maker* a few weeks later, Ono blamed the underground for their breakup. "Now, we're going to try to do things separately for a while. Maybe early next year we might try to do something together. There was such a strong anti-John-and-Yoko thing out there, and it didn't come from middle Americans either. They weren't anti-John-and-Yoko at all. In fact, they felt we were a cute couple, so much in love. The objection from the underground was what really disturbed us."

The week that Lennon was mixing his album, George Harrison was featured on the new single by comedy duo Cheech and Chong. Lifted from their album *Los Cochinos*, 'Basketball Jones' featured Harrison on guitar and contributions from Michelle Philips, Billy Preston, Tom Scott, and Carole King. "George and I were buddies,"

Tommy Chong recalled. "George and I used to smoke quite a bit when we'd meet once in a while at different places. He was in the studio at A&M at the same time we were doing 'Basketball Jones,' so Lou (Adler) asked him to come in and do a little guitar riff for us. And George is George; He literally made that song." Lennon may have had a reputation for razor-sharp wit, but Harrison was the real joker. While he would go on to produce records for Monty Python, Cheech and Chong was the first comedy act to benefit from his playing. The single was a top twenty hit, reaching number 15 on the *Billboard* chart, while the album reached number 3 on the *Billboard* album chart.

While Lennon was being kept busy in New York, McCartney was in Scotland and faced his own problems. The McCartneys had decamped to their farm near Campbelltown in late July, with Wings following soon after, to start rehearsing material for their next album. The accommodation on McCartney's High Park farm was rudimentary, with the single-storey, tin-roofed building just large enough to accommodate the McCartney family. The two Dennys, Henry, and their wives and partners weren't as lucky. Once again, McCartney neglected the welfare of his fellow musicians. Only weeks earlier, Wings were at number-one in the American singles and albums charts. Their latest single, 'Live And Let Die,' looked like a chart-topper. With gold records to their name, Laine, McCullough, and Seiwell must have thought that things were looking up. Although they weren't expecting luxury accommodation, they were appalled by the lodgings when they arrived at the remote location. McCartney had arranged for them to stay at a nearby farm he'd purchased, Low Ranachan. The farmhouse and outbuildings, where Wings members were expected to stay, had no basic amenities. Living the simple life was one thing; being invited to sleep in a recently vacated shippen was quite another. With discontent within the ranks already running high, if this was how members of a chart-topping band were going to be treated by their boss, then mutiny couldn't be ruled out. Consequently, Wings and crew members moved out of the substandard housing offered by the McCartneys, either renting a caravan or a cottage. One thing is sure: they were not living the rockstar life that others in a similar position were enjoying. The first two weeks of August were spent preparing material in a makeshift rehearsal space in a barn at Low Ranachan. Once they'd knocked the songs into shape, they moved to McCartney's Rude Studio to record demos.

Rehearsals were tense, with tensions exacerbated by the poor living conditions they were expected to endure. Despite everything, McCullough was still determined to fit in. However, his way of working irritated McCartney, and McCartney's way of working vexed him. As McCullough recalled: "We were still on this retainer, and we'd been told that as things progressed, we could contribute material, become part of a 'band' as such, but it never ever came to that. We'd rehearsed *Band On The Run* and were due to go to Lagos [to record it], and I can remember it well – we had a row one afternoon. [..] It wasn't a fierce row, just 'Oh stuff it, I'm away home' sort of thing. There were a lot of things said in the press, like there was a terrible rumour I'd pulled a gun on him, that I'd hit him over the head with a bottle – really! But I think we both knew in our hearts it was time for me to go and he left it to me to choose the time of leaving."

Enough was enough. McCullough quit the group and went on a well-deserved holiday to cool his heels. McCullough wasn't the only member of Wings to experience McCartney's wrath. A few days after McCullough left the band, Denny Laine's partner, Jo Jo, gave birth to a son. Laine was clearing out the rented caravan in readiness for their return to London when Jo Jo's waters broke. A frantic drive along winding dirt roads to the nearest hospital followed. However, when Laine returned from the hospital with the news of the birth of his son, rather than being congratulated on becoming a father, he was confronted by the McCartneys, who accused him of leaving a mess. "They seemed far more concerned about that than the baby we had just had," he recalled.

Denny Seiwell also had concerns but had thus far convinced himself to stick with the group. Having completed rehearsals and recording at McCartney's farm, he was due to fly to Lagos on 30th August. But McCullough's recent departure and other issues that had yet to be resolved still played on his mind, and he couldn't bring himself to go. The night he was due to fly to Lagos, McCartney sent a car to pick him up. But Seiwell decided it was time to quit Wings. Like McCullough, Seiwell had had enough of McCartney, not musically but with his unwillingness to put anything down on paper. McCartney's reluctance to commit to any legally binding document is understandable, considering the years of legal wrangling The Beatles partnership had caused. Despite all the talk about Wings being a band, McCartney never treated his fellow bandmates as equals. "We had no contract or even written agreements," Seiwell explained. "And that was the main reason for the decision I made to leave when I did—that, and the fact that we wouldn't be a band anymore, without Henry. I regret doing it that way. And for years, we didn't speak."

It wasn't all bad news. On 30th August, Wings were awarded another gold disc for 'Live and Let Die'. Although it hadn't topped the chart, it was another million-seller, which meant more royalties being deposited in McCartney's bank account. That would have covered the cost of Wings' trip to Lagos and a decent pay rise for the musicians who helped keep McCartney at the topper most of the popper most.

US

WEEK ENDING 4 AUGUST 1973
1. THE MORNING AFTER: MAUREEN MCGOVERN
2. BAD, BAD LEROY BROWN: JIM CROCE
3. LIVE AND LET DIE: WINGS
4. SMOKE ON THE WATER: DEEP PURPLE
5. YESTERDAY ONCE MORE: CARPENTERS
6. DIAMOND GIRL: SEALS & CROFTS
7. TOUCH ME IN THE MORNING: DIANA ROSS
8. BROTHER LOUIE: STORIES
9. WILL IT GO ROUND IN CIRCLES: BILLY PRESTON
10. SHAMBALA: THREE DOG NIGHT

WEEK ENDING 11 AUGUST 1973
1. THE MORNING AFTER: MAUREEN MCGOVERN
2. LIVE AND LET DIE: WINGS
3. BROTHER LOUIE: STORIES
4. TOUCH ME IN THE MORNING: DIANA ROSS
5. BAD, BAD LEROY BROWN: JIM CROCE
6. SMOKE ON THE WATER: DEEP PURPLE
7. LET'S GET IT ON: MARVIN GAYE
8. UNEASY RIDER: CHARLIE DANIELS
9. MONSTER MASH: BOBBY "BORIS" PICKETT AND THE CRYPT-KICKERS

WEEK ENDING 18 AUGUST 1973
1. TOUCH ME IN THE MORNING: DIANA ROSS
2. LIVE AND LET DIE: WINGS
3. BROTHER LOUIE: STORIES
4. THE MORNING AFTER: MAUREEN MCGOVERN
5. LET'S GET IT ON: MARVIN GAYE
6. BAD, BAD LEROY BROWN: JIM CROCE
7. GET DOWN: GILBERT O'SULLIVAN
8. DELTA DAWN: HELEN REDDY
9. UNEASY RIDER: CHARLIE DANIELS
10. FEELIN' STRONGER EVERY DAY: CHICAGO

WEEK ENDING 25 AUGUST 1973
1. BROTHER LOUIE: STORIES
2. LIVE AND LET DIE: WINGS
3. TOUCH ME IN THE MORNING: DIANA ROSS
4. LET'S GET IT ON: MARVIN GAYE
5. THE MORNING AFTER: MAUREEN MCGOVERN
6. DELTA DAWN: HELEN REDDY
7. GET DOWN: GILBERT O'SULLIVAN
8. SAY, HAS ANYBODY SEEN MY SWEET GYPSY ROSE: DAWN
   FEATURING TONY ORLANDO
9. UNEASY RIDER: CHARLIE DANIELS
10. BAD, BAD LEROY BROWN: JIM CROCE

UK

WEEK ENDING 4 AUGUST 1973
1. I'M THE LEADER OF THE GANG (I AM!): GARY GLITTER
2. WELCOME HOME: PETERS AND LEE
3. ALRIGHT, ALRIGHT, ALRIGHT: MUNGO JERRY
4. GOING HOME: THE OSMONDS
5. LIFE ON MARS: DAVID BOWIE
6. 48 CRASH: SUZI QUATRO
7. YESTERDAY ONCE MORE: THE CARPENTERS
8. SPANISH EYES: AL MARTINO
9. TOUCH ME IN THE MORNING: DIANA ROSS
10. RANDY: BLUE MINK

WEEK ENDING 11 AUGUST 1973
1. I'M THE LEADER OF THE GANG (I AM!): GARY GLITTER
2. WELCOME HOME: PETERS AND LEE
3. ALRIGHT, ALRIGHT, ALRIGHT: MUNGO JERRY
4. 48 CRASH: SUZI QUATRO
5. YESTERDAY ONCE MORE: THE CARPENTERS
6. GOING HOME: THE OSMONDS
7. LIFE ON MARS: DAVID BOWIE
8. SPANISH EYES: AL MARTINO
9. YING TONG SONG: GOONS
10. BAD BAD BOY: NAZARETH

WEEK ENDING 18 AUGUST 1973
1. I'M THE LEADER OF THE GANG (I AM!): GARY GLITTER
2. YESTERDAY ONCE MORE: THE CARPENTERS
3. 48 CRASH: SUZI QUATRO
4. WELCOME HOME: PETERS AND LEE
5. SPANISH EYES: AL MARTINO
6. ALRIGHT, ALRIGHT, ALRIGHT: MUNGO JERRY
7. YOU CAN DO MAGIC: LIMMIE AND THE FAMILY COOKIN'
8. DANCING ON A SATURDAY NIGHT: BARRY BLUE
9. YING TONG SONG: GOONS
10. GOING HOME: THE OSMONDS

WEEK ENDING 25 AUGUST 1973
1. YOUNG LOVE: DONNY OSMOND
2. YESTERDAY ONCE MORE: THE CARPENTERS
3. I'M THE LEADER OF THE GANG (I AM!): GARY GLITTER
4. DANCING ON A SATURDAY NIGHT: BARRY BLUE
5. YOU CAN DO MAGIC: LIMMIE AND THE FAMILY COOKIN'
6. SPANISH EYES: AL MARTINO
7. 48 CRASH: SUZI QUATRO
8. WELCOME HOME: PETERS AND LEE
9. SMARTY PANTS: FIRST CHOICE
10. ALRIGHT, ALRIGHT, ALRIGHT: MUNGO JERRY

CHAPTER 9
SEPTEMBER: THE ROAD TO LAGOS

On 30th August, Paul McCartney and his family flew from London to Lagos, Nigeria, to join Denny Laine and recording engineer Geoff Emerick. Once there, the intention was to record the next Wings album in a relaxing, holiday-like environment. They were, however, in for a shock. The trip to Lagos would be anything but relaxing.

Recording overseas was nothing new. McCartney recorded his Ram album in New York in late 1971/early 1972. Several British acts did likewise. Deep Purple recorded their *Machine Head* album in Montreux, Switzerland, in December 1971. Elton John recorded his 1972 album *Honky Château* in France. He recorded its follow up in Jamaica in January 1973 before moving production back to France. The Rolling Stones recorded their album *Goat's Head Soup* in Jamaica in November 1972. Cat Stevens followed the Stones to Jamaica in March '73 to record his *Foreigner* album.

Why were so many British rock acts choosing to record outside of the UK? One reason for all this jet-setting was simply because there was the money to do it and the recording studios to facilitate their rock star fantasies. Indeed, it was a fantasy that McCartney had been contemplating for some time. Speaking to *Beat Instrumental* a few weeks earlier, he said: "[I]t would be easy for us now that we have got the touring and performing bit together, we could do the Bowie (I don't know whether he has seriously done it, by the way), and go off to Marrakesh and record an album."

Like his contemporaries, McCartney was well placed to indulge his fantasies. Why not record in Marrakesh? It would have been a better option than the one he opted for. Unfortunately, EMI didn't have a recording studio there. But that needn't have stopped him. He could have done what Deep Purple and The Rolling Stones did and use a mobile studio.

Another reason for recording outside of Britain was for tax purposes. Deep Purple's Ian Gillan was very open about why his band recorded in Switzerland: "You can avoid paying some tax on your albums, on your royalties, if you've made the album out of the country. It's a very complicated deal, but it's not illegal. The tax people know about it; it's just that if you take advantage of it, you have to record outside the country." An article published in *Billboard* about musicians and their use of recording studios had this to say about recording outside of the United Kingdom. "The move out of the country, that has been made by many of the top artists, is a completely different question. This is primarily one of taxation. This explains the presence of the Rolling Stones in Jamaica and of McCartney in Lagos – not to mention the numerous artists who use American studios."

With help from his in-laws and advisors, the Eastmans, McCartney would have known of the loophole and taken advantage of it. Indeed, when McCartney spoke to Paul Gambaccini about his tax situation, he said that for tax purposes: "We had to record outside of the country. I have to write my songs outside of the country, too. Otherwise the government will say, right, this is a British record, all the money has to come back to Britain. I'm in 98 percent tax then. I get 2p, the government gets 98p. I mean, I don't particularly like it when the US government gets 30¢ and I get 70¢ but it's better than getting 2p in the pound."

As a former colony, Nigeria had plenty of connections with Britain. Not the least of which was an EMI-owned and operated recording studio. Whatever mental picture McCartney had of Lagos bore no relation to reality. Nigeria was still recovering from a civil war with the Republic of Biafra. It had a military dictatorship headed by General Yakubu Gowon, who had played a role in overthrowing Nigeria's civilian government. An oil boom transformed the city of Lagos from a quaint African port into an unmanageable mess, unable to cope with an influx of tens of thousands of people eager to benefit from the jobs created by the oil industry. Besides the ineffectual infrastructure, Nigeria was racked with wealth inequality, corruption, ethnic tension, and military intervention. This heaving mass of chaotic humanity would be home to Wings and their entourage for the best part of a month. What could go wrong?

McCartney did some basic research before deciding to record in Lagos. Vincent Romeo, his manager, was dispatched to inspect Ginger Baker's ARC studio. Baker's Batakota (ARC) studios opened at the end of January 1973. It was a state-of- the-art recording facility with a 16-track recording complex (the first on the African continent), a Helios console, a Studer 16-track tape machine, a 26-channel mixing console, and acoustics designed by Sandy Brown Associates. Romeo would have been impressed, and no doubt reported back to his boss that it more than met his requirements. As EMI would be paying for studio time, and perhaps mindful of the recording costs for Wings' last album, it reminded McCartney that it would be financially prudent to use its studio rather than Baker's more expensive recording facility. McCartney opted for the cheaper studio and got second best.

Whatever expectations he may have had were shattered when faced with reality. Geoff Emerick recalled that EMI Lagos was little more than a large shed. If the exterior was terrible, what would the interior be like? Emerick: "The studio was really small, without any acoustic screens, which we had to have made. There was no drum booth. The microphone supply was a cardboard box just full of old mics. There were half of the amplifiers missing in the eight-track tape machine. And there was a door at the back of the studio, and I'll always remember this, it was a soundproof door, and you opened this door, and at the back of the studio was the pressing plant where they pressed all the records. There was fifty or sixty people all stamping out records at the back of the studio."

Because EMI was parsimonious much of the equipment was familiar to Emerick. It was redundant kit that had been sent from London for use in the colonies. The studio was fitted with a standard EMI console, albeit a smaller model than employed at EMI Studios London, and monitors. The studio had an eight-track tape machine, but only four of its amplifiers worked, which meant that only four of the eight tracks could be played back when overdubbing.

It would have made more sense to record at Baker's ARC studio. It was everything EMI's studio wasn't. Furthermore, Laine knew Baker because he'd been a Ginger Baker's Airforce group member before joining Wings. He also knew he would have been upset when McCartney declined to record at his studio. Baker wasn't the kind of person you wanted to displease, even if you were Paul McCartney. Speaking after the event, Baker said: "I am fuckin' angry. The actual truth of the matter is that *Band On The Run* would never have been recorded if it wasn't for me." Hyperbole, perhaps, but it has been suggested that Baker helped arrange visas for McCartney's party through his partner, Bayo, who was Minister of Information. As Laine recalled: "Ginger Baker had a studio there. We didn't go there for that reason, but Ginger introduced us to some people, so we didn't feel so alone." Also, Baker was possibly the only other European musician in Lagos. Because he had all the right contacts, keeping in with him would have been wise. In unpredictable Lagos, you never knew what might happen or when you might need a reliable, friendly contact. There is little doubt that McCartney exploited Baker's unique position in Lagos. But he treated him in much the same way that he'd treated Seiwell and McCullough, with indifference.

Luckily for the McCartneys, Laine, and Emerick, their accommodation was in a Government Residential District in Ikeja. A remnant of colonialism, these exclusive residential areas were created to cater to white colonial administrators. Now, they catered to wealthy white tourists, visiting rock stars, and Nigerians holding senior administrative posts. The Ikeja district was close to the airport but an hour's drive from the studio.

Recording started on Monday 3rd September. The first song McCartney and Laine attempted was 'Ma Moonia' (the working title for 'Mamunia'). Working at EMI's Lagos studio would have limitations; this acoustic ballad was the obvious choice to start with.

According to Laine, they weren't phased by their new surroundings and continued to work as they always had. They had, after all, spent the previous five weeks rehearsing and recording in equally rough-hewn conditions at McCartney's Scottish farm. EMI's Lagos studio was slightly more advanced than McCartney's Rude studio and almost a home from home. The only difference was the heat and humidity. As Laine recalled, 'Mamunia' was: "The first one we did in Lagos – recorded in the middle of a tropical rainstorm. I don't know if that had any effect on the final result."

The way they worked remained the same, whether or not they were in Africa or Scotland. "It didn't really change, except that before, we would have done the backing tracks as a band. Now it was me on acoustic guitar or keyboards and Paul on drums. We would put the track down that way he could get the drum part first." On this occasion, Laine played percussion, and McCartney played acoustic guitar and sang.

Next to be recorded was 'Band On The Run'. This was a little more complicated to record, meaning it was captured in two parts. McCartney was inspired to write the song by a chance remark that George Harrison made at an Apple business meeting. "He was saying that we were all prisoners in some way, some kind of remark like that. 'If we ever get out of here,' the prison bit … and I thought that would be a nice way to start an album." McCartney used an old trick of combining incomplete fragments to make a whole. 'Band On The Run' comprised three unfinished songs. The slow introduction, "Stuck inside these four walls," was combined with the up-tempo "If we ever get out of here". These two parts were added to a third unfinished but more complete song, with the chorus 'Band on the Run'. Parts one and two were recorded as one complete section that would be edited with the second recorded section, the third part of the song, the edit being covered by Tony Visconti's orchestral arrangement that would be overdubbed later in London.

The basic track for the first section comprised McCartney on drums, Laine on rhythm guitar, and Linda on keyboards. Next, McCartney overdubbed the simple but effective electric guitar parts. Laine recalled that it was McCartney, not him, who played most of the lead guitar on the album: "It was his part. Some people think it's doubled with me and him, but when I listen to it, it doesn't sound that way. Usually, we would double riffs. *Band on the Run* didn't have a lot of guitar solos, except 'Nineteen Hundred and Eighty-Five,' which I played the solo on. I very rarely did solos in Wings."

For the second section, McCartney played drums along with Laine's acoustic rhythm guitar. "Me and him had this kind of feel together musically. We slotted in well together," recalled Laine. "We could read each other, and that came from growing up on the same musical influences. Paul's got a good sense of rhythm, and he doesn't overplay, which I like." The last part to be added while in Lagos was McCartney's bass guitar.

The final song recorded during the first week of sessions didn't appear on the British version of the album but would be added to the American edition and released as Wings' next single. 'Helen Wheels,' a pun on 'hell on wheels,' was a straightforward two-chord rocker. All three members of Wings helped record the drum part. McCartney is a good amateur drummer but struggles with anything that isn't in straight 4/4 time. 'Helen Wheels' has a shuffle beat, simple enough if you're Denny Seiwell, a little trickier if you're not. McCartney got around the problem by creating a three-person drum kit. Linda kept time by counting 1, 2, 3, 4. Denny played the bass drum, and McCartney played the rest of the kit. Next, Laine and McCartney added electric guitars, and Linda her keyboards. McCartney added his lead vocals before all three added backing vocals.

Lennon recorded the basic backing tracks for his latest album in record time – five days. However, overdubbing and mixing would occupy him throughout September. Richard Perry may have criticised him for his way of recording, but he overlooked Lennon's meticulous attention to detail in the later stages of production. Lennon constantly made changes, adjustments, and refinements throughout the overdubbing and mixing stage. On Monday, 3rd September, Lennon was again in studio B at the Record Plant. During this evening's sessions, he added overdubs and edited 'Out Of The Blue'. The following evening, he worked on 'You Are Here' and 'Tight A$'. On 5th September, he mixed and edited 'Aisumasen'. The following evening was dedicated to mixing 'One Day At A Time,' and the day after, he was engaged in remixing 'Meat City'. Several songs mixed this week were revisited and remixed in the coming days and weeks.

On Thursday 6th, Lennon mixed and edited 'One Day At A Time'. The following day, he returned to 'Meat City,' remixing the song for a third time. Still unsatisfied with the results, he returned to the Record Plant on Monday, the 10th, for another go at mixing the song. The remainder of the week was spent mixing or remixing the remaining songs for the album. 'Out Of The Blue' was remixed on the 11th, 'Bring On The Lucie' was remixed on the 12th, 'Tight A$' was mixed on the 13th and remixed on the 14th.

Sunday, the 16th, was long and busy at the Record Plant. A seventeen-hour marathon session created the cutting masters for Lennon's new album, tentatively titled *Out The Blue*. Lennon's *One to One* concert was re-broadcast in America today by DIR (Dig It Radio) Broadcasting as part of the regular King Biscuit Flower Hour

173

series. The show was broadcast nationally by 100 radio stations, and where available, it was broadcast in quadraphonic sound. As with the original concert, all broadcast proceeds went to the One to One charity.

While Lennon, McCartney, and Starr were busy preparing new albums, record companies continued to be concerned about a shortage of materials. October was a crunch month when record companies began stocking up for the Christmas spending spree. In previous months there had been concerns about a shortage of the raw material used to manufacture records. Record companies were receiving reports about the shortage of boards used to produce LP sleeves. Such was the demand for records that pressing plants could not keep up. This, coupled with a shortage of raw materials, meant that the major companies were finding it difficult to sub-contract work to independent firms.

A shortage of materials and a lack of capacity, caused partly by under-investment, sent shock waves through the industry. One way around the problem was to import records from other countries. For big companies like CBS, which had pressing plants in the UK and Europe, it could sub-contract production to one of its pressing plants in another country. However, this would only work if other countries had spare capacity, and it increased costs because records had to be imported. Another problem affecting printing companies was the fast turnaround expected by record companies. Garrod and Lofthouse, a company that manufactured record sleeves, was frustrated by the shortage of materials but conceded that it had no option than to import materials because, Chairman Norman Garrod said, record companies "want sleeves in days, not months." McCartney was one of the recording artists who demanded this kind of service. Garrod and Lofthouse had no option but to acquiesce to his and EMI's requests. Thereby adding to Mr Garrod's woes.

Records sales might have been booming, but that didn't mean everyone enjoyed enormous profits. ABKCO announced that its profits were down, with share dividends halved on the previous year from 81¢ to 41¢. It was also reported that operations for the third quarter ending 30th June resulted in a loss of $69,923. ABKCO had taken a big hit when it lost The Beatles, with additional costs incurred when it sued them. Things would get worse for Klien/ABKCO before getting better. Lennon and Harrison hadn't repaid their loans and were prepared to withhold payment for as long as possible, partly as leverage and partly as revenge. Lennon was being deliberately slow in responding to ABKCO's complaint regarding the unpaid loan and had already received two extensions to file his response.

On 11th September, his lawyers defended his refusal to pay because of the existence of "other litigation" and the interconnected "claims and counterclaims" that "The Beatles Group of Companies" had against ABKCO. Unknown to Klein, Lennon also planned to use litigation to exhaust ABKCO's resources. Despite the statement issued a few weeks previously that The Beatles were close to resolving their partnership problems, there remained a byzantine labyrinth of accounting anomalies to be ironed out. Lennon and Harrison didn't have the spare cash to repay ABKCO, but they could use the courts to hamstring their former manager's attempts to recover the money.

ATV Music also reported lower profits than usual. Associated Television Corporation's subsidiaries, ATV Music and Pye Records, made a significant contribution to gross pre-tax profit for the year ending 25th March 1973, with pre-tax profit up $3 million on the previous year. However, profits dropped slightly to $475,000. Jack Gill, ATV group finance director, blamed the fall in profits on narrower profit margins and a fall-off in income from music publishing due to the expiry of the original contracts with Lennon and McCartney.

Both songwriters had formed their own music publishing companies, but McCartney developed the strongest interest in publishing. Although he was in Lagos recording his next album, with the help of his in-laws, he continued to build his music publishing empire. *Billboard* reported that Frank Coachworth, formally general manager of Chappell Music, had concluded a deal with Lee Eastman to represent McCartney's music publishing activities through the McCartney Music Co.

Unknown to the Eastmans or Frank Coachworth, their boss was, to quote a song from Elton John's soon-to-be-released *Goodbye Yellow Brick Road* album, living his life like a candle in the wind. The mean streets of Lagos were hazardous, even for locals. McCartney had been told not to venture out after dark. Any sensible tourist would have taken the advice and done as they were told. McCartney, however, lived by his own rules and, one evening decided to walk the mile from Laine's rented house to his. Although both houses were in a supposedly safe Government Residential District, he was robbed at knifepoint and relieved of his valuables, including his notebooks of lyrics and cassettes of Wings' recent demo recordings. If the mugging proved one thing, nowhere in Lagos was safe. Even McCartney had to admit it was a stupid thing to do: "They told us at the studio not to go walking late at night, because there was crime and stuff. We just went (sarcastically) 'Yeah, sure!' We were hippies. We thought we were immortal. I've got this – I think it's basically stupidity. I must admit there's an element of stupidity there. When I look at these things afterwards, I think, 'What are you on?' The following morning, he told the studio manager what had happened and was told, 'You're lucky you're a white man. If you were black, you would have been killed.'"

One man living in Lagos who may have been spared by the robbers was Fela Aníkúlápó Kútì. A popular figure with the people of Nigeria, Kútì was a pioneer of Afrobeat, a prolific songwriter, a multi-instrumentalist, a political activist, a thorn in the side of the military government, and a strong advocate for Anti Colonial Nationalism. Kútì suspected McCartney of cultural appropriation and publicly accused him of such. Although McCartney and Laine enjoyed African music and subsequently claimed it influenced the album's mood, they were not there to steal local music.

McCartney arranged to see Kútì perform at a nightclub the musician owned, the Africa Shrine. It would be another unforgettable experience that went from sublime to unnerving. Thanks to some strong local cannabis, McCartney was high as a kite and was moved to tears by the music of Kútì's band Africa '70, who performed 'Why Black Men Dey Suffer'. "I had this fantastic evening, really quite, sort of, wild, experience there," McCartney recalled. "When I heard [the music], due to the circumstances of the evening, I mean, you were right in the depths of Africa here. Talk about the black experience. We were the only white people there, and it was very intense. When this music broke, I ended up weeping. It was one of the most amazing musical moments of my life."

McCartney's euphoria soon disappeared when, during a break, several members of Africa '70 approached him and accused him of stealing their music. Lady Luck smiled on McCartney for a second time. Ginger Baker had accompanied them to the nightclub and intervened. McCartney was formally introduced to Kútì and assured him he was not there to steal African music. "I think old Fela, when he found us in Lagos, thought, 'Hello, why have they come to Lagos?' And the only reason he could think of was that we must be stealing black music, black African music, the Lagos sound, we'd come down there to pick it up," McCartney told Paul Gambaccini. "So I said, 'Do us a favour, we do OK as it is, we're not pinching your music.'"

Kútì temporarily put his concerns aside and invited McCartney on stage at the end of the performance in a public show of unity. A photograph of them smiling and holding hands was printed in the local paper, suggesting everything had been smoothed over. However, Geoff Emerick later recalled that the confrontation scared McCartney, and far from being appeased, Kútì went on the radio to, once again, accuse him of stealing African music.

The experience certainly unsettled McCartney. It was still on his mind when he spoke to Chris Welch of the *Melody Maker* a few weeks after returning to London. McCartney said of Kútì's accusations: "Fela Ransome Kuti accused us of trying to steal black African music. […] There was one and a half weeks of pretty bad vibes. It felt a bit dangerous and raw, and you're not sure how you're going to figure."

If McCartney hadn't been so stoned, he may have been able to comprehend the meaning of the song that moved him to tears. Had he been paying attention, he may have better understood what Kútì was fighting for. As it was, he failed to understand the song's message or Kútì or the continent's colonial past. 'Why Black Men Dey Suffer' is an anti-colonial anthem, a call for post-colonial Nationalism, a cry of dismay at what white men had done to Africa and Africans, and a call for Africans to defy their colonial oppressors and embrace their own culture. McCartney represented everything that Kútì opposed.

A few days later, Kútì visited the studio to further quiz McCartney about his reasons for visiting Lagos. He was played what Wings had been recording to prove that they hadn't stolen any African rhythms. Once again, Ginger Baker intervened to help ease the tension. By way of thanks, McCartney agreed to one day's recording at his ARC studios.

On Monday 17th, Wings decamped to Baker's studio to record the basic tracks for 'Drink To Me'. According to McCartney, he was on holiday in Jamaica and struck up a friendship with the actor Dustin Hoffman who asked if he would write a song about anything, and McCartney said yes. "I just pull it out of the air. I knock a couple of chords off, and it suggests a melody to me. If I haven't heard the melody before, I'll Keep it." McCartney visited Hoffman a couple of days later and was asked if he could write a song about Picasso, who had recently died. Speaking to Paul Gambaccini, McCartney said: "Then we went to Nigeria, and we were working in Ginger's studio, Ginger Baker/ARC Studio in Lagos. It's a nice studio down there. We thought we'd do this Picasso number, and we started off doing it straight. Then we thought, Picasso was kind of far out in his pictures, he'd done all these different kinds of things, fragmented, cubism, and the whole bit. So Ginger, he helped on a few little things of it. At the end, where we go 'Ho, hey, ho.' We did the cutting up there. Then we got Ginger and a couple of people from around the studio and we got little tin cans and filled them with gravel from outside the studio, and used them as shakers, so at the end you hear this (makes shaking gravel noise), and that's Ginger and a big mob of us going (gravel noise again). So we just made it all up and then edited the tape. There were about four or five big edits in it, really."

Towards the end of their stay, Wings were working in the studios when McCartney collapsed. According to Geoff Emerick, it was a Friday afternoon; McCartney was recording a lead vocal when he became breathless. He was taken outside, which didn't help because it was hotter and more humid outside than in the studio, where he crumpled to the ground. Linda suspected a heart attack. McCartney was bundled into the back of a car and driven to the nearest hospital by the studio boss, Odion. He was diagnosed with having suffered a bronchial spasm brought on by too much smoking. The incident shook him, but undeterred he returned to work the following Monday after spending the weekend resting at his villa. The last day in Lagos was spent compiling tapes to take back to London.

Before Wings returned to Britain, EMI held a farewell party with a riverboat cruise and barbeque. Ginger Baker was invited and learned why Wings had recorded at EMI's studio, not his. Baker claimed that at the party, he was approached by the managing director of EMI overseas, who told him of EMI's plans to shut him down. "We're going to screw you because this is our territory. You can't build a studio here – this is EMI territory, and you've got to get that into your head." Baker claimed that EMI had fifty percent of West African recording artists under contract and insisted they record at its studio. In partnership with DECCA, EMI also owned a record-pressing plant, attached to the rear of its studio, and refused to press any records issued by Baker's Associated Recording Company Limited. Thanks to EMI's parsimony and unscrupulous business practices, McCartney, Laine, and Emerick had to record in substandard conditions using second-hand equipment in what was little more than a glorified soundproof shed with a makeshift pressing plant attached.

Even their return to London didn't go as planned. Emerick accompanied the tapes to ensure their safety. However, the flight was cancelled at the last minute because of problems with the aircraft. McCartney's small entourage went to a country club to wait for the aircraft to be repaired while one of their roadies remained at the airport to keep an eye on their luggage and tapes. Wings arrived back in Britain in the early hours of Sunday 23rd. They were tired but had the basic tracks for seven songs in the safekeeping of Geoff Emerick.

As Wings were returning to Britain, Lennon was heading for Los Angeles. According to May Pang, Lennon's decision to leave home was spontaneous. Ono was out of town, which meant he was unencumbered by any feelings of guilt he may have had about leaving. Earlier in the day, he'd met with Harold Seider, a lawyer acting as his business advisor. Seider informed Lennon that he was flying to Los Angeles after their meeting. Lennon decided to join him, taking Pang along with him. On arrival, Lennon and Pang stayed at Seider's apartment on West Harper Avenue. Partially free of Ono, she continued to call him on the phone at least twice a day; Lennon started to take in the varied attractions LA nightlife had to offer. On the 23rd, he and Pang saw Neil Young at the Roxy Theatre. The following night, they returned to the Roxy to watch Richie Havens. Two days later, they were seen at the Roxy, again, where Harrison's friends Cheech and Chong were performing. Around this time, Lennon bumped into The Beatles' former public relations assistant, Andrew Loog Oldham. The former Rolling Stones manager had been living at the house of record producer and co-owner of the Roxy, Lou Adler, in Stone Canyon but was about to return to New York. Oldham handed Lennon the keys to the house and assured him he'd square it with Adler, who was more than happy to have a Beatle housesit for him.

Lennon was in Los Angeles to work on his new album. Capitol Records' head office was at 1750 Vine Street; it would be responsible for organizing the promotion and marketing of the album. Although Apple had been downsized, it still employed Tony King, who had been working on Starr's new album. Having finished work on the delayed *Ringo* album, King was about to fly home when he got a call from Pang asking him to help with Lennon's new album. "Initially, I was nervous because John could be cruel," said King. "John had an edge to him, and you didn't want to get on the wrong side of him because he could cut you down. When we met, I was actually so nervous that I couldn't drive properly. I'd picked them up at a house in Beverly Hills and was driving them to a restaurant. But when we got there, I was so nervous about having John Lennon in my car that I lost the ability to park. And it was an automatic! So, I had to ask him to get out and go inside while I parked. He found this hilarious, and after that, we got on famously."

King was now working for Lennon and would liaise with Capitol on all matters relating to the album's promotion. The first single from Starr's much-delayed album was released in America on the 24th. 'Photograph' b/w 'Down And Out' was released by Apple Records with a picture sleeve and custom labels to favourable reviews. *Record World* said: "Ringo puts out one single a year, and it's usually a winner. From his forthcoming LP comes this strong pop tune penned by Starr and George Harrison. Solid Richard Perry production clinches number one spot." Writing in *Phonograph Record*, Alan Betrock said: "'Photograph' is one of those rare pop records that grows stronger with each play, and will be covered and revived for years to come (I'll lay you 50-1 it appears on the next Andy Williams album)." Andy Williams didn't record 'Photograph', but did record a cover of McCartney's 'My Love.' 'Photograph' was recorded by Engelbert Humperdinck, the singer who kept 'Penny Lane' b/w 'Strawberry Fields Forever' from reaching number 1 in the British singles charts. But more importantly, in its first week of release, *Cash Box* reported that 60% of radio stations surveyed had added 'Photograph' to playlists, where it was competing with new releases by The Carpenters 'On Top Of The World' and Jim Croce 'I Got A Name'. The following week, 'Photograph' had been added to playlists by 95% of the radio stations surveyed and started climbing the charts.

When the single was released in Britain, it received mixed reviews. Reviewed by Downbeat for the *Herald Express*, 'Photograph' was considered: "An unremarkable song, penned by Ringo and George Harrison. Some nice horns break the monotony, but otherwise, this is very run of the mill – except, of course, for the singer's name." Downbeat wasn't the only reviewer to be disappointed by Starr's new single. Ian MacDonald was equally sniffy about it. "'Photograph,' yet another triumph for earache rock, is a totally undistinguished composition from the twin pens of Starkey and Harrison, although calling it a composition is stretching a point. It sounds as if it's been written the way those two aged sisters paint. One starts at the nose and paints backwards, while the other begins at the tail and works forwards. However, they always seem to meet and make the joint convincing... 'Photograph' is a wash-out, let's leave it at that."

Capitol Records' top radio promotion man, Al Coury, was also doing his bit to sell Starr's new album. Speaking to *Record World*, he made much of the fact that the album featured contributions from all of The Beatles: "This will be the first album recorded by any individual Beatle since they split, where the collective talents of The Beatles, all four of them, will be brought back on one album. There are songs on the album that were written by George Harrison, by John Lennon, by Paul McCartney and by Ringo. They all sing and play on individual tracks, and some sing back-ups for Ringo. So I would say it's probably going to be the most important album to come out this fall because it's going to present the collective talents of The Beatles again on one album. It's gotta be a landmark album. I know the package which is now being put together on the West Coast is an incredible package there's a 20-page booklet inside, and the cover is fantastic, it's got Ringo on stage with his name in those typical Broadway show lights." He also announced new albums from Lennon and McCartney. "So, as far as new Beatles product, we're gonna have a lot of dynamite product coming out in the fall. I'm sure Lennon's album is gonna be well greeted; I'm sure Ringo's album is gonna be a milestone for many reasons; and the same with Paul's album." He wasn't wrong.

WEEK ENDING 1 SEPTEMBER 1973
1. BROTHER LOUIE: STORIES
2. LET'S GET IT ON: MARVIN GAYE
3. DELTA DAWN: HELEN REDDY
4. TOUCH ME IN THE MORNING: DIANA ROSS
5. LIVE AND LET DIE: WINGS
6. SAY, HAS ANYBODY SEEN MY SWEET GYPSY ROSE: DAWN
   FEATURING TONY ORLANDO
7. THE MORNING AFTER: MAUREEN MCGOVERN
8. GET DOWN: GILBERT O'SULLIVAN
9. LOVES ME LIKE A ROCK: PAUL SIMON (WITH THE DIXIE
   HUMMINGBIRDS)
10. FEELIN' STRONGER EVERY DAY: CHICAGO

WEEK ENDING 8 SEPTEMBER 1973
1. LET'S GET IT ON: MARVIN GAYE
2. BROTHER LOUIE: STORIES
3. DELTA DAWN: HELEN REDDY
4. SAY, HAS ANYBODY SEEN MY SWEET GYPSY ROSE: DAWN
   FEATURING TONY ORLANDO
5. TOUCH ME IN THE MORNING: DIANA ROSS
6. LOVES ME LIKE A ROCK: PAUL SIMON (WITH THE DIXIE
   HUMMINGBIRDS)
7. LIVE AND LET DIE: WINGS
8. WE'RE AN AMERICAN BAND: GRAND FUNK
9. GYPSY MAN: WAR
10. HERE I AM COME & TAKE ME: AL GREEN

WEEK ENDING 15 SEPTEMBER 1973
1. DELTA DAWN: HELEN REDDY
2. LET'S GET IT ON: MARVIN GAYE
3. SAY, HAS ANYBODY SEEN MY SWEET GYPSY ROSE: DAWN
   FEATURING TONY ORLANDO
4. LOVES ME LIKE A ROCK: PAUL SIMON (WITH THE DIXIE
   HUMMINGBIRDS)
5. WE'RE AN AMERICAN BAND: GRAND FUNK
6. BROTHER LOUIE: STORIES
7. TOUCH ME IN THE MORNING: DIANA ROSS
8. GYPSY MAN: WAR
9. LIVE AND LET DIE: WINGS
10. HERE I AM COME & TAKE ME: AL GREEN

WEEK ENDING 22 SEPTEMBER 1973
1. LET'S GET IT ON: MARVIN GAYE
2. WE'RE AN AMERICAN BAND: GRAND FUNK
3. DELTA DAWN: HELEN REDDY
4. LOVES ME LIKE A ROCK: PAUL SIMON (WITH THE DIXIE
   HUMMINGBIRDS)
5. SAY, HAS ANYBODY SEEN MY SWEET GYPSY ROSE: DAWN
   FEATURING TONY ORLANDO
6. BROTHER LOUIE: STORIES
7. HALF-BREED: CHER
8. HIGHER GROUND: STEVIE WONDER
9. TOUCH ME IN THE MORNING: DIANA ROSS
10. THAT LADY (PART 1): THE ISLEY BROTHERS

WEEK ENDING 29 SEPTEMBER 1973
1. WE'RE AN AMERICAN BAND: GRAND FUNK
2. LET'S GET IT ON: MARVIN GAYE
3. HALF-BREED: CHER
4. LOVES ME LIKE A ROCK: PAUL SIMON (WITH THE DIXIE HUMMINGBIRDS)
5. DELTA DAWN: HELEN REDDY
6. HIGHER GROUND: STEVIE WONDER
7. SAY, HAS ANYBODY SEEN MY SWEET GYPSY ROSE: DAWN FEATURING TONY ORLANDO
8. THAT LADY (PART 1): THE ISLEY BROTHERS
9. MY MARIA: B.W. STEVENSON
10. RAMBLIN MAN: THE ALLMAN BROTHERS BAND

UK

WEEK ENDING 1 SEPTEMBER 1973
1. YOUNG LOVE: DONNY OSMOND
2. DANCING ON A SATURDAY NIGHT: BARRY BLUE
3. YOU CAN DO MAGIC: LIMMIE AND THE FAMILY COOKIN'
4. YESTERDAY ONCE MORE: THE CARPENTERS
5. SPANISH EYES: AL MARTINO
6. I'M THE LEADER OF THE GANG (I AM!): GARY GLITTER
7. LIKE SISTER AND BROTHER: THE DRIFTERS
8. WELCOME HOME: PETERS AND LEE
9. SUMMER (THE FIRST TIME): BOBBY GOLDSBORO
10. SMARTY PANTS: FIRST CHOICE

WEEK ENDING 8 SEPTEMBER 1973
1. YOUNG LOVE: DONNY OSMOND
2. DANCING ON A SATURDAY NIGHT: BARRY BLUE
3. ANGEL FINGERS: WIZZARD
4. YESTERDAY ONCE MORE: THE CARPENTERS
5. SPANISH EYES: AL MARTINO
6. ROCK ON: DAVID ESSEX
7. YOU CAN DO MAGIC: LIMMIE AND THE FAMILY COOKIN'
8. LIKE SISTER AND BROTHER: THE DRIFTERS
9. ANGIE: THE ROLLING STONES
10. PICK UP THE PIECES: HUDSON-FORD

WEEK ENDING 15 SEPTEMBER 1973
1. YOUNG LOVE: DONNY OSMOND
2. ANGEL FINGERS: WIZZARD
3. ROCK ON: DAVID ESSEX
4. DANCING ON A SATURDAY NIGHT: BARRY BLUE
5. ANGIE: THE ROLLING STONES
6. SPANISH EYES: AL MARTINO
7. OH NO NOT MY BABY: ROD STEWART
8. PICK UP THE PIECES: HUDSON-FORD
9. YOU CAN DO MAGIC: LIMMIE AND THE FAMILY COOKIN'
10. THE DEAN AND I: 10 C.C.

WEEK ENDING 22 SEPTEMBER 1973
1. ANGEL FINGERS: WIZZARD
2. BALLROOM BLITZ: THE SWEET
3. ROCK ON: DAVID ESSEX
4. MONSTER MASH: BOBBY (BORIS) PICKETT AND THE CRYPT-KICKERS
5. ANGIE: THE ROLLING STONES
6. OH NO NOT MY BABY: ROD STEWART

7. YOUNG LOVE: DONNY OSMOND
8. DANCING ON A SATURDAY NIGHT: BARRY BLUE
9. SPANISH EYES: AL MARTINO
10. FOR THE GOOD TIMES: PERRY COMO

WEEK ENDING 29 SEPTEMBER 1973
1. EYE LEVEL: SIMON PARK ORCHESTRA
2. BALLROOM BLITZ: THE SWEET
3. ANGEL FINGERS: WIZZARD
4. MONSTER MASH: BOBBY (BORIS) PICKETT AND THE CRYPT-KICKERS
5. ROCK ON: DAVID ESSEX
6. OH NO NOT MY BABY: ROD STEWART
7. ANGIE: THE ROLLING STONES
8. NUTBUSH CITY LIMITS: IKE AND TINA TURNER
9. FOR THE GOOD TIMES: PERRY COMO
10. ALL THE WAY FROM MEMPHIS: MOTT THE HOOPLE

CHAPTER 10
OCTOBER: DR WINSTON O'BOOGIE GOES TOO FAR

Being a rock star can be hard if you don't weaken. As John Lennon approached his 33rd birthday, he continued working on his new album in Los Angeles. For the most part, this appeared to involve spending long hours at the Rainbow Bar and Grill with his rock-star chums. On Friday, 5th October, Lennon was holding court at the Rainbow when Tony King introduced him to Chris Charlesworth of the *Melody Maker*. Part of King's strategy to promote Lennon's new long-player was for him to talk to the press, much of which still considered him a weirdo activist. King's plan was simplicity itself. The press was keen to speak to Lennon, and Lennon was eager to talk to the media. "I went upstairs into the VIP area of the Rainbow where I met Tony King, who I knew because he used to work for Elton John," recalled Charlesworth. "He told me he was now working for John Lennon, and he asked me, 'Do you want to meet him?' 'Of course I want to meet John!' I replied. Tony led me over to where John was sitting, drinking, and talking with some friends. Following the introductions, John began quizzing me about life in London, what was happening on the London rock scene, how Paul (McCartney) was, what the weather was like, what the government was like, how much a pint of milk cost, and what the royal family was doing. I got the impression that he seemed to be very isolated, or rather, he had chosen to isolate himself. It was almost as if he was homesick, though he would later deny that. He was just curious about what was going on back home."

Back home, Paul McCartney took a leaf out of his former bandmate's book and took things easy. Although he had basic tracks for the bulk of Wings new album, there was still a lot of work to do to finish it. Particularly as he had set his sights on a December release date. Wings still had to record 'Jet,' 'Bluebird' and 'Nineteen Hundred And Eighty-Five,' record overdubs, and mix the album. They also had to finish 'Helen Wheels,' which would be rush-released as a single before the month was out. While McCartney was relaxing, Emerick's first job was to transfer the eight-track tapes recorded in Lagos onto sixteen-track tapes to facilitate overdubbing. This done, 'Helen Wheels' was mixed in the first week of October at AIR studios, London.

One of the first to hear 'Helen Wheels' was McCartney's brother, Mike McGear. He wasn't impressed. The brothers had never seen eye-to-eye about music, according to McGear: "Paul and I have always been brutally honest with each other." He knew when his opinion wasn't welcomed and when to keep quiet. "When I know my opinion's not going to be a good one, I just keep quiet, and he knows. I mean, it can hit a bit hard when someone's put their whole thing into something and really believes in it and the other person doesn't like it. Like that 'Helen Wheels' single. I went down to the studio and there they were, Paul and Wings, all dancing around. Paul was saying 'isn't it great' and bopping up and down and I just had to sit down and say nothing because it did absolutely nothing to me. It was a nice little pop tune but not where that man's head's at at all. He's a very clever boy, so to waste it on that seemed a shame."

While 'Helen Wheels' wasn't as successful as Wings' previous two singles, it still reached the top ten in America and a respectable number 12 in Britain. Furthermore, when it was included on the American version of *Band On The Run*, it helped push the album to number 1. McCartney wasn't keen on adding singles to albums or, for that matter, taking singles from albums. If it had been good enough for The Beatles, it was good enough for Wings. But if it meant selling extra units, he was in. It was Capitol Records ace radio plugger, Al Courly, who persuaded him to add 'Helen Wheels' to the American version of the album. "We got a call from one of the Capitol executives saying 'Paul, you know we took 'Money' off the Pink Floyd album (*Dark Side Of The Moon*) and after it became a hit single the album did so many extra units. What do you say if we put 'Helen Wheels' and we'll do so many extra units'. So I phoned him back the next day and told him it sounded OK to me."

The following day, Wednesday the 3rd, McCartney and Laine attempted to record the backing track for 'Jet.' Unhappy with the results, it was put to one side to be re-recorded later. Next, they reverted to proven ways of recording and started work on 'Bluebird'. A backing track comprising two acoustic guitars and a guide vocal by McCartney resulted from today's session. Thursday 4th, Wings recorded a Linda McCartney track that, like 'Seaside Woman,' would remain unreleased. Linda wrote 'Oriental Nightfish' while in Lagos. Not quite a song, nor quite an instrumental, it has spoken passages by Linda that sit in between lengthy, partly improvised, instrumental sections.

Wings ended the week by recording the backing track for 'Nineteen Hundred and Eighty-Five'. At this stage, the working title was 'Piano Thing,' suggesting it was far from finished. Indeed, McCartney never got around to fleshing out his opening statement. Speaking to Paul Gambaccini, he confessed: "You see, with a lot of songs I do, the first line is it. It's all in the first line, and then you have to go on and write the second line. With this one, it was 'No one ever left alive in nineteen hundred and eighty-five'. That's all I had of that song for months." Recording 'Nineteen Hundred and Eighty-Five' was a straightforward task. McCartney played piano and sang a guide vocal before adding drums. The rest of the instruments were overdubbed later, including Laine's lead guitar,

Tony Visconti's orchestral arrangement, Linda's keyboards, and McCartney's bass and vocal.

On Saturday 6th, Lennon and Pang travelled to Las Vegas with radio host Elliot Mintz to watch Fats Domino and Frankie Valli and The Four Seasons. Mintz had been tasked with booking the tickets for the trip and had made a rookie mistake by booking a flight with no first-class seating. As Tony King had noted, Lennon had an edge to him, and you didn't want to get on his wrong side. Lennon was never comfortable in public settings. Having to sit with the common people put Mintz in Lennon's bad books. Pang recalled that Lennon berated Mintz, saying, "Don't ever put me in this fucking position again!"

When they arrived in Las Vagas, they booked into Caesar's Palace Hotel, where Lennon met his hero, Fats Domino, before taking his seat. Once again, he started drinking. The more he drank, the louder he got. By the time Frankie Valli came on stage, Lennon had attracted the attention of the hotel's security, who eyed him with growing concern. Tony King, who had joined the Lennon party, maintains that when Valli came on stage, Lennon started heckling the singer, shouting, "Get your cock out, Frankie!" Lennon left before he was thrown out. When Beverly Madid interviewed him for *Record World*, he confirmed that he had visited Las Vagas and offered an apology, of sorts, to Valli. "I also appeared in Las Vegas, but only on the floor. It's a wonderful town. And I won too. I have to apologize to Frankie Valli. I'm not going to say what I did, but it's alright, Frank. I was going to send you a note. But this will do." Lennon was so uncomfortable at the thought of having to mix with the hoi polloi on the return flight home, that he opted to drive back to Los Angeles with Tony King.

On Monday 8th, Lennon spent the afternoon being interviewed by Chris Charlesworth for the *Melody Maker*. (The interview was published in the 3rd November issue.) In New York, lacquers for Lennon's new single 'Mind Games' b/w 'Meat City' were produced at the Cutting Room and sent to Apple in London for processing. While Lennon was interviewed for *Melody Maker*, his former bandmate was busy recording overdubs for 'Bluebird'. Most of the session was spent adding percussion, backing vocals, and a new lead vocal. The percussion was played by Remi Kabaka, a Nigerian who had played with Laine in Ginger Baker's Airforce. Despite Fela Kútì's protests, Kabaka was the only African to play on the album, and he was recorded in London, not Lagos.

On Tuesday, McCartney and Laine remade 'Jet'. They recorded drums and rhythm guitar before moving on to overdub more guitar parts. This time, they nailed the track and were keen to keep working late into the night to finish it. Unknown to them, there was a problem with the tape. In the early 1970s, manufacturers of recording tape changed the formula of the glue that held the oxide on the surface of the tape. That's why some old master tapes must be baked before use to ensure the oxide remains on the tape. Very rarely, faulty tapes would start shedding oxide during a recording session. This is what happened during the session for 'Jet'. Emerick noticed that the cymbals were losing top end or treble. He asked the assistant engineer, Pete Sweetenham, to check the tape machine, where he found a pile of oxide next to the tape heads. Every time the tape passed over the record/playback heads, it got worse, and the process was irreversible. Eventually, the tape would be unusable. Emerick decided not to tell McCartney because it would have ended what was otherwise a very creative session. Luckily for Emerick, Wings agreed to end the session before the tape failed. The session over, Emerick made a copy on a good tape and prepared it for the next session.

Wednesday 10th, Wings recorded overdubs for 'Nineteen Hundred and Eighty-Five,' 'Let Me Roll It,' and 'Picasso's Last Words'. This session continued into the early hours of Thursday morning, with McCartney adding drums and replacing his guide vocal to 'Picasso's Last Words'. Friday was spent recording vocals for 'No Words' and adding new lead and backing vocals to 'Picasso's Last Words'. This week's final job was for Emerick to produce rough mixes of everything they had worked on since returning to London and compile a tape for McCartney to listen to.

On Thursday, the 11th, Lennon returned to the Roxy, this time to watch his hero, Jerry Lee Lewis. It would be another event-filled night. Although Lennon entered the room once the lights had dimmed, he was quickly spotted by both the audience and the irascible pianist. Lewis started a rant about how The Beatles and Rolling Stones were shit and couldn't play rock 'n' roll. Lennon was in a buoyant mood and heckled Lewis, which resulted in him flouncing off stage.

Lennon made his way backstage to make peace with the Killer. Lewis recalled: "It was in about 1973 or 1974, and we had been playing the Roxy Theatre in Los Angeles. John and a couple of guys were sitting up in the balcony above us, and I don't know what they were smoking, but my sax player kept stretching up to try and sniff a little of it. Next thing I knew, John was on his knees in front of me trying to kiss my boots! When he stood up, he said: 'Thanks, Killer, for showin' me how to rock 'n' roll.' My son, Junior, was with me and he started elbowing me. When John left, Junior said: 'Daddy, do you know who that was?' I just laughed and said: 'Yeah, son, I know who that was.'"

The record industry continued prosecuting bootleggers, in its attempt to stamp them out. On the 13th, *Cash Box* reported that Arpad Joseph Loecsey had been fined $10,000 ($70,345.05) and given three years' summary probation for manufacturing and distributing pirate copies of albums by The Beatles, John Lennon, George Harrison, Paul and Linda McCartney and Wings, Traffic, Badfinger and more. Loecsey's firm, Audio Specialties Distributors, had been raided in January by FBI agents and the LA Police Dept., who seized more than 75,000 allegedly pirated 8-track cartridge tapes, a quantity of allegedly pirated cassette tapes, and duplicating equipment capable of producing 5,000 to 10,000 tapes a day. Loecsey was in seriously hot water. Not only did he have the FBI on his back, but to make matters worse, in March, the Internal Revenue Service filed a tax lien (a legal claim against the assets of a person or business that fails to pay taxes owed) for $333,000 ($2,342,490.00) with the Los Angeles County Recorders Office against him. Stan Gortikov, president of RIAA, commented on the case, saying, "This decision acknowledges that Los Angeles law enforcement truly means business. RIAA is truly grateful for the expedient action taken by our local law enforcement agencies against tape piracy."

Joseph Loecsey was getting lots of press coverage for all the wrong reasons. Despite his enormous success, George Harrison did a remarkable job of avoiding publicity. Since the initial surge of excitement following the release of his new album, he'd been conspicuous by his absence. He'd popped up and popped off just as quickly. Such was the interest in The Beatles that *Living In The Material World* had topped the charts without Harrison having to lift a finger. He didn't give interviews or make promo films or public appearances. The success of *Living In The Material World* rested solely on the quality of the music, a few adverts in the music press, and plenty of airplay.

Although he was out of sight, he kept himself busy working on music in the privacy of his home studio and those of his rock star friends. Having finished *Little Malcolm and His Struggle Against the Eunuchs*, Harrison started work with Splinter on their debut album. Recording began at Apple Studios before relocating to F.P.S.H.O.T.. Basic tracks for 'The Place I Love,' 'Gravy Train,' 'Somebody's City,' 'China Light' and 'Drink All Day (Got To Find Your Way Home)' were finished by late '73. At that point, Harrison began looking for a distributor for his new label – Dark Horse.

Harrison wasn't the only musician to move to Henly-On-Thames, although he was by far the highest-profile resident of the town. Alvin Lee, lead guitarist with Ten Years After, had moved into Hook End Manor, a few miles from Friar Park. Like Harrison, he installed a state-of-the-art recording studio where he made his album *On The Road To Freedom* with Mylon LeFevre. One of the songs he recorded was Harrison's 'So Sad (No Love Of His Own),' which featured Harrison on guitar and backing vocals. When interviewed by *Cash Box* about the album, Lee explained how he came to record the song: "We got George Harrison to write a song for the album when we ran into him at a local pub. We said, Hey, George! What are you up to? You want to write a song for us, and he said OK. It was all very sociable and easygoing. There were no hassles." Not only did Harrison provide a song, but he also helped record it. Speaking to the *Melody Maker*, Mylon LeFevre recalled their recording regime: "We'd come in here [to record] about dark," he said. "We'd go on until about 4 p.m. the next afternoon, thinking it was still dark outside. We'd been up two days doing things in here, and George Harrison would be asleep for two days, and he'd come over. He'd be ready and raring to go, and we'd get into it again." Harrison added dobro to their wistful interpretation of his desolate break-up song. Issued as a single, 'So Sad (No Love Of His Own)' received mixed reviews. *Circus* magazine described it as a "genuine country tearjerker". However, the *NME* considered it "disappointingly Harrison-esque".

'So Sad (No Love Of His Own)' was pertinent and prophetic. The Harrisons marriage was in no better shape than the Lennons. While Lennon had left home for the bright lights of Los Angeles, Harrison, the homebody, was content to wander his garden and invite musicians over to play with him. Harrison invited Ronnie Wood and his wife Krissie to stay at Friar Park for the month to hang out and record. Wood had already started work on his début album at his home in Richmond Hill, where a constant flow of hangers-on, actors, and musicians passed through his door. In his autobiography, Wood said: "Whoever came over would bring their instrument or they'd pick up whatever they could find lying around, and we'd play." Harrison was a regular guest at Wood's house and wrote the verse section of what became 'Far East Man' during a visit. Wood wanted the song for his album and asked him to finish it. Harrison added a middle-eight and completed the lyrics while driving to Wood's house. When he arrived, Wood was wearing a tee shirt with the wording 'Far East Man' – The Faces had recently completed a tour of the Far East – that became the title.

Wood recorded his version, with Harrison contributing vocals and playing slide guitar. Wood's version has a busier slide guitar part, which Harrison would refine for his recording. The song's minor chords and jazzy inversions suited Wood to a tee. A consummate sidesman with a knack of complementing a melody with tasteful licks, it was tailor-made for him. As fun as it may have been to record and socialize with a member of the Faces, it soon turned sour and complicated.

Guitarists were buzzing around Patti Harrison like bees around honey. If it wasn't Eric Clapton, it was Ronnie Wood. Harrison was no better. He'd already had an affair with Ringo Starr's wife; now, according to Wood, he had an affair with his. According to Wood: "Krissie had a short fling with George, they holidayed in Portugal. Remember, I'd pinched Krissie from Eric, and later, after Pattie and Eric split up, I had a lovely thing going with Pattie. We loved to go to Paradise Island on many occasions, where Sam Clapp gave us his home and hospitality. So Eric and I have always had this kind of sparring thing about girls we've known, and if you look at it sort of like a jigsaw puzzle, you can see how our lives have been fit together over the years."

In her memoir, Patti confirmed that George had an affair with Krissie. "He didn't want to go on holiday with me and ended up going to Spain, supposedly to see Salvador Dali, with Ronnie Wood's wife, Krissie. I was desperately hurt: another of my friends was sleeping with George. When I challenged him, he denied it and tried once again to make me feel as though I was paranoid." George was no saint. But neither was Patti.

This bizarre love triangle, or should it be a bizarre love pentagon, became public knowledge when Wood told the press: "My romance with Pattie Boyd is definitely on. Things will be sorted out in a few days. Until then, I naturally can't say very much. We're going to talk it out between us and hope to get a happy arrangement. Meanwhile, Pattie has gone back to her home and will be talking to George about it. I won't be seeing her today."

Publicly, however, the Harrisons gave the impression that all was well. When asked about the statement, George replied: "Whatever Ronnie Wood has got to say about anything, certainly about us, it has nothing to do with Pattie or me. Got that! It has nothing to do with us her or me!" Patti remained silent. A few weeks later, Krissie, who happened to be in Los Angeles at the same time as George, said: "As far as I am concerned, nothing has changed between us. I love Ronnie, and he loves me. In fact, I refuse to believe his statement is serious. I haven't seen George in ages. The four of us have been friends for a long time." The following year, Harrison was interviewed by Alan Freeman for BBC radio, who asked if he had any downfalls in assessing friendships. Harrison's reply was cryptic; he played the first verse of 'Far East Man'. He was, of course, addressing Ronnie Wood, the cryptic reply going unnoticed by most listeners. As impassive as his assessment was, 'Far East Man' was a contemplation on friendships and relationships thrown into turmoil by infidelity.

Besides having his private life splashed all over the pages of the tabloid press, the only other stories about Harrison concerned rumours of him working with two unlikely American singers. The first of these was Barbra Streisand. Speculation had it that he was writing songs for her new album. Neither of the albums Streisand released in 1973 appear to have involved Harrison, nor did they feature any of his songs. The other was Andy Williams. Rumours about Harrison contributing guitar to his album were reported by American music industry magazines, including *Billboard*, which ran an article on Williams' *Solitaire* album that quoted the singer: "Middle of the Road music has changed drastically in the past two years," Williams said. "Easy Listening radio now plays predominantly the softer new rock records, not cover versions by MOR artists. My Columbia albums of hit covers have all made money, but I feel it's time for me to move along with the market." Harrison's music was veering towards soft rock. His work with Splinter was an early indicator of his direction of travel. The article made much of the fact that Williams' album was produced by Richard Perry, "who has achieved outstanding results with an artist roster including Streisand, Nilsson, Carly Simon and Tiny Tim."

By referencing Perry, they were, of course, alluding to his recent work with Starr and the almost Beatles reunion. It continued: "Some of Perry's friends who played on the Williams dates were George Harrison and Nicky Hopkins." There is no evidence that Harrison or Hopkins played on Williams' album. The press speculation may have stemmed from little more than Williams' recording of Harrison's 'That Is All' from his recently released *Living In The Material World* album.

Whatever was happening in their private lives, publicly, all four Beatles continued to go from one success to another. Ringo Starr's current single was racing up the American and Canadian charts. Capitol placed an advert in *Billboard* with the headline "Ringo Fever Grips Canadian Playlist". "'Ringo fever' has hit hard for Beatle drummer Starr as smash PHOTOGRAPH has been the top morsel desired by both major and secondary Canadian outlets. Stations were grabbing tapes, private servicing, and unofficial exclusives while the parts were being pressed in both American and Canadian plants. CHUM's (Toronto) Dave Charles, jumped with an initial 20 position, CFTR's (Toronto) Paul Godfrey has leaned on high playlist rotation, CKLG's Roy Hennessey (Vancouver) has Ringo staunchly numbered. Says CHUM's Charles, 'It may well be the record of the year.'" Forget the hyperbole; 'Photograph' was making steady progress on the charts. It entered the *Billboard* chart at number 74 before moving to number 60. By its third week, it had jumped into the top thirty at number 29 before ending the month in the top twenty at number 18.

Like George Harrison, all Ringo had to do was put out a record and watch it climb the charts. However, his fellow Apple Records recording artist, Yoko Ono, had to work at it. She made it clear to *Billboard* that her album was as much a statement of intent as it was about feminism. "I would hope this album will be the one which prevents me from being known only as Mrs, John Lennon," she said. She had been fighting against patriarchy, a system that made it difficult for women to be recognised as artists and musicians, all her life. Marrying Lennon had increased her profile but also placed other restrictions on her. The release of her new album was a move into a new creative space that she did not want to share with her husband. While referring to her artistic identity, it could also be read as an acknowledgement that her relationship with her husband was coming to an end. Lennon could try and paper over the cracks in his marriage as much as he liked. Ono was less circumspect. She was going to tell it like it was. After all, her new album was about women taking control of their lives. *Feeling The Space* is a concept album about the way men undermine women and how they can combat it. Gone was the screaming and groaning of her earlier albums. Gone, also, were the side-long, avant-garde compositions that tested the patience of the most dedicated fan. Instead, there were conventional pop songs written by a woman for women. Ono was stepping out of the shadow cast by her husband, out from the dark corners of the underground and avant-garde art community, and into the bright light of the mainstream. "The album is probably a bit more commercial than anything I have ever done before," she said. "But I want to reach as wide an audience as possible through airplay and touring. Making things slightly more commercial and still not completely compromising seems the best way to reach people."

Ono also announced plans for a solo tour, a "five or six [date] concert tour to include major cities for later this fall." Lennon would not be accompanying her. Instead, her all-male band, so much for feminism, comprised the same session musicians who played on her album. According to *Billboard*, this was "a rather unusual situation in the music business."

While Ono was busy promoting her new record, her husband was preparing to record his second album in as many months. Lennon announced his plan to record an album of rock 'n' roll oldies with Phil Spector to Pang. She claims she voiced concerns about working with the maverick producer. But Lennon brushed them aside. According to Lennon, he was tired of writing songs and wanted to be a singer. "I've had enough of this 'be deep and think,'" he explained. "Why can't I have some fun?" Lennon may have convinced himself this was the case. But it was only partly true. He was legally obliged to record three songs published by Big Seven for his next album.

As the writer of 'Come Together,' a track from The Beatles' Abbey Road album, Lennon was sued for copyright infringement. Big Seven Music Corp., owned by Morris Levy (the man who had tried, unsuccessfully, to copyright the phrase 'rock'n'roll'), claimed that Lennon had appropriated lyrics from Chuck Berry's 'You Can't Catch Me'. Lennon's habit of borrowing from other songs to kick-start his own had caught up with him. 'Come Together,' originally intended as a campaign song for Timothy Leary, displayed more than a passing resemblance to Berry's primal rocker. Although Lennon's lawyers agreed that both songs shared similar lyrics, they argued that the meaning had been substantially changed, and there was no case to answer. The case dragged on for over two years, during which time Lennon spent almost as much time in the courts as he did in the studio. Growing tired of Levy's litigation, Lennon instructed his lawyers to settle out of court.

On Friday, the 12th details of the agreement were formally put into the legal record in New York. The deal with Levy stipulated that "John Lennon agrees to record three songs by Big Seven publishers on his next album. The songs [he] intends to record at this time are 'You Can't Catch Me,' 'Angel Baby,' and 'Ya Ya,' [and he] reserves the right to alter the last two songs to any other songs belonging to Big Seven." Other clauses stated that Lennon would use his influence to cause Apple to licence to Big Seven three songs from the Apple non-Beatles catalogue. Failure to comply with this by 31st December 1974 would result in Lennon recording another two songs published by Big Seven.

Lennon had never recorded cover versions for any of his his albums. Now he was legally obligated to do just that, but how could he work them into a new album without it looking like a compromise. His only option was to recorded seven more oldies and issue an entire album of cover songs. First, he had to persuade Spector to take on the job. Lennon had his people contact Spector's people and arrange a meeting. Lennon and Pang were invited to Spector's house, where they were kept waiting. Spector liked to play mind games with people; keeping them waiting was one of his tricks. His next was to accuse Pang of being one of Klien's untrustworthy people. Lennon reassured him that Pang could be trusted, and when Spector eventually calmed down, they discussed Lennon's plans for the album. This involved giving the eccentric producer total control of the project.

Spector played Lennon like a fish. First, he gave him the impression that he'd do it and then that he wouldn't. "On the Rock 'n' Roll [album] it took me three weeks to convince him that I wasn't going to co-produce with him, and I wasn't going to go in the control room, I was only, I said I just want to be the singer, just treat me like Ronnie [Spector]. We'll pick the material, I just want to sing, I don't want anything to do with production or writing or creation, I just want to sing. So I finally convinced him." True to his word, Lennon let Spector have total control, including hiring the studios and musicians.

McCartney was keen to finish work on his album and arranged to meet Tony Visconti to discuss string arrangements. "It started with a phone call," Visconti explained. "He said, 'I like the T. Rex tracks you produced. Did you write those strings for the T. Rex tracks?' He's talking about 'Cosmic Dancer' and 'Get It On'. I said, 'Yes, I did'. He goes, 'Can you read and write music?'. I said, 'Yes, I can'. He said, 'Well, I've recorded this song, and he told me the background in Nigeria, and he said, 'I want some string writing on it, and I like that simple kind of strings, that very tasty strings that you've written.' This was a Sunday. He says 'Can you come over to my house in Saint John's Wood and we can go through it. I've got a piano.' And so I did. I took Mary with me because she was friends with Paul and Linda." McCartney knew exactly the kind of string arrangements he wanted. What he couldn't do was write them down. Previously, he would have worked with George Martin, who would transcribe his ideas onto manuscript paper. The process was similar this time, but as Visconti explained, McCartney sang his ideas onto cassette tape. "Paul and I were at the piano, and he played little bits of 'Band On The Run' on this little Philips cassette player, and he had a second cassette player, and he played the backing track from 'Band On the Run,' and he'd sing a part over it and say, 'I want the strings to do this.' He'd sing something, and the brass to do this. And I had to return that cassette to him, he wouldn't let me keep it. So anyway, I took it home and said, 'When is the session?' And he said, 'I want it in two days.' And it was a good nine or ten arrangements on it. Some were complicated, like 'Drink To My Health' (sic). The Picasso song. That was a big deal., That was a big Motown style arrangement, which he didn't dictate. He said do your thing on this. That was the one where I did my thing. But in 'Jet' he had that line (sings melody) he wanted that on saxes."

Before Visconti's string arrangements were recorded, Wings spent Monday 15th mixing Linda's 'Oriental Nightfish' and compiling a sixteen-track tape of the master backing tracks for Wednesday's overdub session. While this was taking place, the *NME* sent Julie Webb to interview Wings, but as McCartney and

Laine were preoccupied, Linda fielded most of the questions. The interview comprised the usual inquiries about Linda's role in the band and the events of recording the album in Lagos. If the departure of Seiwell still hurt, the McCartneys were more forgiving of McCullough. Linda said she was pleased to hear he was back working with Joe Cocker. She also intimated that his loss wasn't felt as much because he wasn't a founding member of the band. "I think that's what he was always happier with," she said. "You see, we threw the band together to get back on stage. We didn't really know Henry, and he didn't know us. We had Seiwell, Laine, Paul, and myself and thought we'd like a lead guitar player to take some of the weight off. Somebody mentioned Henry; he came to one rehearsal, and we said, 'OK, we'll have you.' It worked out great on the road, though." Linda's attitude appears to mirror that of her husband. McCullough was never fully integrated into the band. Whether or not it was conscious or subconscious, he was considered a sidesman who could, and would, be replaced when necessary. Seiwell, however, was deemed to be a full member of the band, which is why his last-minute decision not to travel to Lagos hit them so hard.

Wednesday's overdub session involving sixty musicians had to be planned with military precision. "I hardly slept for two days," Visconti recalled. "I also had to book and strategize the session, starting with the sixty musicians needed for the title track, 'Band On The Run,' down to the string quartet for 'No Words'. The very first thing we did was the interlude between the first and second parts of 'Band On The Run'; it proved to be very difficult because the first section is in an entirely different tempo from the next. We just kept doing take after take until we got the transition to work smoothly. Only some of the sixty musicians were wearing headphones, so it was a genuine job of conducting to bring them in and to keep them together."

With the orchestral arrangements recorded, they turned their attention to recording the brass section. 'Jet' was the first song the four-strong brass section worked on. Having copied the faulty tape onto a new one, it was safe to run it through the tape machine without fear of it shedding precious oxide. Overdubs for 'Jet' completed, it was Howie Casey's turn to add a saxophone solo to 'Bluebird' and 'Jet.' However, the solo McCartney wanted for 'Jet' was partly out of his instrument's range. Visconti solved the problem by having an alto saxophone play the first part, and Casey play the second on a tenor saxophone. The remainder of the week was spent perfecting vocals for 'Band On The Run,' 'Mamunia,' and 'Mrs. Vandebilt'. All that remained was to mix the album. But even that was complicated by external forces that continued to dog the album.

While McCartney finished *Band On The Run*, Lennon held his first session with Spector. Mal Evans had returned to Los Angeles and was on hand to act as Lennon's road manager, social secretary, and minder. It would be a demanding and, at times, dangerous role. It was also rewarding. As Evans recalled: "It was fascinating because John was talking to me like a songwriter, and that was incredible. For the first time, John and I really communicated, whereas, when it was the four of them, John was always the hardest to talk to." On the evening of the 17th, Lennon headed to A&M Studios on LaBrea Avenue to cut 'Bony Moronie'. Assembled that evening were fifteen top LA session players, including Hal Blaine, Larry Carlton, Steve Cropper, Jim Horn, Barry Mann, Jim Keltner, and Phil Spector. Lennon's dream had come true. He was standing in Ronnie's shoes and would have to deliver. Like her, he would quickly discover how tedious Spector's recording process was and how manic the producer could be. Spector was hardly in control of himself, let alone a roomful of musicians. Ronnie had started divorce proceedings the previous year. It was messy and revealed what the man behind the shades and wigs was really like. In her divorce testimony, Ronnie said that Spector had: "imposed his will on [me] by the use of force and threats." If Lennon wanted Spector to treat him like Ronnie, he would be in for a shock.

Spector would arrive at the session each night dressed in a different outfit. This may have been his way of expressing different sides of his personality. Later, he would be diagnosed as schizophrenic. Although, he claimed: "I take medication for schizophrenia, but I wouldn't say I'm schizophrenic … I have a bipolar personality … I'm my own worst enemy. I have devils inside that fight me." He also had anger management issues that would result in blazing fights with musicians. He was drinking heavily, which, Dan Kessel claimed, was "an anger cushion, just being real bugged about a lot of things and wanting to sort of cushion the nervous system." If this combination of personal issues wasn't enough, the fact that he carried a loaded handgun should have set alarm bells ringing. The man was in no fit state to produce an album. Let alone an album as chaotic and ill-disciplined as this one. He may have controlled the project, finances, etc., but he did not control Lennon.

Spector's preferred way of working was to routine a group of musicians using his tried and trusted formula. He would gather the musicians and then have just the rhythm section play while the engineers got the sound he wanted. Then, he'd repeat the process with different sections of the band. If your idea of fun is listening to the same song played over and over again for hours, then A&M Studios was the place to be. The process quickly wears thin, particularly if you have a low boredom threshold like Lennon. Lennon soon found a way to while away the long hours while he waited to sing, and it wasn't doing the *Los Angeles Times* crossword.

The Lennon/Spector show wasn't the only one in town, but it was, perhaps, the most fascinating. Joni Mitchell was recording her *Court And Spark* album in an adjacent studio and popped in to see what was happening. Larry Carlton, who was booked to play on tonight's session with Lennon, also appeared on Mitchell's album. She may have looked in to see how he was getting on but spent most of her time making eyes at Lennon. Either way, she proved to be anything but a calming influence. While flirting with Lennon, which embarrassed him, she annoyed Spector so much that the session ended early. Distractions aside, they managed to capture a solid performance of 'Bony Moronie' and would repeat the process with another song the following night.

Tonight's session started two hours later than previously, running from 9pm to midnight. According to Pang, the atmosphere in the studio had already changed from the previous evening. "The musicians who had been cool and professional with each other on the first evening greeted each other like long-lost army buddies who had suddenly been recalled to fight one more war. Everyone seemed almost too relaxed, too jolly." It was a portentous insight. After only two days, the sessions were already unravelling. To relieve the boredom of Spector's relentless recording technique, and with Lennon intent on having fun, the sessions took on a party atmosphere. Drummer Jim Keltner recalled that a typical night at the studio would descend into disorder, with Lennon the lead hedonist. "He was drinking too much, and as the evening progressed, John would get a little out of control – the whole thing would deteriorate." It wasn't only Lennon; most of the musicians were drinking to relieve their boredom, but at least they maintained a level of self-control. Joni Mitchell returned to enjoy the spectacle, which did little to lighten the mood. Spector attempted to retain control but was fighting a losing battle. Eventually, a bored and drunken Lennon snapped and smashed a set of headphones on the recording console. In less time than it took to record The Beatles' debut album, all control had been lost.

Remarkably, Lennon recorded a vocal for 'Be My Baby,' purring, growling, groaning, and screaming his way through take after take of Ronnie's finest two minutes and forty seconds. Only tonight, the song meandered on for over six uninspired minutes. Under Spector's maniacal eye, Lennon discovered how difficult it was to repeatedly deliver a convincing performance to a roomful of semi-intoxicated session players who'd seen and heard it all before. Surprisingly, the session was a partial success. Somehow, they'd managed to record a song. But the night's drama was only beginning to unravel.

At the end of the session, an intoxicated Lennon was bundled into a car, accompanied by Spector, his bodyguard, George, and Jim Keltner; and driven back to Lou Adler's house. By the time they arrived, Lennon was uncontrollable. Spector suggested pumping him full of black coffee to sober him up. It did little good. Lennon was swearing and shouting, and the more Spector tried to calm him, the more argumentative and violent he became. As unpredictable as he was, Spector took command of the situation and dragged Lennon off to bed with assistance from his bodyguard. But Lennon wouldn't go quietly and fought like a man possessed. The only thing Spector and his bodyguard could think of was to bind Lennon with neckties to stop him from harming himself or others. No sooner had Spector left the scene than Lennon broke free of his makeshift bonds and stood at the top of the stairs screaming, "Yoko, you slant-eyed bitch, you wanted to get rid of me. All this happened because you wanted to get rid of me."

Chasing Pang out of the house, he trashed Adler's plush pad. By the time Pang managed to raise Tony King on the phone, Lennon was wandering the streets bellowing like a banshee. King managed to calm him, eventually putting the drunken Beatle to bed. But Lennon hadn't finished. He insisted that Pang call Spector so he could sack him. The night's escapade made Lagos look like a walk in the park. Unsurprisingly, the next evening's session was cancelled while both parties cooled their heels.

Recording started again on the 22nd with the tracking of 'Sweet Little Sixteen'. Earlier in the day, Lennon gave an interview to *Record World*. Tony King planned to rebrand Lennon as something other than a political firebrand and artistic fruitcake. The interview was titled 'Moving on With John Lennon'. So far, so good. But where had Lennon moved to? Indeed, the old Lennon was absent. He seemed evasive, untalkative, and uninterested in promoting himself or the *Mind Games* album. When asked, "Can you talk about some of the things in the album [*Mind Games*]?" he replied: "No, that's too heavy. I can't tell you what it's goin' be. They're just songs." Asked about what influenced the album, he said: "No, it's called the dregs. No, it's really half and halfs, bits from before, bits from after."

Was he nursing the mother of all hangovers? Perhaps he was having an off day? If recent events were anything to go by, he was depressed. It would explain the excessive drinking and the lack of interest he showed in talking about himself and his work. Whatever it was, he was hardly selling the album. The rest of the interview was a little better. It covered politics, performing, plans for JohnandYoko, and his current recording project. None of which seemed to inspire him. When asked who was producing the album he was currently recording, he said: "Phil Spector and that makes me even more nervous." Nervous, insecure, depressed, drunk, whatever Ono had planned when she kicked him out, it couldn't have been this.

The following night's session was cancelled, resuming on the 24th with 'Just Because'. Once again, Lennon hit the bottle, but that was all. Punches were not thrown. For some reason, Spector recorded Lennon's drunken singing, which he'd replace the following year. The only word to describe tonight's performance is pitiful. Mac Rebennack was booked to play keyboards for the session and recalled how everyone was hell-bent on indulging Lennon's excesses. "Instead of sayin', 'Hey man, you're fuckin' up your own date,' they let it happen. It was the first time in my life that I ever felt sorry for the producer. There was nothin' that Spector could do. He would try and dole out the lush to John – and the cat would have it smuggled in. The next night, Phil would get somebody to make sure that John didn't drink more than a certain amount. The cat wouldn't cut 'til he had his taste. But when he had his taste, he couldn't cut!" Later, Lennon confirmed that his rock 'n' roll friends were part of the problem, not the solution. "When I've been drunk or disembodied in one way or another, there're always friends and hangers-on who sit around applauding as they hand me more and more stuff to kill myself with. It's like Bob Dylan says in that song, 'pull you down in the hole that he's in.' But whenever I say these things, I'm careful not to blame other people."

There was one friend who was concerned about him. Roy Cicala, hired to engineer the sessions, phoned Ono to tell her what was happening. "Yoko, you have to come out here," he told her. "John is in need. You're the only one that can come out and help him." Ono was having none of it. As far as she was concerned, he'd made his bed, and now he would have to sleep in it. Recalling the conversation she had with Cicala, she said: "All that time, I was getting a very bad reputation, that I would not let anybody come near him … He called me one day and said, 'Yoko, you have to come and pick him up.' I said, 'What are you talking about? All this time, you guys were thinking that I'm holding him up and you can't get near him. So now it's your turn. Do it! You take care of him.'" Spector couldn't help Lennon. Neither could Pang. Roy Cicala was a great engineer and had shown concern, but he couldn't help either. The only person who could help was Ono. She did eventually relent and went to Los Angeles for a week to try and talk some sense into her estranged husband. It didn't do much good. By now, it was too late. Lennon was hanging out with some heavy drinkers, all of whom encouraged his bad habits. They were rock 'n roll people born to be the news. And the news was, they were all drunks.

A playback session for the following day was cancelled. Two more sessions followed, where backing tracks were recorded, but Lennon didn't contribute vocals during either session. On Friday 26th, Spector had the band record the backing track for 'A Love Like Yours (Don't Come Knocking Every Day),' originally recorded by Martha and the Vandellas and later covered by Ike and Tina Turner (produced by Phil Spector). The following night, they recorded the backing track for 'Born To Be With You,' originally by The Chordettes. Four months earlier, Dave Edmunds had a hit with a Spector-esque version of the song in the UK. Lennon was a fan of Edmunds' earlier hit 'I Hear You Knocking' and may have heard his version, which prompted him to try the song.

While all this drunken chaos was happening, in New York, Lennon's immigration lawyer, Leon Wildes, filed US District Court suits on 17th and 24th October, claiming the government used the immigration laws to deport Lennon because of his opposition to US policy on Indochina and the old possession of marijuana chestnut. The suits sought to determine whether the Lennons were, or had been, under federal surveillance and subject to wiretapping, whether Lennon's case was prejudged, and whether the INS purposefully overlooked marijuana convictions in other cases. A week later, on Wednesday, 29th, Wildes urged the US Board of Immigration Appeals to allow Lennon to remain in the United States while earlier lawsuits related to his deportation case were being settled by federal court. "Conceivably, that could take years," board chairman Maurice Roberts said at a hearing. Wildes countered, "I believe there will be no adverse effect on the United States if John Lennon hangs around and publishes a few more songs." Unfortunately, Wildes' views were not shared by the INS lawyer, Vincent Schaino, who argued that an earlier March ruling by immigration judge Ira Fieldsteel that Lennon should be deported because he had stayed longer than legally permitted should be upheld.

While Lennon ran wild in Los Angeles, Apple/EMI rushed to release Paul McCartney and Wings' new single. Released in Britain on the 19th, 'Helen Wheels' b/w 'Country Dreamer' found favour with the critics for its no-nonsense simplicity. *Disc* said it was "A good rocking single from the prolific pen of Mr. McCartney – and a surefire chart entry." While John Peel likened it to Canned Heat: "A bit of a rocker from the Wings, recorded, no doubt, in Nigeria or wherever it was that they all went to record. It's based on an old

John Lee Hooker riff - something like that on Canned Heat's 'On The Road Again.'"

In America, *Billboard* reviewed the single: "Driving rock tune showing a marked change of pace from the artist's last two releases. Catchy chorus and play on words in title combined with excellent guitar work make this a sure bet to follow on the back of McCartney's last several disks." *Cash Box* said of the single: "The title may be a play on words ("Hell On Wheels?"), but it fits. The lady may be, but this track most certainly is. A savage rocker from a band that has become more proficient at rock with each outing, this one looks to be a major pop success and another in the long line of Paul McCartney hits that looks to be getting only longer as time goes by." The single also found favour with *Record World* who wrote: "Following up two straight number one records is an easy task for super Paul. Rock and rolling number should drive to number one in a matter of weeks."

Wings made a film to promote the song, combining shots of them driving in McCartney's Rolls Royce with footage of the trio mining in a studio. The production took the best part of a working week, which meant that work mixing the album couldn't start until Thursday 25th. While Lennon had recorded the backing tracks for his *Mind Games* album in five days, he'd spent several weeks mixing and re-mixing songs. McCartney had spent weeks recording but was forced to mix the album in three days. The reason for this was Gerry Bron, the owner of Bronze Records and former Bonzo Dog Doo-Dah Band manager. Bron had a reputation for being thrifty, particularly with studio costs, and strict with contracts. Bron had booked Emerick to work with one of his bands, Tempest, and would not let him delay the start date, even if he was working for Paul McCartney. In Emerick's words, attempting to mix the album in three days was ridiculous. The job was even more difficult because neither AIR Studios nor EMI Studios were available. McCartney booked into the smaller Kingsway Studios, which wasn't as well equipped, resulting in additional equipment being hired. Luckily, many of the instruments had been recorded with effects in place, which made the mixing process a little quicker. As ridiculous as the task was, the mix was completed in the early hours of the 29th. All that remained was to compile a cutting tape, cut the lacquers, take the cover photograph, design the cover, and press the records. All of this had to be achieved in the next four weeks.

McCartney had been thinking about the cover concept for some time. He knew he wanted something modern and contemporary that echoed the idea of something as old- fashioned as a Hopalong Cassidy prison break. Hipgnosis had been producing cutting-edge designs for years and had recently made one of its most straightforward and visually striking designs for Pink Floyd's *Dark Side Of The Moon*. Based in Denmark Street, London, they got the job. Usually, they were employed to come up with a concept for the artwork. On this occasion, their client already had the concept; all they had to do was follow his instructions. McCartney provided Hipgnosis with a list of celebrities he would like to feature on the cover; all Hipgnosis had to do was call their agents to see if they were available. The idea had been used before, but rather than cut-outs, as had been employed for *Sgt. Pepper's Lonely Hearts Club Band*, McCartney used real celebrities to give a contemporary rather than nostalgic feel.

Clive Arrowsmith was booked to take the photo. Previously, he'd been the art director for the British television show Ready Steady Go. He also had Beatle connections, having attended the Liverpool College of Art with Lennon. He'd only recently changed his career to photography, which would lead to another unforeseen slip-up.

On Sunday, the 28th, McCartney's band of celebrities gathered for lunch at an Italian restaurant in Knightsbridge before heading to Osterley Park for the photo shoot. A small film unit was also on hand to capture the event for posterity. Once everyone had changed into their hired convict costumes, they stood against a brick wall, illuminated with a hired spotlight. The first problem Arrowsmith encountered was that the spotlight wasn't bright enough. This meant he'd have to use a much longer exposure time of two seconds. "Two seconds may not sound like a long time, however, they did have a party before the shoot and everyone was very much the worse for wear, but still enjoying each others company to say the least," Arrowsmith recalled. "Trying to get everyone to stay still and play the part of escaping prisoners was proving extremely difficult, amid the laughter, jokes and substance haze; I arranged them all together so they could lean against each other and the wall. Now, because they had all become a little unsteady on their feet, Denny Lane fell over a couple of times laughing hysterically – everyone was having a great time. I had to have a megaphone to get their attention, I had even positioned myself up to the top of a ladder, next to the spotlight and barked instructions persistently, which the most part everyone ignored, until I finally snapped and screamed 'Stay Still!'"

More by luck than judgment, Arrowsmith ended up with four usable photos for the cover. "I only managed to shoot two rolls of film, which is only 24 exposures in total," he explained. "The group couldn't hold the pose for long, some would be still in one frame and others would be moving in another, the real worry was that there wouldn't be a shot where everyone was still and sharp. My woes did not end there; once the film came back, it had a strong, warm yellow cast, but thankfully, there were four frames where everyone was sharp. I showed them to Paul and he loved them, I never mentioned the golden hue to him until a few years later when I was photographing the back cover for Wings At The Speed of Sound." McCartney likes to embrace mistakes and luckily for Arrowsmith he liked the unintentional warm glow that resulted from his error. It was too late to re-shoot the cover, so nothing could be done about it anyway.

For the back cover, Arrowsmith took some "super passport crook pictures" of Paul, Linda, and Denny, which were placed with fake files, rubber stamps, and coffee cups on his refectory table. The idea was to make it look like a spymaster after the band on the run. Hipgnosis added another twist to the cover by using an alternative shot with the photos of Paul, Linda, and Denny in a different order for the American sleeve. It also added 'Helen Wheels' to the side two track listing.

The 29th saw Lennon's new single 'Mind Games' b/w 'Meat City' released in America. Record World gave it a positive review: "Long awaited single from Lennon is one of his best songs in the post-Beatle period. Title tune from forthcoming album should be on top in no time." *Billboard* said of the single: "Vocal overdubs and swaying strings combine in John's assertion that positive thoughts are the answer to happiness. He espouses chanting the Mantra and peace on earth." *Cash Box* said: "John comes through with his most powerful recorded effort in some time. Top flight vocal performance backed by that steady, yet driving, tempo accentuates some great lyrics, all in making for a great song. Definitely Top 5 within a matter of weeks."

In Britain, the single was released on 9th November. Pete Jones reviewed it for *Record Mirror*, saying: "Soul-stirring stuff, really. Some reviewers find this intensity, slow mind-numbing intensity, gets on their collective wick, but I find it hypnotic and built with skill. John still has one of the most instantly recognisable voices in the world. The strings add lushness to his gruffness." A review in a rival paper was by one of those for whom this kind of thing got on their wick. Reviewing Elvis Presley's 'Raised On Rock' and Lennon's 'Mind Games' under the subheading 'Bummers of the Week,' they tore both to shreds. "It's always rather harrowing to watch one of the architects of modern rock making a complete toadstool of himself, but sad to relate, that's more or less what's happened. 'Mind Games' hauls out references to 'the search for the grail,' 'the spirit,' and 'the karmic circle' while asserting that 'love is the answer.' Musically, it's quite charming, but the sublime dreadfulness of the lyrics leads the listener to the inescapable conclusion that Hari Georgeson's been dropping God pills in

Lennon's cocoa." Not everyone thought it dreadful. Writing in the *NME*, Chris Charlesworth said: "A medium-paced rock (sic) with a repetitive commercial chorus line of 'Love is the answer.' Very full backing with swirling organ and heavy bass drum work. Dramatic but not over-powering."

Lennon might have been disappointed by the mixed reviews. He had, however, set himself up for a fall with the brilliance of his first two albums. Following them with the poorly received *Some Time In New York City* didn't help. However, there was better news for McCartney. In America, 'Live and Let Die' was certified gold by the RIAA. Another million seller and another gold disc to hang on the office wall.

US

WEEK ENDING 6 OCTOBER 1973
  1. HALF-BREED: CHER
  2. LOVES ME LIKE A ROCK: PAUL SIMON (WITH THE DIXIE
     HUMMINGBIRDS)
  3. LET'S GET IT ON: MARVIN GAYE
  4. WE'RE AN AMERICAN BAND: GRAND FUNK
  5. HIGHER GROUND: STEVIE WONDER
  6. THAT LADY (PART 1): THE ISLEY BROTHERS
  7. RAMBLIN MAN: THE ALLMAN BROTHERS BAND
  8. ANGIE: THE ROLLING STONES
  9. DELTA DAWN: HELEN REDDY
  10. KEEP ON TRUCKIN' (PART 1): EDDIE KENDRICKS

WEEK ENDING 13 OCTOBER 1973
  1. HALF-BREED: CHER
  2. RAMBLIN MAN: THE ALLMAN BROTHERS BAND
  3. LET'S GET IT ON: MARVIN GAYE
  4. HIGHER GROUND: STEVIE WONDER
  5. ANGIE: THE ROLLING STONES
  6. THAT LADY (PART 1): THE ISLEY BROTHERS
  7. LOVES ME LIKE A ROCK: PAUL SIMON (WITH THE DIXIE
     HUMMINGBIRDS)
  8. MIDNIGHT TRAIN TO GEORGIA: GLADYS KNIGHT AND THE PIPS
  9. KEEP ON TRUCKIN' (PART 1): EDDIE KENDRICKS
  10. WE'RE AN AMERICAN BAND: GRAND FUNK

WEEK ENDING 20 OCTOBER 1973
  1. ANGIE: THE ROLLING STONES
  2. HALF-BREED: CHER
  3. RAMBLIN MAN: THE ALLMAN BROTHERS BAND
  4. LET'S GET IT ON: MARVIN GAYE
  5. MIDNIGHT TRAIN TO GEORGIA: GLADYS KNIGHT AND THE PIPS
  6. THAT LADY (PART 1): THE ISLEY BROTHERS
  7. KEEP ON TRUCKIN' (PART 1): EDDIE KENDRICKS
  8. HIGHER GROUND: STEVIE WONDER
  9. HEARTBEAT - IT'S A LOVEBEAT: THE DEFRANCO FAMILY
     FEATURING TONY DEFRANCO
  10. PAPER ROSES: MARIE OSMOND

WEEK ENDING 27 OCTOBER 1973
  1. MIDNIGHT TRAIN TO GEORGIA: GLADYS KNIGHT AND THE PIPS
  2. ANGIE: THE ROLLING STONES
  3. HALF-BREED: CHER
  4. RAMBLIN MAN: THE ALLMAN BROTHERS BAND
  5. KEEP ON TRUCKIN' (PART 1): EDDIE KENDRICKS
  6. LET'S GET IT ON: MARVIN GAYE
  7. PAPER ROSES: MARIE OSMOND
  8. HEARTBEAT - IT'S A LOVEBEAT: THE DEFRANCO FAMILY
     FEATURING   TONY DEFRANCO
  9. THAT LADY (PART 1): THE ISLEY BROTHERS
  10. HIGHER GROUND: STEVIE WONDER

WEEK ENDING 6 OCTOBER 1973
1. EYE LEVEL: SIMON PARK ORCHESTRA
2. BALLROOM BLITZ: THE SWEET
3. MONSTER MASH: BOBBY (BORIS) PICKETT AND THE CRYPT-KICKERS
4. MY FRIEND STAN: SLADE
5. NUTBUSH CITY LIMITS: IKE AND TINA TURNER
6. ANGEL FINGERS: WIZZARD
7. FOR THE GOOD TIMES: PERRY COMO
8. LAUGHING GNOME: DAVID BOWIE
9. JOYBRINGER: MANFRED MANN'S EARTH BAND
10. ROCK ON: DAVID ESSEX

WEEK ENDING 13 OCTOBER 1973
1. EYE LEVEL: SIMON PARK ORCHESTRA
2. MY FRIEND STAN: SLADE
3. BALLROOM BLITZ: THE SWEET
4. NUTBUSH CITY LIMITS: IKE AND TINA TURNER
5. MONSTER MASH: BOBBY (BORIS) PICKETT AND THE CRYPT-KICKERS
6. LAUGHING GNOME: DAVID BOWIE
7. FOR THE GOOD TIMES: PERRY COMO
8. DAYDREAMER/PUPPY SONG: DAVID CASSIDY
9. JOYBRINGER: MANFRED MANN'S EARTH BAND

WEEK ENDING 20 OCTOBER 1973
1. EYE LEVEL: SIMON PARK ORCHESTRA
2. DAYDREAMER/PUPPY SONG: DAVID CASSIDY
3. MY FRIEND STAN: SLADE
4. NUTBUSH CITY LIMITS: IKE AND TINA TURNER
5. MONSTER MASH: BOBBY (BORIS) PICKETT AND THE CRYPT-KICKERS
6. LAUGHING GNOME: DAVID BOWIE
7. BALLROOM BLITZ: THE SWEET
8. FOR THE GOOD TIMES: PERRY COMO
9. GOODBYE YELLOW BRICK ROAD: ELTON JOHN

WEEK ENDING 27 OCTOBER 1973
1. DAYDREAMER/PUPPY SONG: DAVID CASSIDY
2. EYE LEVEL: SIMON PARK ORCHESTRA
3. MY FRIEND STAN: SLADE
4. SORROW: DAVID BOWIE
5. CAROLINE: STATUS QUO
6. GOODBYE YELLOW BRICK ROAD: ELTON JOHN
7. FOR THE GOOD TIMES: PERRY COMO
8. LAUGHING GNOME: DAVID BOWIE
9. NUTBUSH CITY LIMITS: IKE AND TINA TURNER
10. A HARD RAIN'S GONNA FALL: BRYAN FERRY

CHAPTER 11
NOVEMBER: ANOTHER DAY, ANOTHER LAWSUIT

The Beatles' contract with ABKCO may have ended in March, but the fallout from its termination, like their attempt to dissolve the original partnership agreement, limped on. On 3rd November, Lennon, Harrison, Starr, Apple Corps, and thirteen other companies in the group filed an action in the High Courts of Justice, London, against ABKCO, claiming damages for misrepresentation. As part of their writ, they argued that the 8th May 1969 contract was invalid because they did not fully understand its nature and effect. This was only partly true because Lennon and Harrison had signed an affidavit in February 1971 confirming that it had been explained to them. If Lennon, Harrison, and Starr didn't understand the nature of the contract, McCartney did. The *Daily Telegraph* reported that McCartney had brought a High Court action to break up The Beatles' partnership precisely because he did not trust Mr Klein with his stewardship. This was public knowledge and would further undermine Lennon's, Harrison's, and Starr's claim that they didn't know what they were signing. The writ also stated that ABKCO was not entitled to a commission because it committed fundamental breaches of its duties and that its demands for the commission were either erroneous or overblown. Lawyers also argued that ABKCO could not sue several companies named in its writ because they did not trade in America. These included Apple Publishing, Apple Films: Subafilms, Harrisongs, Startling Music: Python Music, Singsong Music, and Ono Music, all of Savile Row London. This still left companies incorporated in the United States, including Apple Records Inc. of New York, Apple Records Inc. of California, Apple Music Publishing Co. Inc., Apple Films Inc., and Apple Music Inc.

Paul Gambaccini asked McCartney what he thought of the other Beatles lawsuit against Klein. "Of course I loved that," he said. "My God, I hope they win that one. That's great. You see, apart from - everything that came down, all the little personal conflicts, the reason why I felt I had to do what I had to do, which ended up specifically as being I had to sue the other three, was that there was no way I could sue Klein on his own, which is what I wanted to do. It took me months to get over the fact."

Naturally, Klein retaliated. One week after Lennon, Harrison, and Starr sued him in London, he countered by suing them in New York. Now, both parties were fighting legal battles on two fronts on different continents. Both sides wanted vengeance, but Harold Seider claimed that Klein always thought he would get them back. On 8th November, ABKCO sued six New York and three California corporations affiliated with The Beatles, all the individual Beatles, Ono and Michael Boreham, an English solicitor representing The Beatles other than McCartney. That action alleged forty-two counts with ABKCO seeking judgment for commissions owing and to accrue in the future, repayment of loans, and compensation for services rendered. In total, ABKCO sought almost $19 million ($130,390,495.50). Count 42 against all defendants was for conspiracy, breach of contract, and fraud, for which ABKCO sought an additional $34 million, which included $10 million in punitive damages. ($233,330,360.36)

This transatlantic legal battle dragged on for another three years and was only settled with help from an improbable source. The person who played the most significant part in resolving this mess was the very person who was vilified for supposedly breaking up The Beatles, Yoko Ono. According to Klein, it was her "Kissinger-like negotiating brilliance" that ended the dispute, which, in the final year of litigation, cost ABKCO $1,200,000 ($6,426,052.72). One assumes Apple Corps shelled out a similar sum in legal fees. Both parties eventually settled out-of-court, with Apple Corps paying ABKCO $5,009,200 ($26,824,486.09) and ABKCO paying "certain Apple associates" the sum of $800,000 ($4,284,035.15).

McCartney's 1970 lawsuit to dissolve The Beatles' partnership which resulted with the official receiver holding most of their income proved to be beneficial. "As it turns out, it was the best thing because that got the receiver in there and froze the money and gave everybody time to think about it," recalled McCartney. It gave The Beatles time to think about future outcomes and meant that Apple Corps had a massive pot of cash to draw on once the partnership agreement dispute was resolved. However, it must have been galling for all four Beatles to think that Klein ended up with even more of their money.

According to Albert Pergam, an attorney representing the Apple/Beatles group of companies, the $5,009,200 was paid by Apple Corps Ltd. The $800,000 payment by ABKCO was divided between Harrisongs Ltd., Richard Starkey, Apple Films Ltd., and Apple Records Inc. in California. As for the conspiracy charges brought against all four Beatles, the charges against McCartney and his lawyer were dismissed by the Appellate Division of the Supreme Court of New York State in June 1976. McCartney had been proved right again. But at what cost? As a director of Apple Corps, his share of the payment to ABKCO came to $1,252,300. And that didn't include his share of Apple's legal fees. That had to hurt.

While all this was going on, Apple Records released three new albums. Ringo Starr's much-delayed *Ringo* album was released on 2nd November. Buoyed by the success of 'Photograph', which in the first week of November was sitting at number 11 on the *Billboard* chart, and the continued interest in the much talked about Beatles reunion, the album received widespread praise.

Cash Box suggested it was a unique work of genius. "Ringo continues to develop his own identity in this fascinating Richard Perry produced LP which features the sensational hit single 'Photograph'. The artistry on this album is the most unique in the history of pop music. All of the ex-Beatles, The Band, Marc Bolan, David Bromberg, Nicky Hopkins, Billy Preston, Steve Cropper, and a host of the finest studio men in the world combine to make each track a masterpiece," it gushed. "John Lennon's 'I'm The Greatest' is a gem as is Randy Newman's 'Hold On'. In fact, every cut on the LP is distinguished by the individual genius of Ringo and the collective talents of his friends."

Billboard was equally fulsome in its praise. "Just the best Ringo album ever. We all know already that 'Photograph' has got to be a No. 1 single this month, right? Rest of the album is comparably enjoyable. Richard Perry and his cadre of superstar session helpers have created another stunning production package. Highly varied song selection with Ringo, Harrison, McCartney, and Lennon all on tap as musicians and writers." Reading between the lines, both reviewers were as impressed by the calibre of players as with Starr himself. Admittedly, the *Cash Box* reviewer drew attention to the "individual genius of Ringo," but even that was qualified by the "collective talents of his friends." Ringo's star might have been shining brightly, but its brilliance depended on all the other stars surrounding him. Remove any of the supporting cast, and Ringo's "individual genius" fades ever so slightly.

This point was raised when the British music paper *Disc* reviewed the album. "With such a fine array of artists to assist Ringo, one would question just how much he had to do towards the record, but from accounts he appears to have contributed a great deal." Ringo, however, was more honest in his appraisal of his role in making the album. At a press conference held after the album's release, he was asked, "Did you and Richard Perry do the mixing?" To which Starr replied: "Yes. Well, he is the producer and I just sit there and say, 'Well, I'd like the drums a bit louder.' I tend to say things like that, but he does the producing."

Ringo's most significant contribution was his ability to gather a stellar supporting cast around him. He'd repeat the process with his next album, albeit with less satisfying results. He would return to the concept fifteen years later with his All-Starr Band, which sustained the remainder of his solo career.

Most reviews highlighted the fact that *Ringo* was a collaborative effort. Like the American reviews, Peter Jones's review for *Record Mirror* concluded by alluding to the quality of the musical mates Starr called on to help make the album. "So good ole Ringo has delivered the goods again. He's no great shakes as a singer, but he has the personality to win through ... and the sort of mates who guarantee that there's always something happening in the instrumental background."

Ringo, the stalwart Beatle, the soul of the party Beatle, the easy-going Beatle, was another recurring trope. Reviewing the album for the *Village Voice*, Robert Ades summarised the consensus: "Ringo Starr finally begins to look like he's going to live up to his last name. It's not a masterpiece, but as Perry puts it: 'Ringo transcends music!' The funny-looking kid at the drums no doubt has learned that personality is his chief talent. And here that comes across better than anything Perry's done since Tiny Tim."

Perhaps more importantly, Ringo's fans liked the record. Teresa Slade liked it so much that she felt compelled to write to *Record Mirror* and share her delight with its readers. "I am sitting here, listening and absorbing the truly magical sounds of a man of the past, present, and future, in musical talents. Superb production, understanding and simply written words, mass vocal backing, and the most talented top stars ever combine to make Ringo the album of the year."

Having received largesse from his rock star buddies, Starr passed on the baton by helping the brother of Scottish singer Lulu. Her brother, Billy Lawrie, had recorded a version of 'Roll Over Beethoven' for Polydor in 1969. It wasn't a hit, and he remained silent until late '73 when he returned with a single and album for RCA. His return to recording was marked by the help of some celebrity friends, not the least of whom was Ringo Starr, who lived on the same road as Lulu and Maurice Gibb. *Record Mirror* reported that Starr wrote the first verse of 'Rock and Roller' with Lawrie at four in the morning, possibly during one of Ringo's house parties. The recording also featured Maggie Bell, Stone The Crows, and the Average White Band brass section. Pete Jones reviewed it for *Record Mirror* and liked it. It sounded like an outtake from the recent *Ringo* album crossed with something from the Lennon-produced Harry Nilsson album, and he suggested it had a chance at charting. It didn't.

Lawie's flop was evidence that not everything Starr touched turned to gold. Ringo's latest movie, *Son Of Dracula*, also flopped. But for every action, there is an equal and opposite reaction. When it came to property, he was in for a windfall. Having recently moved into the Lennons' Ascot estate, he'd put his Highgate mansion up for sale. Starr bought the property in 1969 for £70,000 (£969,625.52) and sold it four years later for £200,000. (£2,073,135.14) He'd sold at the right time. House prices in Britain peaked in October 1973, up 50.4%. Being a drummer, he knew that timing was everything. Starr received more good news one week after his *Ringo* album was released, it was awarded a gold disc by RIAA for sales of 1 million dollars.

A brace of John Lennon and Yoko Ono albums was released alongside Starr's album. Had the Lennons not been going through a creative and personal spat, they could have been released as a joint double album. They shared the same pool of musicians, the same production values, and similar themes. Lennon had participated in Ono's album, and Ono had participated in Lennon's. But despite the shared genus and similarities, the twain did not meet on this occasion. Ono's was the more political of the two records, focusing, as it does, on feminism. Lennon's album appeared less political but nevertheless featured 'Bring On the Lucie (Freda Peeple),' 'Mind Games,' and 'Nutopian International Anthem'. The latter is a jokey silent protest.

This time, Lennon and Ono sugar-coated their politics. The in-your-face Yippie-influenced, hard-driving rock of Elephant's Memory Band was replaced with something more sedate and sophisticated. Even mainstream industry-facing publications like *Cash Box* gave Ono's album a positive review. "A devastating collection of powerful music and meaningful lyrics spotlight Yoko's latest Apple LP, which may very well prove to be her biggest seller to date. ... A fine musical package, the LP speaks the praise of Yoko's arrangement, writing, and production." *Billboard* also liked what it heard. "Ms. Ono has produced not only her most commercial LP but her best with this often melodic set of tunes concerning women. From the subservience of her sex in 'Growing Pain' to women's development in 'Women Power'. Singing is excellent."

Ono may have forsworn avant-gardism for popularism, but she needed publicity if her album would be heard and bought by more than the already converted cognoscenti. Luckily, it was coming thick and fast. In Britain, the *Sunday Mirror* devoted an entire page to an exclusive interview with Ono. In it, she claimed that the separation from her husband was purely professional. "We have decided on two separate careers and are both now immersed in our own work," she said. "I am going to see if I can be a success without John, which is perhaps what I should have done from the start." She was right. Having created JohnandYoko, it would be challenging to reverse the process. Without Lennon, Ono's success would have always been limited. That had nothing to do with her ability, skill, intelligence, and everything to do with being a woman. Women who did make it in the arts were few and far between. It could be argued that they were successful because specific rich and powerful men in the film and music industry chose them and made them stars. It was, after all, primarily men who controlled the means of production.

If reviews for her album were anything to go on, the chances of Ono becoming a success on her own looked promising. The only stumbling block was her insistence on performing live. The *Mirror* reported that she was planning a European tour with the impresario Jimmy Vaughan. "Till now, I couldn't work away from the USA when I wanted to because of John. This seemed kind of unfair. There were several things I couldn't do then. Now they're possible. I will be coming to Europe and bringing a band with me. First, I'll tour Germany and Britain."

Ono had recently performed at Kenny's Castaways in New York to mixed reviews. Vicki Wickham reviewed one of Ono's New York performances for the *Melody Maker*. If it was anything to go by, Ono would need to fine-tune her stage act and take singing lessons before touring Europe. "The club's atmosphere is great but small, and the sound system from where I was sitting made it impossible to hear more than the occasional lyric. This was a great pity because lyrics, poetry and innovative topics is what Yoko is all about, and this was lost. Yoko is improving performance-wise. Her chat between numbers was unnecessarily macabre and not too relevant to 'entertainment' but her stage presence was fine. To sum-up. The evening was fine. But can Yoko sing? NO." Jim Melanson reviewed a show for *Billboard* and came to a similar conclusion. "As a music celebrity, Miss Ono definitely has the recognition others lack. But, whether it is deserved remains to be seen. If there was an unwitting victim in this performance, one had to wonder whether it was Miss Ono herself or the audience."

Since she began her relationship with Lennon, Ono had received acres of negative press coverage. Turning that around was a remarkable feat. But she would always be the sort of performer you either loved or hated. There was little middle ground for her to occupy, and this would always limit her appeal and chances of commercial success. She was an interesting conceptual and visual artist, but no Carly Simon, Aretha Franklin, or Barbara Streisand. Try as she might, she would always be the wife of John Lennon and, in musical if not artistic terms, perceived as the lesser talent.

Lennon's *Mind Games* album also received mixed reviews, which ran the gamut from fawning to disappointed. *Billboard's* review was the former. It claimed that *Mind Games* was: "The finest set put together by Lennon since *Imagine*, running the complete gamut of his talents as singer and songwriter from the hard rock of 'Tight A$' and 'Out the Blue' to beautiful acoustic material such as 'Intuition'. For those who thought this artist was running out of gas, the cohesiveness and skill in this LP should quickly change their minds."

Rolling Stone's Jon Landau disagreed. Although he thought *Mind Games* was a return to the form of *Plastic Ono Band*, as far as he was concerned, the lyrics lacked insight and passion. "Lennon has come up with his worst writing yet," he said. "With lines like, 'A million heads are better than one/So come on, get it on,' a listener can only accept or reject them. I've done the latter." He continued his review by saying: "*Mind Games* reveals another major artist of the Sixties lost in the changing social and musical environment of the Seventies, helplessly trying to impose his own gargantuan ego upon an audience that has already absorbed his insights and is now waiting hopefully for him to chart a new course."

Cash Box aligned itself with *Billboard*, claiming: "Genius is almost impossible to define, but somehow it's very easily recognizable, and it is genius that sparkles from each and every cut of John's latest LP. Highlighted by the hit single title track, the album bears the unmistakable stamp of one of the most influential pop superstars of all time." It also claimed that 'Nutopian International Anthem' was "introspective," which makes one wonder if the reviewer bothered to listen to the album or was trying to be funny. They gushed: "'Aisumasen (I'm Sorry),' and 'Tight A$' are particularly fine and underscore the consummate production and arrangement artistry so evident on each cut."

In Early November, Lennon arranged to have a television advert made to promote his *Mind Games* album on American television. The 30-second advert starts with 'Land Of Hope And Glory'; a door opens and reveals Tony King dressed as Queen Elizabeth II sitting on a throne holding a copy of the album. The idea originated with King, who had recorded himself impersonating the Queen. (There's an in-joke here that is not unlike the one about *Queen* magazine in the film *A Hard Day's Night*.) King played the recording for Lennon, who thought it hilarious. A few days later, Lennon informed King that he wanted to do a television commercial in which King played the role of HMQ. The advert was filmed in Santa Monica with Lennon, who can be heard snickering in the background, and Elton John in attendance. What middle America made of it is anyone's guess. Lennon, however, was proud of his handiwork. When he spoke with Andrew Tyler of the *NME*, he asked: "Did I tell you about the commercial we've done for the new album? Hah. It's great. We have the Queen plugging the record for us. It starts inside the house with a gate swinging open, over a red carpet, and then inside. It's all done in very good taste, Your Majesty. It's a friend of mine in drag, as it were. There's 'Land Of Hope And Glory' and someone says (in a plummy warbling voice) 'I've been asked to do this commercial. It relates to a gramophone record...' and it goes on like that. I'm hoping her Majesty will be able to laugh at it. A few vodkas and it was all over."

A week had passed since the last session for Lennon's oldies album. Despite the embarrassing drunken session that ended with Spector and his bodyguard securing Lennon with neckties, the boozy duo continued to paint the town red and cause trouble. On 7th November, they went to the Whiskey a Go Go to watch Bobby 'Blue' Bland in concert. This time, it was Spector who disgraced himself. Tired and emotional, he was reportedly thrown out of the venue for repeatedly heckling the support act. Two days later, Lennon's 'Mind Games' single was released in the UK, and to promote it, he gave a series of interviews to Nicky Horne of Capital Radio, Charlie Gillett of BBC Radio 1, and Walter Bachauer of RIAS Germany. Robert Hilburn of the *Los Angeles Times*, Patrick Snyder-Scumpy and Jack Breschard for *Crawdaddy*, Ivor Davis for the *Daily Express*, and Caroline Boucher for *Disc* also interviewed Lennon. During the interviews, Lennon revealed that he'd been writing songs and that some of his new material might end up on the album. Lennon may have been referring to 'Here We Go Again,' a song he'd written and made demo recordings of in October. When he recorded his demos, he had yet to finish the lyrics, which Spector helped him complete.

While most of the interviews went well, there were days when Lennon's abrasive side surfaced. When Patrick Snyder-Scumpy and Jack Breschard interviewed him, he appeared tetchy and eccentric. At one point in the interview, he used a ventriloquist's dummy, like Anthony Hopkins in the film *Magic*, to answer their questions. They had caught him on another bad day. If he wasn't suffering from a hangover, he was tormented by guilt. A letter he wrote to Derek Taylor, Apple's former press officer, from Lou Adler's house indicates his state of mind. Typically bizarre and full of Lennonisms, he wrote: "Yoko and me are in hell." If Lennon was in hell, it was partly his own making. Ono appeared far more stable. Unlike her husband, she controlled her life, career, and emotions. She was also still able to control her husband.

The slightest incident could bring out Lennon's inner demons. A seemingly innocent lunch date with David Cassidy was all it took for Lennon to be overcome with jealousy. He accused Pang of flirting with the heartthrob, of being a liar and a gold-digger. His angst and anger were only made worse by a telephone call with Ono, who, despite preparing to go on stage in New York, managed to stir things up between her husband and Pang. Ono knew her husband only too well. She could read him like a book and twist him around her little finger. A skilled puppet master, she continued to micro-manage him from afar. It was all too much for Pang, who recalled: "I didn't know what to do. I knew how complex and paranoid John was; I knew how complex and unpredictable Yoko could be. I was no match for either of them."

Publicly, Lennon was in denial. Speaking to Ivor Davis of the *Daily Express*, he said: "I'm not saying I'm not neurotic anymore, but I can handle it better, and I don't need to get ulcers and a heart attack. If I'm at a sad movie, I'll cry... women cry, but men are not supposed to show their emotions." Showing one's emotions is one thing; not being able to control them is another. In private, Lennon was acting like a spoilt toddler who needed validation from mummy otherwise he'd scream and scream and scream until he was sick. May Pang was stuck in the middle, an isolated victim to the left of her a radical feminist to the right.

News that the Lennons were no longer cohabiting reached the INS, which notified Leon Wildes, intimating that the separation may affect Lennon's application for permanent residence. If Lennon was no longer living with Ono, who had permanent residence status, there was no reason why he couldn't be deported. Their split was big news on both sides of the Atlantic. The *Evening Standard* published an article that offered conflicting evidence of their relationship status. According to the article, Ono claimed they were separated because of their engagements. It also claimed that Lennon was quoted as saying that there was no longer any serious relationship between them without offering a direct quote from him. Years later, Pang contended that one reason Lennon went back to Ono was because she'd persuaded him that it would help his deportation case if they were at least seen to be a happy, loving couple.

While Lennon was trying to sort out his life and record a new album, his former bandmates continued to rack up significant sales worldwide. *Billboard* reported that McCartney's *Red Rose Speedway* and Harrison's *Living in a Material World* had achieved gold record status in Australia with sales of over 550,000, making them instant gold records. *Cash Box* reported that Toshiba EMI Co., the Japanese branch of EMI, had published its accounts for the period 1st October 1972 to 30th September 1973 with total sales of 14,784,000,000 yen or $56,860,000 ($414,482,194.26), and profits before tax of 1,049,000,000 yen or $4,030,000 ($29,376,771.77). The increase in sales was attributed to The Beatles and George Harrison. Capitol Records executives were rubbing their hands in America, expecting another bumper Christmas. Phil Caston, national marketing director for Capitol, said: "It looks like it's going to be a blockbuster Christmas season for us. We have new product from Ringo Starr, Paul McCartney, John Lennon, Steve Miller and

The Band. Good sales are directly attributable to having good product and we're going to be very hot this Christmas."

Bumper Christmas or not, the future for record labels and music fans looked uncertain, with further price rises on the cards. The cost of long-playing records was forecast to increase, with Columbia Records the first of the majors to put up its prices from $6.98 ($50.88) to $7.98 ($58.17). For now, Capitol Records had no immediate plans to increase its prices. Although Starr's album had a higher retail price than comparable titles issued by Capitol, it stated that the higher list price of $6.98 was because of the booklet packaged along with the album. In Britain, prices for albums remained steady at around £2.50 (£47.00), with chain stores such as Comet discounting them to anything from £1.70 (£31.00) for the *McCartney* album to £1.95 for *Imagine*.

With *Band On The Run* finished McCartney's attention shifted to recruiting new members for Wings and recording more of Linda's songs for the much talked about Suzy and The Red Stripes album. McCartney had been watching a young Scots guitarist, Jimmy McCulloch. He had been a member of the band Thunderclap Newman, who scored a UK number 1 hit with the Pete Townshend produced 'Something in the Air'. After Thunderclap Newman disbanded, he drifted in and out of several bands before joining Stone The Crows in 1972. The guitarist lived close to Wings roadie Ian Horne, who told McCulloch that McCartney was looking for a new guitarist and that his name was on the list. McCulloch, however, was already under contract to Robert Stigwood, which would create complications later. But for now, he was free to record with Wings and was invited to join the band on a trip to Paris to work on a batch of Linda McCartney songs. They were joined by drummer Davy Lutton, who had been in Eire Apparent with Henry McCullough. His stint with Wings was brief, and rather than join McCartney, he decided to join T. Rex, staying with them until 1976.

The latest incarnation of Wings arrived in Paris on either the 13th or 20th of November – sources differ. However, contemporary reports state that The Osmonds were booked into the George V at the same time as Wings and that the two groups met. Wings decamped to the George V Hotel on the Champs-Elysées, with the McCartneys occupying three rooms at this luxury hotel. Once everybody had settled in, Wings set off for Pathe Marconi studios in Boulogne-Billancourt (near Paris). Wings might have arrived at the studio on time, but their equipment was held up at customs, forcing them to borrow equipment from Les Variations before starting work at approximately 12:45 am Thursday morning on Linda's 'Wide Prairie'. The rest of Thursday was spent recovering from the previous night's recording session. In the early evening,

McCartney was interviewed by *Paris Match & Francais* before Wings returned to Pathe Marconi studios to record Linda's 'I Got Up'. Also recorded during this brief visit to Paris was the instrumental 'Zoo Gang' and 'Luxi,' a jingle for Radio Luxembourg. 'Zoo Gang' was recorded as part of McCartney's recent publishing deal with ATV, which included an agreement from McCartney to write the theme music for the ATV series. The television series was screened from April to May of the following year. 'Luxi' featured a vocal from Laine that consisted of 'I heard it on Luxi,' with Paul and Linda McCartney calling out song titles for the soon-to-be-released *Band On The Run* album. Sounding like a cross between the Glitter Band and Sweet, it is about one and a half minutes too long for a jingle, and it's unclear whether the station used it.

Meanwhile, Lennon continued to enjoy LA's nightlife. On the 21st, he and Harry Nilsson attended Anne Murray's Thanksgiving party at the Troubadour. Like the Rainbow Bar and Grill, it quickly became his preferred venue of choice. Mingling with Helen Reddy, Neil Diamond, Mickey Dolenz, and Alice Cooper, he enjoyed a turkey dinner and several glasses of wine. The following week, on 28th November, Lennon, Spector, and assorted musicians returned to A&M Studios to continue work on the oldies album. Remarkably, Spector coaxed a usable rendition of 'To Know Her Is To Love Her' from the assembled drunken rabble of session players, and Lennon delivered a respectable vocal. While the recording went as planned, the session ended with two guests, Harry Nilsson, and Keith Moon, urinating on the recording console. This was the final straw for the owners of A&M studios. Lennon may have started as a VIP, but having guests pee on expensive recording equipment ensured he was no longer welcome. As Spector was theoretically in charge of every aspect of the recording sessions, he was responsible for the damage. Lennon wrote a note explaining the culprits and who should pay for the repair. "Phil, Should you not know, it was Harry and Keith who pissed on the console! Tell Jerry to bill Capitol for the damage, if any? I can't be expected to mind adult rock stars, nor can May. Besides, she works for me, not A&M. 'I'm about to piss off to Record Plant because of this crap."

Lennon was back at the Troubadour two days later with Elton John. They had gone to watch Dr. John, who had recently played on a Lennon session. Towards the end of the show, Lennon and John joined the Doctor on stage for two songs, 'Cold, Cold, Cold' and 'Mama Don't Know'. The *Los Angeles Free Press* was on hand to review the event: "Speaking of the Troubadour, I stopped by last Friday night to catch Dr. John's set one more time, and I (and the rest of the audience) received an unexpected treat. For both the second and third shows that evening, a few of Dr. John's friends stopped by to jam. The results were far from together, but the energy and excitement made for one of the most fun rock and roll parties I have ever stumbled upon. The 'friends' who played during the second set were John Lennon, Elton John, and Bobby Womack. Those dropping in for the third set were Cher, Joni Mitchell, and Bonnie Bramlett."

While Lennon was jamming with Dr. John, Paul McCartney, and Wings released their new album *Band On The Run* in Britain. Unlike previous releases, it received mostly positive reviews. Peter Harvey wrote a lengthy and somewhat rambling review in the form of a letter for *Record Mirror* that once again referenced The Beatles. There was no escaping the Fabs' long shadow. "Dear Paul (Linda and Denny too), Felt I had to write and tell you how much your new elpee sounds like that old group you used to play with, The Beatles. I know it's all in the past now and perhaps you'd all much rather forget your identity, but honest, there isn't a track that doesn't send me into a shiver of nostalgia for those Fab Four days. I've got a sneaky feeling that you Paul had an inkling of this when you returned from making the album in Nigeria. Still, down to the music. That was what I really wanted to congratulate you on. The songs are as good as anything you have written and much more thoughtful than those on your last album."

Reviewing the album for the *NME*, Charles Shaar Murray wrote: "The ex-Beatle least likely to re-establish his credibility and lead the field has pulled it off with a positive masterstroke of an album entitled *Band On The Run. Band On The Run* is a great album. If anybody ever puts down McCartney in your presence, bust him in the snoot and play him this. He will thank you for it afterwards." *Disc* gave the album a four-star review and highlighted McCartney's continuing development of his own individual sound. "On the whole this is a superb album. There are flashes of that McCartney magic, and I prefer this even to *Red Rose Speedway*. Paul says it was fun to make – and it's fun to listen to. An outstanding album, with a lot more of Paul's individual sound than his previous albums have had – and for my money there can't be enough."

Jon Landau wrote a lengthy review for *Rolling Stone* that praised the album: "*Band On The Run* finds McCartney walking a middle ground between autobiographical songwriting and subtle attempts to mythologize his own experience through the creation of a fantasy world of adventure — perhaps remotely inspired by his having recently written 'Live and Let Die'. He does it by uniting the myth of the rock star and the outlaw, the original legendary figure on the run. I'm surprised I like *Band On The Run* so much more than McCartney's other solo albums because, superficially, it doesn't seem so different from them. Its superiority derives from a subtle shifting and rearrangement of elements running through all of his post-Beatles music, a rounding out of ideas that had previously been allowed to stand half-baked, often embarrassingly so. *Band On The Run* is no collection of song fragments (*McCartney, Ram*), nor a collection of mediocre and directionless songs (*Wild Life, Red Rose Speedway*). *Band On The Run* is a carefully composed, intricately designed personal statement that will make it impossible for anyone to classify Paul McCartney as a mere stylist again."

Robert Hilburn reviewed the album alongside Lennon's *Mind Games* for the *Los Angeles Times* and was one of the few reviewers who wasn't impressed. "Unlike some artists whose records seem to improve with repeated listenings (i.e. The Rolling Stones), McCartney's albums normally offer all their strengths initially. Thus, time has not led me to think any better of McCartney's *Ram*, *Wild Life* and *Red Rose Speedway* than I did in my original moments of disappointment. For some reason, I can predict rather easily that *Band On The Run* won't be remembered as anything more than a slight return in a what has been a steady declining artistic barometer for McCartney. But it is, however slight, an upturn, the first since he began his solo career. *Band On The Run* isn't a good enough album to live up to the old expectations we had about McCartney but it may well be the most consistent album, particularly in craftsmanship contained in some highly effective mood pieces. As in Lennon's album, the lyrics are less important than the performance, but there is far more control and discipline here than in McCartney's other solo works. If he could only find something fresh to write about, he might be on his way again." Also released around this time was a cover version of 'One More Kiss' by MIM. Released on the Bradley's Record label, it flopped.

WEEK ENDING 3 NOVEMBER 1973
1. MIDNIGHT TRAIN TO GEORGIA: GLADYS KNIGHT AND THE PIPS
2. ANGIE: THE ROLLING STONES
3. KEEP ON TRUCKIN' (PART 1): EDDIE KENDRICKS
4. HALF-BREED: CHER
5. PAPER ROSES: MARIE OSMOND
6. HEARTBEAT - IT'S A LOVEBEAT: THE DEFRANCO FAMILY FEATURING
   TONY DEFRANCO
7. RAMBLIN MAN: THE ALLMAN BROTHERS BAND
8. LET'S GET IT ON: MARVIN GAYE
9. SPACE RACE: BILLY PRESTON
10. ALL I KNOW: ART GARFUNKEL

WEEK ENDING 10 NOVEMBER 1973
1. KEEP ON TRUCKIN' (PART 1): EDDIE KENDRICKS
2. MIDNIGHT TRAIN TO GEORGIA: GLADYS KNIGHT AND THE PIPS
3. ANGIE: THE ROLLING STONES
4. HEARTBEAT - IT'S A LOVEBEAT: THE DEFRANCO FAMILY FEATURING
   TONY DEFRANCO
5. PAPER ROSES: MARIE OSMOND
6. PHOTOGRAPH: RINGO STARR
7. SPACE RACE: BILLY PRESTON
8. HALF-BREED: CHER
9. ALL I KNOW: ART GARFUNKEL
10. TOP OF THE WORLD: CARPENTERS

WEEK ENDING 17 NOVEMBER 1973
1. KEEP ON TRUCKIN' (PART 1): EDDIE KENDRICKS
2. MIDNIGHT TRAIN TO GEORGIA: GLADYS KNIGHT AND THE PIPS
3. HEARTBEAT - IT'S A LOVEBEAT: THE DEFRANCO FAMILY FEATURING
   TONY DEFRANCO
4. PHOTOGRAPH: RINGO STARR
5. SPACE RACE: BILLY PRESTON
6. PAPER ROSES: MARIE OSMOND
7. TOP OF THE WORLD: CARPENTERS
8. ANGIE: THE ROLLING STONES
9. JUST YOU 'N' ME: CHICAGO
10. I GOT A NAME: JIM CROCE

WEEK ENDING 24 NOVEMBER 1973
1. PHOTOGRAPH: RINGO STARR
2. KEEP ON TRUCKIN' (PART 1): EDDIE KENDRICKS
3. TOP OF THE WORLD: CARPENTERS
4. SPACE RACE: BILLY PRESTON
5. HEARTBEAT - IT'S A LOVEBEAT: THE DEFRANCO FAMILY FEATURING
   TONY DEFRANCO
6. MIDNIGHT TRAIN TO GEORGIA: GLADYS KNIGHT AND THE PIPS
7. JUST YOU 'N' ME: CHICAGO
8. PAPER ROSES: MARIE OSMOND
9. GOODBYE YELLOW BRICK ROAD: ELTON JOHN
10. THE LOVE I LOST (PART 1): HAROLD MELVIN AND THE BLUE NOTES

WEEK ENDING 3 NOVEMBER 1973
1. DAYDREAMER/PUPPY SONG: DAVID CASSIDY
2. EYE LEVEL: SIMON PARK ORCHESTRA
3. SORROW: DAVID BOWIE
4. LET ME IN: THE OSMONDS
5. CAROLINE: STATUS QUO
6. GOODBYE YELLOW BRICK ROAD: ELTON JOHN
7. GHETTO CHILD: DETROIT SPINNERS
8. MY FRIEND STAN: SLADE
9. TOP OF THE WORLD: THE CARPENTERS
10. FOR THE GOOD TIMES: PERRY COMO

WEEK ENDING 10 NOVEMBER 1973
1. DAYDREAMER/PUPPY SONG: DAVID CASSIDY
2. LET ME IN: THE OSMONDS
3. SORROW: DAVID BOWIE
4. DYNA-MITE: MUD
5. TOP OF THE WORLD: THE CARPENTERS
6. EYE LEVEL: SIMON PARK ORCHESTRA
7. CAROLINE: STATUS QUO
8. GHETTO CHILD: DETROIT SPINNERS
9. FOR THE GOOD TIMES: PERRY COMO
10. GOODBYE YELLOW BRICK ROAD: ELTON JOHN

WEEK ENDING 17 NOVEMBER 1973
1. I LOVE YOU LOVE ME LOVE: GARY GLITTER
2. LET ME IN: THE OSMONDS
3. DAYDREAMER/PUPPY SONG: DAVID CASSIDY
4. SORROW: DAVID BOWIE
5. DYNA-MITE: MUD
6. WHEN I FALL IN LOVE: DONNY OSMOND
7. TOP OF THE WORLD: THE CARPENTERS
8. PHOTOGRAPH: RINGO STARR
9. DO YOU WANNA DANCE?: BARRY BLUE
10. GHETTO CHILD: DETROIT SPINNERS

WEEK ENDING 24 NOVEMBER 1973
1. I LOVE YOU LOVE ME LOVE: GARY GLITTER
2. LET ME IN: THE OSMONDS
3. PAPER ROSES: MARIE OSMOND
4. DYNA-MITE: MUD
5. SORROW: DAVID BOWIE
6. WHEN I FALL IN LOVE: DONNY OSMOND
7. DO YOU WANNA DANCE?: BARRY BLUE
8. MY COO-CA-CHOO: ALVIN STARDUST
9. TOP OF THE WORLD: THE CARPENTERS
10. PHOTOGRAPH: RINGO STARR

CHAPTER 12
DECEMBER: WELCOME TO THE
THREE DAY WEEK

As December dawned, a growing energy crisis enveloped the world. Twelve days before Christmas, Prime Minister Edward Heath announced that from midnight on 31st December, commercial consumption of electricity would be limited to three consecutive days each week. Come the New Year, Britain would be plunged into darkness and a three-day week. The situation was not as dire in America. But it, too, was experiencing an energy crisis. While America avoided power cuts and rationing, the crisis was such that Apple and Capitol Records decided to turn off Ringo Starr's flashing billboard on Sunset Strip. The billboard spelt out the letters of Ringo's name one by one, a little like Blackpool illuminations, but not as impressive. From late November, Ringo's billboard would only be illuminated from 4:30 p.m. to 1:00 a.m..

Ringo wasn't the only ex-Beatle effected by the crisis. The billboard for Paul McCartney and Wings *Band On The Run* LP was to have been illuminated. But to save electricity, phosphorescent glow-in-the-dark paint was used instead.

As dire as things were, Starr and McCartney could take solace from their new records. On 3rd December, Apple released Starr's latest single, 'Your Sixteen,' b/w 'Devil Woman'. Starr's previous single, 'Photograph,' was still riding high on the charts, as was his album, which would be awarded a gold record the following week. *Cash Box* reviewed 'You're Sixteen' saying: "Ringo is digging the '50s and you know what? This track is simply fantastic and perfect for the '70s. Not only is the vocal perfect and steady, for this delightful easy-going rocker, but the music is the perfect complement. And one Paul McCartney is featured on a mouth sax solo. Can't miss the top of the pops."

On the same day, Paul McCartney and Wings latest album *Band On The Run* was released in America. Unlike the British counterpart, it included the current hit single 'Helen Wheels'. *Billboard* began its review by focusing on 'Jet' "a song with strong overtones of The Beatles – more so than on any previous McCartney effort with a band. The vocal overdubs, the thumping drums and the solid guitar strumming, sparked with voice popping in and then disappearing, reminds one of the sophisticated kinds of tunes The Beatles created in the studio. This LP, cut in London and Lagos, is artistically an impressive work. McCartney and Linda team on the simple, innocuous tune, 'Bluebird' and their harmonic construction turns the tune into an infectious listening experience. There's an interesting sax solo but the musician isn't credited. 'Mrs. Vanderbilt' is another head-bobbing fun tune. Concern and care are the hallmarks of this outstanding package."

McCartney's package was outstanding, and such was demand that in just two days it racked up sales of $1 million and was awarded a gold disc. If creatively McCartney's solo releases had been considered disappointing, commercially, every album he'd released, either as Paul McCartney, Wings or Paul McCartney and Wings, had achieved gold record status in America. Two weeks after McCartney was awarded a gold disc for *Band On The Run*, Ringo Starr, received a gold disc for his *Ringo* album.

Not every release on the Apple label turned to gold. Available concurrently with these releases was Badfinger's *Ass* album. Its cover was telling. It showed a donkey chasing a distant carrot, which has been claimed to allude to the band's feeling that Apple had misled them. The album should have been released in September but was delayed until November because of problems with Apple over publishing and payment of mechanical licences. Apple was also late paying royalties to the band, which led to concerns about its ability to pay future royalties. Badfinger had already signed a new deal with Warner Brothers Records, and while Warner Brothers had issued a single 'Love Is Easy' in Britain, the delayed release of *Ass* caused the band's first album for their new label to be delayed too.

With the release of *Ass*, Apple Records stopped functioning as a bona fide record label. All existing acts signed to the label were let go, and Apple became little more than another artist-owned label putting out albums and singles by its owners. John Beland, who had signed to Apple Records only months earlier, recalls being informed that "everything at Apple was frozen". *Ass* peaked at 122 on the *Billboard* chart and a few years later could be found in deletion/cut-out bins in record stores across America. The album didn't sell because Apple/Capitol was focusing its attention on the solo Beatles releases. Apple Records didn't even have an American office, which meant there was no support. Having lost Badfinger to Warner Brothers, would they have spent money supporting a band that had moved to pastures new.

While activities relating to non-Beatle acts were put on ice, Lennon, McCartney, and Starr were full steam ahead. Back in Blighty, McCartney had given a round of interviews to the music weeklies before taking his family on holiday to Jamaica and, when news of his visa came through, America. When asked by *Melody Maker* about the lacklustre performance of 'Helen Wheels' on the British singles chart, McCartney pulled his usual trick and feigned indifference. "We don't have a policy on singles. We're a bit vague on all that," he claimed. "All we need is for someone to say, 'that'll make a good single,' and we bung it out. We're a bit haphazard. But they all seem to sell quite well."

Haphazard was one way to describe Wings' run of singles. They encompassed everything from political rants to children's nursery rhymes. Yet despite claiming he had no policy for single releases, McCartney did reveal that he kept a close eye on musical trends on both sides of the Atlantic. "The British market is a bit funny at the moment. I mean 'Eye Level' and next week, Gary Glitter or Donny Osmond. It's quite a big teenybopper market. Yet Gary, Dave Cassidy and the Osmonds don't do anything in America. And big acts here don't do well there."

The worst thing McCartney could do was try and compete with Gary Glitter or Donny Osmond. Nevertheless, the top three singles in the first week of December were by 'Glam Rockers', Slade, Garry Glitter and Alvin Stardust, all of whom had a big teenybopper following.

Record Mirror, *Disc* and *Sounds* published interviews with the McCartneys promoting Wings' new album in the following weeks. Denny Laine was conspicuous by his absence but was interviewed by *Disc* to promote his latest solo album, *Ah Laine*, and talk about the current state of Wings. He came across as depressed, discouraged and confirmed the inkling that had been circulating for some time, that he and his bandmates were little more than hired hands. "I'm kind of the odd job man in this group," he said. "I look on *Band On The Run* as definitely their album. We're not a group anymore. I'm one of the three, or I'm an individual. If it was Wings, I'd feel more part of it." If what Laine said is true, any semblance of band unity had gone with McCullough and Seiwell. That's if it had existed at all.

Disc also reported that Laine wasn't overjoyed with his new album and no longer felt 'part' of it. The departure of McCullough and Seiwell seems to have hit Laine hardest. His downbeat assessment of what Wings had become and the *Band On The Run* album was hardly a ringing endorsement for McCartney as a boss or Wings as a group. Nevertheless, whatever had brought about Laine's dark mood, he remained loyal to the McCartneys.

While McCartney and Starr were busy promoting their new records, Lennon resumed work on his *Back To Mono* album. Having been thrown out of A&M studios, on 3rd December sessions moved to the Record Plant. At this session, he'd record a new original composition that he'd alluded to in interviews given a few weeks earlier. 'Here We Go Again' was the only original song Lennon recorded during this time with Spector. Why he recorded it makes no sense. It wasn't a rock 'n' roll oldie and didn't fit the album's concept. Lennon claimed that he didn't like having songs in the archives, where 'Here We Go Again' would remain for the next thirteen years. Did he have other plans for it? Or did he record it to keep Spector happy and give the musicians something other than oldies to get their teeth into.

The music press on both sides of the Atlantic continued to review the *Mind Games* album. In Britain, Ray Coleman, writing in the 8th December issue of *Melody Maker*, claimed that comparisons with his previous albums were not valid because of the unpredictable nature of his solo career. He also remarked upon the effect America, or rather the American State machine, had on Lennon and his writing. "Battered by America's curious logic and sheer hard-heartedness seem[s] to have spurred him to write incisively, and the track 'Mind Games' is one that grows into a gem the more it is played." He continued: "Musically or melodically this may not be a stand-out album, but if you warm to the rasping voice of Lennon and, like me, regard him as the true fulcrum of much of what came from his old group, then like any new Lennon album, it will be enjoyable and even important."

Radio Luxembourg broadcast a telephone interview Lennon gave to Tony Prince the following day. Besides talking about his new album, the conversation covered the rumours about the state of the his marriage. As far as Prince, and possibly most people listening, was concerned the Lennons' marriage was made in heaven. When asked if he could clarify the situation, Lennon toed the line and preserved the narrative he'd been propagating for the last four years. The rumours were unfounded, and any speculation about his relationship with Pang was false. "We have a couple of people working for us, and some of them are male and some of them are female. There are a couple of females and a couple of males and May happens to know about copyright and she handles the copyright situation. So, I was given May and Yoko was given John and Nadya. I've got May and Mal, the old Beatles road manager and so, when I'm being seen around, it looks like I'm going dancing, or something."

Lennon's account contradicted Ono's. She, at least, was more open. Previously, the Lennons had shared a narrative because it was important to them. It was a story they wanted to share with the world. Whether it was as part of their peace campaign or creating the myth of JohnandYoko, they were two people, one mind. That had changed. So, too, had the stories. A week after Lennon's interview with Tony Prince, the *Sunday People* published an article titled 'Lennon and Yoko Part'. In the article by Joylon Wilde, Ono is quoted as saying: "It could be we loved too much. Maybe we spent too much time together. In many ways, ours was an unnatural relationship." She went on to say: "This way is better. We're both having a rest from one another, and we're not at each other's throats." It was clear that they both needed a break and their own space. Although their relationship hadn't completely broken down, it would need a lot of work to make it good again. Ono said they moved into the Dakota because it gave them more personal space, but it hadn't worked out. "I guess we've reached a point in our lives when we need to be away from each other completely. It may be temporary, or it may be… who knows. But whatever happens, it will be for the best." Whatever was happening to the Lennons, they were no longer in a simpatico relationship. If anything, Lennon was in denial, while Ono had at least accepted the situation.

With or without Ono, Lennon's life wasn't getting any better. His marriage was on the rocks, and his deportation case was very much on his mind, so much so that he used his interview with Tony Prince to ask the Queen for a pardon. Lennon was asked if he wanted his MBE back, to which he replied: "No, I want a pardon for being bust in England. That's the cause of the whole problem, the whole immigration problem. So listen, Her Majesty, I think I've done more good for Britain than harm. Will you just give me a nice pardon, okay, and then I can just travel around again?" By the following year the campaign to get Lennon a royal pardon began to gather some momentum. The following January, the *NME* ran an article, 'Please, your Majesty, can our John have a Free pardon?'. Besides pleading Lennon's case, the main thrust of the piece was an interview with Andrew Tyler in which Lennon restated his claim that a bent copper framed him, that he was followed and had his telephone tapped by the FBI. He asked again for a pardon from the Queen and promoted his new album. "I was thinking of writing to the Queen, you know. I hope she reads *NME*. Yeah. I was after a pardon for being planted by the cops and being hassled for three years and everything that happened. That's one way to solve the problem. That so-called bust I was involved in has left me with a criminal record. That's the legal reason they're trying to throw me out. If that was taken away, there'd be nothing they could do. And now the real answer is for me to get a pardon… but because I'm a naughty boy, I don't suppose they want to give me one."

He was right; the chances of the Queen granting him a pardon were non-existent. The last royal pardon to be granted had been eighty-nine years earlier, in 1884. It wouldn't have worked anyway. Free pardons only release a person from the effect of a penalty or a consequence of a sentence; they do not overturn the conviction, which remains after the pardon. In the eyes of the law, Lennon's status would have remained unchanged. Nevertheless, it was a nice try and got Lennon some publicity.

Publicity wasn't a problem. Lennon, McCartney, and Starr were still big news for national and local newspapers alike. Local newspapers on both sides of the Atlantic published reviews of their latest albums. Jack Lloyd gave the Ringo album a positive review in the *Philadelphia Inquirer* but singled out Richard Perry for assembling the right people and material. While he considered the album a gem and Ringo the real star, he thought the drummer was riding on the coattails of "far more talented people". Writing in the *Miami Herald*, David Marsh asked how much of the energy and excitement generated on the album was substantial. He concluded, "I have a bleak feeling that the *Ringo* album is too good to be true." In the *Los Angeles Times*, Robert Hilburn was given an entire page to review *Band On The Run* and *Mind Games*. Under the headline 'John and Paul: Artistic Barometer Is Up', he compared the albums with Lennon's coming out on top. "A rating on the albums? Lennon, even with some problems, YES. McCartney, even with the encouraging signs, MAYBE."

In Britain, local newspapers echoed many of the themes discussed by their American counterparts. The *Cambridge Evening News* ran a review of all three solo Beatles albums by John Kelleher in which he wrote, "How does one choose when faced with three first-class albums – unless one can afford them all?" It was a problem that many Beatles fans faced. But Kelleher was on hand to offer advice and concluded that Ringo's was the most heralded of the three, Lennon's the most serious, and McCartney's was the trump card in the pack. "Not much he's done so far since the split has pleased everyone – this time around he seems to have struck a fine balance between raw power and charming melody and he might have done the trick."

Not all reviews were as positive. Readers of the *Torquay Herald Express* may have been discouraged from purchasing a copy of *Ringo*. Far from being heralded, the review began: "*Ringo* is a competent drummer and singer, but I'm afraid he lacks drive that could have made this album great." Neither heralded nor great, it was, instead, disappointing: "With such a star-studded credit list including the three other ex-Beatles, Marc Bolan, Billy Preston and Klaus Voorman, the sleeve is more interesting than the music!"

Good, bad or indifferent, reviews made little difference to sales. In the second week of December, Lennon, McCartney and Starr had albums in the top fifty. *Band On The Run* had entered the UK albums chart at number 45 and was facing some stiff competition, not least from his old band and bandmates. The Beatles *1962 – 66* was up eight places at number 24, *1967 – 70* was up fourteen places at number 22, *Ringo* was at number 16 down from number 9 – and *Mind Games* was at number 13, up thirty-one places. The ex-fabs were also up against Roxy Music, David Bowie (three albums in the top fifty), Black Sabbath, The Who, Elton John, The Carpenters, Slade, Pink Floyd and Max Bygraves – yes, that Max Bygraves – who also had three albums in the top fifty.

In Los Angeles, Lennon continued to work on his *Back To Mono* sessions, albeit spasmodically. On Monday, 10th December, Lennon, Spector, and their drunken crew of session players were booked into the Record Plant. However, the session was cancelled. The session was rebooked for the following night when the most alarming incident occurred. Everything was proceeding as normal, or what was considered normal for these sessions. Lennon recorded the Chuck Berry song 'You Can't Catch Me' and listened to a playback with Spector's mother, Pang and Mal Evans. However, things quickly got out of hand. As usual, Lennon and Spector were drunk and decided to take a break with Evans in the studio's Las Vegas room. Lennon thought jumping on Evans for a piggyback ride would be fun, just as he had the best part of a decade earlier.

Evans was a big man but not as fit as he once was. Spector joined in. Poor old Mal had two fully grown, drunk men to bear. Recalling what happened next, Evans said: "Phil goes a little too far, he karate chopped me on the nose, my spectacles went flying, and I got tears in my eyes I can tell you. I turned around in a real temper and told Phil, 'Don't ever lay another finger on me, man.'" Spector then pulled out his handgun and fired a shot right under Evans' and Lennon's noses. The report could be heard in the control room. Pang heard the shot and ran into the green room, where Evans and John stared at Phil. As Pang recalled: "John rubbed his ears. Finally, he said sternly, 'Listen, Phil, if you're goin' to kill me, kill me. But don't fuck with me ears. I need 'em.'"

Any sober person who had a pistol pulled on them, even if the person with the gun was their producer, would have sacked them and employed a more stable individual to make their record. Unbelievably, Spector wasn't sacked, and sessions picked up again on the Friday when Lennon recorded 'My Baby Left Me'. Once again, the session descended into drunken horseplay with Lennon and Spector chasing one another around the control room; this time, Spector's weapon of choice was cake rather than a pistol. Oh, how the studio owners must have loved hosting these sessions. If it wasn't urine on the recording consul, it was cake trampled into the carpets. Not that Lennon cared. He could afford it more than most. His latest album, *Mind Games*, was certified a million-dollar seller by the RIAA based on its first four weeks of sales.

Lennon and Spector took a two-week break from recording, with sessions starting again on 29th December at Gold Star Recording Studios for a playback session. The sessions over, Spector disappeared into the night, taking the tapes with him. Lennon never saw the maverick producer again and would have to wait months before retrieving the recordings.

Like Lennon, Starr was awarded a gold record for his album *Ringo*, which he could add to his growing collection, which included a recent gold disc for his single 'Photograph'. Despite solid sales, overall record and tape sales were hit by increased costs, inflation, and wage stagnation. *Billboard* noted a slackening interest in cassette sales, but 8-track tapes were still selling well. LP sales remained steady, but price increases had "turned off the consumer". John Cohen, president of Cleveland- based Disc Records, suggested that: "The kids pick up *Ringo*, look at the change in list and even with our discount, walk out without it; probably asking themselves why a John Lennon bears a suggested list of $5.98 and Ringo's album is $1.00 more." The answer was that *Ringo* had a gatefold sleeve and a book; *Mind Games* didn't. Someone had to pay for the extra packaging, and, as always, the consumer picked up the tab. However, Ben Karol, a partner in King Karol, a record store in New York, saw things differently: "If somebody wants to buy the Ringo Starr album badly enough, then they will, whether it's four, five or $6.98." Karol did state that albums with an increased list price of $1.00 or more might be losing "around 25 per cent" over-all sales from those consumers who opted for a standard-priced album in its place. But as he pointed out, if kids wanted the *Ringo* album, they'd buy it, whatever it cost. And with plenty of discount stores to choose from, provided they didn't mind shopping around, the chances were that they could pick up a copy for less than its recommended list price.

Records weren't the only thing Starr was selling. He had been busy making a success of his furniture and interior design company ROR. The company was formed in 1968 with Robin Cruikshank when Cruikshank's company, Robin Ltd., aligned itself with The Beatles' Apple Corps. Cruikshank had generated quite a reputation for himself and had designed furniture for Starr's house in north-west London. In 1971, Starr appeared on the BBC children's television programme *Blue Peter* to discuss his furniture designs and promote an exhibition of ROR's work at Liberty of London. ROR had some high-profile clients, including a $10 million contract to design the interior of the Mushrif Palace in Abu Dhabi and to furnish Prime Minister Edward Heath's private rooms at 10 Downing Street, London. "We have been designing furniture for Mr Heath for quite some time," explained Cruikshank. As a token of his appreciation, Starr designed a unique one-of-a-kind mirror and gifted it to Heath. "Ringo designed the mirror and gave it to Mr Heath as a present. I rather think he likes it", said Cruikshank. ROR also designed a mirror for Harry Nilsson's bathroom. It featured two etched glass mirrors, one of an oak tree and the other of a hangman's noose. It disturbed the singer so much that he asked for it to be replaced.

Although McCartney was on holiday with his family, he could still appear on British television thanks to videotape. Before they left for the warmth of Jamaica, Paul and Linda recorded an episode of *Disney Time* for broadcast by the BBC on Boxing Day. *Disney Time* was an annual celebration of all things Disney that ran between 1961 and 1998. It was a regular holiday schedule filler that promoted Disney films presented by a celebrity host. McCartney is a big fan of animated films and had produced an animated-live action film of Wings' recent European tour. Appearing on *Disney Time* was all good light entertainment fun intended for children, most of whom didn't have the faintest idea who he was. All they were interested in was watching clips from their favourite Disney films. Sandwiched between *Holiday On Ice* and *Casino Royalle*, the McCartneys' presentation skills were somewhat wooden, according to one reviewer. The *Coventry Evening Telegraph* said: "Paul McCartney and his missus gave the latter programme a novelty touch by saying their lines without moving their lips or changing their lugubrious expression." Praise indeed.

While McCartney was doing his best to come across as clean and wholesome, Denny Laine received some unwanted publicity when he appeared before the beak for possession of cannabis. On 19th December, Laine and his girlfriend, Joanne Patrie, were fined £100 for possession of cannabis at London's Marlborough Street court. Laine claimed that a fan had given him the cannabis. Well, if it worked for McCartney. Laine and Patrie had been targets of police stop and search while in Hyde Park, and the drug was found in Miss Patrie's jeans. The fine and conviction for possession of cannabis would make it difficult for Laine to obtain an American visa. When one door opens, another closes. But there was better news for McCartney.

Despite his several convictions for possession of cannabis, McCartney had been granted a visa to enter America. If nothing else, it exposed the INS's hypocritical attempt to deport Lennon, who had two fewer convictions than McCartney. A few days after arriving in America, McCartney gave an interview saying: "We were visiting Jamaica for the holidays when news came through we'd got our visa. So we came here to visit with the Eastmans, Linda's folk. And we should be O.K. on other visits as long as we keep our noses clean, as they call it" McCartney was out of the country and probably would have been unaware that Laine hadn't kept his nose clean or that there were renewed visa problems on the horizon. He did, however, outline his plans for the following year, which included a spring tour of America. Thanks to Laine that would have to be postponed. "We got to put a band together first," he explained, "do a few other things, and then we can come on tour."

Those other things included recording an album with his brother, Mike, and work on Linda's Suzy and The Red Stripes project. Asked about a Beatles reunion, his usually relaxed public persona slipped, revealing displeasure and annoyance: "Let's get this thing straight. We have broken up as a band. As far as a reunion, no one is holding us apart. The idea is not to get together as The Beatles ever again. But looking forward, as soon as our business matters settled, I'd like to see us work together on a loose basis, and I think we will."

The prospects of a Beatles reunion had not abated. The tiresome question, "Will The Beatles reform," continued to dog them whenever they were interviewed. A few days later, a quote by Lennon, taken from his interview with Robert Hilburn for the *Los Angeles Times*, was picked up by the news wire services and widely reported. Asked about the possibility of a reunion, Lennon told Hilburn, "Well, it's possible."

WEEK ENDING 1 DECEMBER 1973
1. TOP OF THE WORLD: CARPENTERS
2. PHOTOGRAPH: RINGO STARR
3. GOODBYE YELLOW BRICK ROAD: ELTON JOHN
4. SPACE RACE: BILLY PRESTON
5. KEEP ON TRUCKIN' (PART 1): EDDIE KENDRICKS
6. JUST YOU 'N' ME: CHICAGO
7. MIDNIGHT TRAIN TO GEORGIA: GLADYS KNIGHT AND THE PIPS
8. THE LOVE I LOST (PART 1): HAROLD MELVIN AND THE BLUE NOTES
9. HEARTBEAT - IT'S A LOVEBEAT: THE DEFRANCO FAMILY
    FEATURING TONY DEFRANCO
10. THE MOST BEAUTIFUL GIRL: CHARLIE RICH

WEEK ENDING 8 DECEMBER 1973
1. TOP OF THE WORLD: CARPENTERS
2. GOODBYE YELLOW BRICK ROAD: ELTON JOHN
3. THE MOST BEAUTIFUL GIRL: CHARLIE RICH
4. JUST YOU 'N' ME: CHICAGO
5. PHOTOGRAPH: RINGO STARR
6. SPACE RACE: BILLY PRESTON
7. THE LOVE I LOST (PART 1): HAROLD MELVIN AND THE BLUE NOTES
8. HELLO IT'S ME: TODD RUNDGREN
9. KEEP ON TRUCKIN' (PART 1): EDDIE KENDRICKS
10. LEAVE ME ALONE (RUBY RED DRESS): HELEN REDDY

WEEK ENDING 15 DECEMBER 1973
1. THE MOST BEAUTIFUL GIRL: CHARLIE RICH
2. GOODBYE YELLOW BRICK ROAD: ELTON JOHN
3. TOP OF THE WORLD: CARPENTERS
4. JUST YOU 'N' ME: CHICAGO
5. TIME IN A BOTTLE: JIM CROCE
6. HELLO IT'S ME: TODD RUNDGREN
7. LEAVE ME ALONE (RUBY RED DRESS): HELEN REDDY
8. PHOTOGRAPH: RINGO STARR
9. THE JOKER: THE STEVE MILLER BAND
10. IF YOU'RE READY (COME GO WITH ME): THE STAPLE SINGERS

WEEK ENDING 22 DECEMBER 1973
1. THE MOST BEAUTIFUL GIRL: CHARLIE RICH
2. GOODBYE YELLOW BRICK ROAD: ELTON JOHN
3. TIME IN A BOTTLE: JIM CROCE
4. LEAVE ME ALONE (RUBY RED DRESS): HELEN REDDY
5. HELLO IT'S ME: TODD RUNDGREN
6. THE JOKER: THE STEVE MILLER BAND
7. TOP OF THE WORLD: CARPENTERS
8. JUST YOU 'N' ME: CHICAGO
9. IF YOU'RE READY (COME GO WITH ME): THE STAPLE SINGERS
10. NEVER, NEVER GONNA GIVE YA UP: BARRY WHITE

WEEK ENDING 29 DECEMBER 1973
1. TIME IN A BOTTLE: JIM CROCE
2. THE MOST BEAUTIFUL GIRL: CHARLIE RICH
3. LEAVE ME ALONE (RUBY RED DRESS): HELEN REDDY
4. THE JOKER: THE STEVE MILLER BAND
5. GOODBYE YELLOW BRICK ROAD: ELTON JOHN
6. HELLO IT'S ME: TODD RUNDGREN
7. TOP OF THE WORLD: CARPENTERS

8. SHOW AND TELL: AL WILSON
9. SMOKIN' IN THE BOY'S ROOM: BROWNSVILLE STATION
10. NEVER, NEVER GONNA GIVE YA UP: BARRY WHITE

UK

WEEK ENDING 1 DECEMBER 1973
1. I LOVE YOU LOVE ME LOVE: GARY GLITTER
2. MY COO-CA-CHOO: ALVIN STARDUST
3. PAPER ROSES: MARIE OSMOND
4. WHEN I FALL IN LOVE: DONNY OSMOND
5. DYNA-MITE: MUD
6. WHY, OH WHY, OH WHY: GILBERT O'SULLIVAN
7. YOU WON'T FIND ANOTHER FOOL LIKE ME FT. LYN PAUL THE NEW SEEKERS
8. LAMPLIGHT: DAVID ESSEX
9. DO YOU WANNA DANCE?: BARRY BLUE
10. LET ME IN: THE OSMONDS

WEEK ENDING 8 DECEMBER 1973
1. I LOVE YOU LOVE ME LOVE: GARY GLITTER
2. PAPER ROSES: MARIE OSMOND
3. YOU WON'T FIND ANOTHER FOOL LIKE ME FT. LYN PAUL THE NEW SEEKERS
4. MY COO-CA-CHOO: ALVIN STARDUST
5. LET ME IN: THE OSMONDS
6. DYNA-MITE: MUD
7. LAMPLIGHT: DAVID ESSEX
8. ROLL AWAY THE STONE: MOTT THE HOOPLE
9. WHY, OH WHY, OH WHY: GILBERT O'SULLIVAN
10. DO YOU WANNA DANCE?: BARRY BLUE

WEEK ENDING 15 DECEMBER 1973
1. MERRY XMAS EVERYBODY: SLADE
2. I LOVE YOU LOVE ME LOVE: GARY GLITTER
3. MY COO-CA-CHOO: ALVIN STARDUST
4. YOU WON'T FIND ANOTHER FOOL LIKE ME FT. LYN PAUL THE NEW SEEKERS
5. PAPER ROSES: MARIE OSMOND
6. I WISH IT COULD BE CHRISTMAS EVERY DAY: WIZZARD
7. LAMPLIGHT: DAVID ESSEX
8. ROLL AWAY THE STONE: MOTT THE HOOPLE
9. STREET LIFE: ROXY MUSIC
10. WHY, OH WHY, OH WHY: GILBERT O'SULLIVAN

WEEK ENDING 22 DECEMBER 1973
1. MERRY XMAS EVERYBODY: SLADE
2. I LOVE YOU LOVE ME LOVE: GARY GLITTER
3. YOU WON'T FIND ANOTHER FOOL LIKE ME FT. LYN PAUL THE NEW SEEKERS
4. I WISH IT COULD BE CHRISTMAS EVERY DAY: WIZZARD
5. MY COO-CA-CHOO: ALVIN STARDUST
6. PAPER ROSES: MARIE OSMOND
7. THE SHOW MUST GO ON: LEO SAYER
8. LAMPLIGHT: DAVID ESSEX
9. ROLL AWAY THE STONE: MOTT THE HOOPLE
10. STREET LIFE: ROXY MUSIC

WEEK ENDING 29 DECEMBER 1973
1. MERRY XMAS EVERYBODY: SLADE
2. I LOVE YOU LOVE ME LOVE: GARY GLITTER
3. YOU WON'T FIND ANOTHER FOOL LIKE ME FT. LYN PAUL THE NEW SEEKERS
4. I WISH IT COULD BE CHRISTMAS EVERY DAY: WIZZARD
5. MY COO-CA-CHOO: ALVIN STARDUST
6. PAPER ROSES: MARIE OSMOND
7. THE SHOW MUST GO ON: LEO SAYER
8. LAMPLIGHT: DAVID ESSEX
9. ROLL AWAY THE STONE: MOTT THE HOOPLE
10. STREET LIFE: ROXY MUSIC

SELECT DISCOGRAPHY

UK SINGLES
23.03.73   'My Love' / 'The Mess'—Apple—R 5985
25.05.73   'Give Me Love (Give Me Peace On Earth)' / 'Miss O'Dell'—Apple—R 5988
01.06.73   'Live And Let Die' / 'I Lie Around'—Apple—R 5987
19.10.73   'Photograph' / 'Down And Out'—Apple—R 5992
26.10.73   'Helen Wheels' / 'Country Dreamer'—Apple— R 5993
15.11.73   'Mind Games' / 'Meat City'—Apple—R 5994

UK ALBUMS
19 04.73   1962-1966—Apple—PCSP 717
19 04.73   1967-1970—Apple—PCSP 718
03.05.73   Red Rose Speedway—Apple—PCTC 251
22.06.73   Living In The Material World—Apple—PAS 10006
06.11.73   Mind Games—Apple—PCS 7165
23.11.73   Ringo—Apple—PCTC 252
30.11.73   Band On The Run—Apple—PAS 10007

US SINGLES
09.04.73   'My Love' / 'The Mess'—Apple—1861
07.05.73   'Give Me Love (Give Me Peace On Earth)' / 'Miss O'Dell'—Apple—1862
18.06.73   'Live And Let Die' / 'I Lie Around'—Apple—1863
24.09.73   'Photograph' / 'Down And Out'—Apple—1865
12.11.73   'Helen Wheels' / 'Country Dreamer'—Apple—1869
29.10.73   'Mind Games' / 'Meat City'—Apple—1868
03.12.73   'You're Sixteen' / 'Down And Out'—Apple—1870

US ALBUMS
02.04.73   1962-1966—Apple—SKBO 3403
02.04.73   1967-1970—Apple—SKBO 3404
30.04.73   Red Rose Speedway—Apple—SMAL-3409
30.05.73   Living In The Material World—Apple—SMAS 3410
02.11.73   Mind Games Apple—Apple—SW 3414
02.11.73   Ringo—Apple—SWAL-3413
03.12.73   Band On The Run—Apple—SO-3415

SOURCES
NEWSPAPERS AND MAGAZINES

Austin American-Statesman, 6 July 1974
Beat Instrumental, September 1973
Beat Instrumental, October 1974
Billboard, 13 January 1973
Billboard 3 February 1973
Billboard 10 March 1973
Billboard, 21 April 1973
Billboard 5 May 1973
Billboard, 12 May 1973
Billboard, 2 June 1973
Billboard, 16 June 1973
Billboard, 30 June 1973
Billboard, 21 July 1973
Billboard, 11 August 1973
Billboard, 25 August 1973
Billboard, 29 September 1973
Billboard, 27 October 1973
Billboard, 3 November 1973
Billboard, 10 November 1973
Billboard, 17 November 1973
Billboard, 28 January 1978
Birmingham Post, 7 July 1973
Boston Globe, 5 May 1974
British GQ, 6 March 2021
Cash Box 3 March 1973
Cash Box, 14 April 1973
Cash Box 28 April 1973
Cash Box, 5 May 1973
Cash Box, 9 June 1973
Cash Box, 30 June 1973
Cash Box, 21 July 1973
Cash Box, 13 October 1973
Cash Box, 3 November 1973
Cash Box, 10 November 1973
Cash Box, 17 November 1973
Cash Box, 8 December 1973

Daily Express, 17 November 1973
Daily Mirror, 3 April 1973
Daily Mirror, 13 April 1973
Daily Mirror, 26 May 1973
Daily Mirror, 12 July 1973
Daily Mirror, 27 Nov 1973
Daily Mirror, 1 Dec 1973
Daily Mirror, 15 Apr 2009
Des Moines Tribune, 22 June 1974
Disc, 14 April 1973
Disc, 21 April 1973
Disc, 28 April 1973
Disc, 9 June 1973
Disc, 4 August 1973
Disc, 27 October 1973
Disc, 24 November 1973
Evening Post, 12 May 1973
Evening Standard, 1 August 1973
Fort Lauderdale News, 17 June 1974
Guardian, The, 18 May 1973
Harrow Observer, 11 May 1973
Herald Express, 2 October 1973
Independent, The, 7 December 2005
Lakeland Ledger, 19 May 1981
Liverpool Echo, 1 January 1973
Liverpool Echo, 22 May 1973
Liverpool Echo, 8 June 1973
Liverpool Echo, 28 June 1973
Liverpool Daily Post 4 April 1973

Liverpool Daily Post, 11 May 1973

Liverpool Daily, Post 19 May 1973

Los Angeles Free Press, 7 December 1973

Los Angeles Times, 5 June 1973

Los Angeles Times, 5 June 1973

Los Angeles Times, 16 December 1973

Melody Maker, 27 January 1973

Melody Maker 6 September 1975

Melody Maker 22 September 1973

Melody Maker, 3 November 1973

Melody Marker, 1 December 1973

Miami Herald, 22 May 1974

Music Week, 26 May 1973

Music Week, 21 July 1973

Newcastle upon Tyne Evening Chronicle, 18 July 1973

NME, 2 December 1972

NME, 28 April 1973

NME, 9 June 1973

NME, 9 June 1973

NME, 28 July 1973

NME, 22 September 1973

NME, 3 November 1973

NME, 19 January 1974

Newsday, 28 October 1973

Philadelphia Inquirer, The, 25 April 1973

Phonograph Record, April 1973

Player, October 2007

Record Mirror, January 6, 1973

Record Mirror, 7 April 1973

Record Mirror, 5 May 1973

Record Mirror, 29 May 1973

Record Mirror, 9 June 1973

Record Mirror, 16 June 1973

Record Mirror, 14 July 1973

Record Mirror, 21 July 1973

Record Mirror, 1 December 1973

Record Mirror, 15 December 1973

Record World, 7 April 1973

Record World, 2 June 1973

Record World, 6 October 1973

Record World, 13 October 1973

Record World, 3 November 1973

Record World, 17 November 1973

Rolling Stone 23 May 1974

Rolling Stone, 19 July 1973

Rolling Stone, 3 January 1974

Rolling Stone, 31 January 1974

Rolling Stone, 23 November 1977

San Bernardino County Sun, The, 22 September 1974

Shepherds Bush Gazette Hammersmith Post, 31 May 1973

Sounds, 2 December 1972

Sounds, 7 April 1973

Sunday Mirror, 11 Feb 1973

Sunday Mirror, 11 Nov 1973

Uncut, May 2012

Village Voice, The, 8 November 1973

Books

Badman, Keith, The Beatles After The Break-Up

Badman, Keith, The Beatles: Off The Record 2

Baker, Ginger, Hellraiser

Blaney, John, Brinsley Schwarz In Their Own Words

Boyd, Patti, Wonderful Tonight

Craske, Oliver, The Life And Music Of Ravi Shankar

Davies, Hunter, The John Lennon Letters

Doggett, Peter, You Never Give Me Your Money The Battle for the Soul of The Beatles

Emerick, Geoff, Here, There and Everywhere

Gambaccini, Paul, Paul McCartney In His Own Words

Goldman, Albert, The Lives Of John Lennon

Granados, Stefan, Those Were the Days – The Beatles Apple Organization

King, Tony, The Taste Maker

Kozinn, Allan and Sinclair, Adrian , The McCartney Legacy: Volume 1: 1969 – 73

Madinger, Chip and Raile, Scott, Lennonology

McGee, Garry, Band on the Run: A History of Paul McCartney and Wings

Miles, Barry, Many Years From Now

Robowsky, Mark, He's A Rebel Phil Spector: Rock & Roll's Legendary Producer

Shankar, Ravi, Raga Mala: The Autobiography of Ravi Shankar

Southall, Brian, Pop Goes to Court: Rock 'n' Pop's Greatest Court Battles

Spector, Ronnie with Waldron, Vince, Be My Baby

The Editors Of The Rolling Stone, The Ballad Of John And Yoko

Wiener, Jon, Gimme Some Truth The John Lennon FBI Files

Wildes, Leon, John Lennon vs. The USA

Womack, Kenneth, Living The Beatles Legend: On The Road With The Fab Four – The Mal Evans Story

Wood, Ronnie, Ronnie

OTHER SOURCES

Stuart Grundy and John Tobler, The Record Producers
FBI document White House 16 June 1973
BBC Ps as Bs (Playlists as Broadcast) sheets 18th June - 22nd
June
BBC Radio interview with John Mitchell
Rock Cellar, In and Out of Wings: Denny Seiwell On His
Friendship with Paul McCartney and Wings' Underrated 1971-
1973 Era By Jeff Slate 12 February 2019
BBC Nationwide, 17 September 1973

www.rayconnolly.co.uk
www.theguardian.com
www.beatlesbible.com
www.johnlennon.com
www.youtube.com
www.beatlesinterviews.blogspot.co.uk
www.the-paulmccartney-project.com
www.rocksbackpages.com
www.washingtonpost.com
www.beatlesbible.com
www.clivearrowsmith.org

www.ingramcontent.com/pod-product-compliance
Lightning Source LLC
Chambersburg PA
CBHW051210090426
42740CB00022B/3449